*Three
Comedies of*
**W. SOMERSET
MAUGHAM**

### THE CIRCLE

"In *The Circle* we find all of Maugham's good guidelines—his smartness of dialogue, sense of a situation, and skill at indicating character."

—*Saturday Review*

"*The Circle* sets a new and higher standard in Mr. Maugham's performance as a playwright."

—*The New Republic*

### OUR BETTERS

"A scorching satire on the American colony in London....The idle rich are always targets for the satirist, but when you have the idle rich doing their idling in a country that does not belong to them and does not want them you have found a chance for a dramatist like Somerset Maugham to write an excoriating comedy. *Our Betters* is just that."

—*The New York Times*

### THE CONSTANT WIFE

"A deft and sparkling comedy...a play written with wit and sprightliness—Mr. Maugham just about at his best. *The Constant Wife* is a light comedy of high order. It is the best play of its kind that has come from England in a long time."

—*The New York Times*

Published by Washington Square Press

*Published by Pocket Books

# Three Comedies of
# W. SOMERSET MAUGHAM

*The Circle*
*Our Betters*
*The Constant Wife*

**WSP** WASHINGTON SQUARE PRESS          NEW YORK

# THREE COMEDIES OF W. SOMERSET MAUGHAM

A *Washington Square Press* edition

1st printing......................January, 1969

L

Published by Washington Square Press,
a division of Simon & Schuster, Inc., 630 Fifth Avenue, New York, N.Y.

WASHINGTON SQUARE PRESS editions are distributed in the
U.S. by Simon & Schuster, Inc., 630 Fifth Avenue, New
York, N.Y. 10020 and in Canada by Simon & Schuster
of Canada, Ltd., Richmond Hill, Ontario, Canada.

## CONTENTS

# THE

# CIRCLE

# CHARACTERS

Clive Champion-Cheney

Arnold Champion-Cheney, M.P.

Lord Porteous

Edward Luton

Lady Catherine Champion-Cheney

Elizabeth

Mrs. Shenstone

A Footman and a Butler

———

*The action takes place at Aston-Adey, Arnold Champion-Cheney's house in Dorset.*

# ACT ONE

SCENE: *A stately drawing-room at Aston-Adey, with fine pictures on the walls and Georgian furniture. Aston-Adey has been described, with many illustrations, in* COUNTRY LIFE. *It is not a house, but a place. Its owner takes a great pride in it, and there is nothing in the room which is not of the period. Through the French windows at the back can be seen the beautiful gardens which are one of the features.*

*It is a fine summer morning.*

ARNOLD *comes in. He is a man of about thirty-five, tall and good-looking, fair, with a clean-cut, sensitive face. He has a look that is intellectual, but somewhat bloodless. He is very well dressed.*

ARNOLD (*calling*): Elizabeth! (*He goes to the window and calls again.*) Elizabeth! (*He rings the bell. While he is waiting he gives a look round the room. He slightly alters the position of one of the chairs. He takes an ornament from the chimney-piece and blows the dust from it.*)

(*A* FOOTMAN *comes in.*)

---

Oh, George! See if you can find Mrs. Cheney, and ask her if she'd be good enough to come here.

FOOTMAN: Very good, sir.

(*The* FOOTMAN *turns to go.*)

ARNOLD: Who is supposed to look after this room?

FOOTMAN: I don't know, sir.

ARNOLD: I wish when they dust they'd take care to replace the things exactly as they were before.

FOOTMAN: Yes, sir.

ARNOLD (*dismissing him*): All right.

(*The* FOOTMAN *goes out. He goes again to the window and calls.*)

ARNOLD: Elizabeth! (*He sees* MRS. SHENSTONE.) Oh, Anna, do you know where Elizabeth is?

(MRS. SHENSTONE *comes in from the garden. She is a woman of forty, pleasant and of elegant appearance.*)

ANNA: Isn't she playing tennis?

ARNOLD: No, I've been down to the tennis court. Something very tiresome has happened.

ANNA: Oh?

ARNOLD: I wonder where the deuce she is.

ANNA: When do you expect Lord Porteous and Lady Kitty?

ARNOLD: They're motoring down in time for luncheon.

ANNA: Are you sure you want me to be here? It's not too late yet, you know. I can have my things packed and catch a train for somewhere or other.

ARNOLD: No, of course we want you. It'll make it so much easier if there are people here. It was exceedingly kind of you to come.

ANNA: Oh, nonsense!

ARNOLD: And I think it was a good thing to have Teddie Luton down.

ANNA: He is so breezy, isn't he?

ARNOLD: Yes, that's his great asset. I don't know that he's very intelligent, but, you know, there are occasions when you want a bull in a china shop. I sent one of the servants to find Elizabeth.

ANNA: I daresay she's putting on her shoes. She and Teddie were going to have a single.

ARNOLD: It can't take all this time to change one's shoes.

ANNA (*with a smile*): One can't change one's shoes without powdering one's nose, you know.

(ELIZABETH *comes in. She is a very pretty creature in the early twenties. She wears a light summer frock.*)

ARNOLD: My dear, I've been hunting for you everywhere. What *have* you been doing?

ELIZABETH: Nothing! I've been standing on my head.

ARNOLD: My father's here.

ELIZABETH (*startled*): Where?

ARNOLD: At the cottage. He arrived last night.

ELIZABETH: Damn!

ARNOLD (*good-humouredly*): I wish you wouldn't say that, Elizabeth.

ELIZABETH: If you're not going to say Damn when a thing's damnable, when are you going to say Damn?

ARNOLD: I should have thought you could say, Oh, bother! or something like that.

ELIZABETH: But that wouldn't express my sentiments. Besides, at that speech day when you were giving away the prizes you said there were no synonyms in the English language.

ANNA (*smiling*): Oh, Elizabeth! It's very unfair to expect a politician to live in private up to the statements he makes in public.

ARNOLD: I'm always willing to stand by anything I've said. There *are* no synonyms in the English language.

Elizabeth: In that case I shall be regretfully forced to continue to say Damn whenever I feel like it.

(Edward Luton *shows himself at the window. He is an attractive youth in flannels.*)

Teddie: I say, what about this tennis?

Elizabeth: Come in. We're having a scene.

Teddie (*entering*): How splendid! What about?

Elizabeth: The English language.

Teddie: Don't tell me you've been splitting your infinitives.

Arnold (*with the shadow of a frown*): I wish you'd be serious, Elizabeth. The situation is none too pleasant.

Anna: I think Teddie and I had better make ourselves scarce.

Elizabeth: Nonsense! You're both in it. If there's going to be any unpleasantness we want your moral support. That's why we asked you to come.

Teddie: And I thought I'd been asked for my blue eyes.

Elizabeth: Vain beast! And they happen to be brown.

Teddie: Is anything up?

Elizabeth: Arnold's father arrived last night.

Teddie: Did he, by Jove! I thought he was in Paris.

Arnold: So did we all. He told me he'd be there for the next month.

Anna: Have you seen him?

Arnold: No! He rang me up. It's a mercy he had a telephone put in the cottage. It would have been a pretty kettle of fish if he'd just walked in.

Elizabeth: Did you tell him Lady Catherine was coming?

Arnold: Of course not. I was flabbergasted to know he was here. And then I thought we'd better talk it over first.

Elizabeth: Is he coming along here?

Arnold: Yes. He suggested it, and I couldn't think of any excuse to prevent him.

TEDDIE: Couldn't you put the other people off?

ARNOLD: They're coming by car. They may be here any minute. It's too late to do that.

ELIZABETH: Besides, it would be beastly.

ARNOLD: I knew it was silly to have them here. Elizabeth insisted.

ELIZABETH: After all, she *is* your mother, Arnold.

ARNOLD: That meant precious little to her when she—went away. You can't imagine it means very much to me now.

ELIZABETH: It's thirty years ago. It seems so absurd to bear malice after all that time.

ARNOLD: I don't bear malice, but the fact remains that she did me the most irreparable harm. I can find no excuse for her.

ELIZABETH: Have you ever tried to?

ARNOLD: My dear Elizabeth, it's no good going over all that again. The facts are lamentably simple. She had a husband who adored her, a wonderful position, all the money she could want, and a child of five. And she ran away with a married man.

ELIZABETH: Lady Porteous is not a very attractive woman, Arnold. (*to* ANNA) Do you know her?

ANNA (*smiling*): Forbidding is the word, I think.

ARNOLD: If you're going to make little jokes about it, I have nothing more to say.

ANNA: I'm sorry, Arnold.

ELIZABETH: Perhaps your mother couldn't help herself —if she was in love?

ARNOLD: And had no sense of honour, duty, or decency? Oh, yes, under those circumstances you can explain a great deal.

ELIZABETH: That's not a very pretty way to speak of your mother.

ARNOLD: I can't look on her as my mother.

ELIZABETH: What you can't get over is that she didn't think of you. Some of us are more mother and some of us more woman. It gives me a little thrill when I think that she loved that man so much. She sacrificed her name, her position and her child to him.

ARNOLD: You really can't expect the said child to have any great affection for the mother who treated him like that.

ELIZABETH: No, I don't think I do. But I think it's a pity after all these years that you shouldn't be friends.

ARNOLD: I wonder if you realize what it was to grow up under the shadow of that horrible scandal. Everywhere, at school, and at Oxford, and afterwards in London, I was always the son of Lady Kitty Cheney. Oh, it was cruel, cruel!

ELIZABETH: Yes, I know, Arnold. It was beastly for you.

ARNOLD: It would have been bad enough if it had been an ordinary case, but the position of the people made it ten times worse. My father was in the House then, and Porteous—he hadn't succeeded to the title—was in the House too; he was Under-Secretary for Foreign Affairs, and he was very much in the public eye.

ANNA: My father always used to say he was the ablest man in the party. Every one was expecting him to be Prime Minister.

ARNOLD: You can imagine what a boon it was to the British public. They hadn't had such a treat for a generation. The most popular song of the day was about my mother. Did you ever hear it? "Naughty Lady Kitty. Thought it such a pity ..."

ELIZABETH (interrupting): Oh, Arnold, don't!

ARNOLD: And then they never let people forget them. If they'd lived quietly in Florence and not made a fuss the scandal would have died down. But those constant actions between Lord and Lady Porteous kept on reminding everyone.

TEDDIE: What were they having actions about?

ARNOLD: Of course my father divorced his wife, but Lady Porteous refused to divorce Porteous. He tried to force her by refusing to support her and turning her out of her house, and heaven knows what. They were constantly wrangling in the law courts.

ANNA: I think it was monstrous of Lady Porteous.

ARNOLD: She knew he wanted to marry my mother, and she hated my mother. You can't blame her.

ANNA: It must have been very difficult for them.

ARNOLD: That's why they've lived in Florence. Porteous has money. They found people there who were willing to accept the situation.

ELIZABETH: This is the first time they've ever come to England.

ARNOLD: My father will have to be told, Elizabeth.

ELIZABETH: Yes.

ANNA (*to* ELIZABETH): Has he ever spoken to you about Lady Kitty?

ELIZABETH: Never.

ARNOLD: I don't think her name has passed his lips since she ran away from this house thirty years ago.

TEDDIE: Oh, they lived here?

ARNOLD: Naturally. There was a house-party, and one evening neither Porteous nor my mother came down to dinner. The rest of them waited. They couldn't make it out. My father sent up to my mother's room, and a note was found on the pincushion.

ELIZABETH (*with a faint smile*): That's what they did in the Dark Ages.

ARNOLD: I think he took a dislike to this house from that horrible night. He never lived here again, and when I married he handed the place over to me. He just has a cottage now on the estate that he comes to when he feels inclined.

ELIZABETH: It's been very nice for us.

ARNOLD: I owe everything to my father. I don't think he'll ever forgive me for asking these people to come here.

ELIZABETH: I'm going to take all the blame on myself, Arnold.

ARNOLD (*irritably*): The situation was embarrassing

enough anyhow. I don't know how I ought to treat them.

ELIZABETH: Don't you think that'll settle itself when you see them?

ARNOLD: After all, they're my guests. I shall try and behave like a gentleman.

ELIZABETH: I wouldn't. We haven't got central heating.

ARNOLD (*taking no notice*): Will she expect me to kiss her?

ELIZABETH (*with a smile*): Surely.

ARNOLD: It always makes me uncomfortable when people are effusive.

ANNA: But I can't understand why you never saw her before.

ARNOLD: I believe she tried to see me when I was little, but my father thought it better she shouldn't.

ANNA: Yes, but when you were grown up?

ARNOLD: She was always in Italy. I never went to Italy.

ELIZABETH: It seems to me so pathetic that if you saw one another in the street you wouldn't recognize each other.

ARNOLD: Is it my fault?

ELIZABETH: You've promised to be very gentle with her and very kind.

ARNOLD: The mistake was asking Porteous to come too. It looks as though we condoned the whole thing. And how am I to treat him? Am I to shake him by the hand and slap him on the back? He absolutely ruined my father's life.

ELIZABETH (*smiling*): How much would you give for a nice motor accident that prevented them from coming?

ARNOLD: I let you persuade me against my better judgment, and I've regretted it ever since.

ELIZABETH (*good-humouredly*): I think it's very lucky that Anna and Teddie are here. I don't foresee a very successful party.

ARNOLD: I'm going to do my best. I gave you my

promise and I shall keep it. But I can't answer for my father.

ANNA: Here is your father.

(MR. CHAMPION-CHENEY *shows himself at one of the French windows.*)

C.-C.: May I come in through the window, or shall I have myself announced by a supercilious flunkey?

ELIZABETH: Come in. We've been expecting you.

C.-C.: Impatiently, I hope, my dear child.

(MR. CHAMPION-CHENEY *is a tall man in the early sixties, spare, with a fine head of grey hair and an intelligent, somewhat ascetic face. He is very carefully dressed. He is a man who makes the most of himself. He bears his years jauntily. He kisses* ELIZABETH *and then holds out his hand to* ARNOLD.)

ELIZABETH: We thought you'd be in Paris for another month.

C.-C.: How are you, Arnold? I always reserve to myself the privilege of changing my mind. It's the only one elderly gentlemen share with pretty women.

ELIZABETH: You know Anna.

C.-C. (*shaking hands with her*): Of course I do. How very nice to see you here. Are you staying long?

ANNA: As long as I'm welcome.

ELIZABETH: And this is Mr. Luton.

C.-C.: How do you do? Do you play bridge?

TEDDIE: I do.

C.-C.: Capital. Do you declare without top honours?

TEDDIE: Never.

C.-C.: Of such is the kingdom of heaven. I see that you are a good young man.

TEDDIE: But, like the good in general, I am poor.

C.-C.: Never mind; if your principles are right, you can play ten shillings a hundred without danger. I never play less, and I never play more.

Arnold: And you—are you going to stay long, father?
C.-C.: To luncheon, if you'll have me.

(Arnold *gives* Elizabeth *a harassed look.*)

Elizabeth: That'll be jolly.
Arnold: I didn't mean that. Of course you're going to stay for luncheon. I meant, how long are you going to stay down here?
C.-C.: A week.

(*There is a moment's pause. Everyone but* Champion-Cheney *is slightly embarrassed.*)

Teddie: I think we'd better chuck our tennis.
Elizabeth: Yes. I want my father-in-law to tell me what they're wearing in Paris this week.
Teddie: I'll go and put the rackets away.

(Teddie *goes out.*)

Arnold: It's nearly one o'clock, Elizabeth.
Elizabeth: I didn't know it was so late.
Anna (*to* Arnold): I wonder if I can persuade you to take a turn in the garden before luncheon.
Arnold (*jumping at the idea*): I'd love it.

(Anna *goes out of the window, and as he follows her he stops irresolutely.*)

I want you to look at this chair I've just got. I think it's rather good.
C.-C.: Charming.
Arnold: About 1750, I should say. Good design, isn't it? It hasn't been restored or anything.
C.-C.: Very pretty.
Arnold: I think it was a good buy, don't you?
C.-C.: Oh, my dear boy, you know I'm entirely ignorant about these things.

ARNOLD: It's exactly my period ... I shall see you at luncheon, then.

(*He follows* ANNA *through the window.*)

C.-C.: Who is that young man?

ELIZABETH: Mr. Luton. He's only just been demobilized. He's the manager of a rubber estate in the F.M.S.

C.-C.: And what are the F.M.S. when they're at home?

ELIZABETH: The Federated Malay States. He joined up at the beginning of the war. He's just going back there.

C.-C.: And why have we been left alone in this very marked manner?

ELIZABETH: Have we? I didn't notice it.

C.-C.: I suppose it's difficult for the young to realize that one may be old without being a fool.

ELIZABETH: I never thought you that. Everyone knows you're very intelligent.

C.-C.: They certainly ought to by now. I've told them often enough. Are you a little nervous?

ELIZABETH: Let me feel my pulse. (*She puts her finger on her wrist.*) It's perfectly regular.

C.-C.: When I suggested staying to luncheon Arnold looked exactly like a dose of castor oil.

ELIZABETH: I wish you'd sit down.

C.-C.: Will it make it easier for you? (*He takes a chair.*) You have evidently something very disagreeable to say to me.

ELIZABETH: You won't be cross with me?

C.-C.: How old are you?

ELIZABETH: Twenty-five.

C.-C.: I'm never cross with a woman under thirty.

ELIZABETH: Oh, then, I've got ten years.

C.-C.: Mathematics?

ELIZABETH: No. Paint.

C.-C.: Well?

ELIZABETH (*reflectively*): I think it would be easier if I sat on your knees.

C.-C.: That is a pleasing taste of yours, but you must take care not to put on weight.

(*She sits down on his knees.*)

ELIZABETH: Am I bony?
C.-C.: On the contrary.... I'm listening.
ELIZABETH: Lady Catherine's coming here.
C.-C.: Who's Lady Catherine?
ELIZABETH: Your—Arnold's mother.
C.-C.: Is she?

(*He withdraws himself a little and* ELIZABETH *gets up.*)

ELIZABETH: You mustn't blame Arnold. It's my fault. I insisted. He was against it. I nagged him till he gave way. And then I wrote and asked her to come.

C.-C.: I didn't know you knew her.

ELIZABETH: I don't. But I heard she was in London. She's staying at Claridge's. It seemed so heartless not to take the smallest notice of her.

C.-C.: When is she coming?

ELIZABETH: We're expecting her in time for luncheon.

C.-C.: As soon as that? I understand the embarrassment.

ELIZABETH: You see, we never expected you to be here. You said you'd be in Paris for another month.

C.-C.: My dear child, this is your house. There's no reason why you shouldn't ask whom you please to stay with you.

ELIZABETH: After all, whatever her faults, she's Arnold's mother. It seemed so unnatural that they should never see one another. My heart ached for that poor lonely woman.

C.-C.: I never heard that she was lonely, and she certainly isn't poor.

ELIZABETH: And there's something else. I couldn't ask

her by herself. It would have been so—so insulting. I asked Lord Porteous, too.

C.-C.: I see.

ELIZABETH: I daresay you'd rather not meet them.

C.-C.: I daresay they'd rather not meet me. I shall get a capital luncheon at the cottage. I've noticed you always get the best food if you come in unexpectedly and have the same as they're having in the servants' hall.

ELIZABETH: No one's ever talked to me about Lady Kitty. It's always been a subject that everyone has avoided. I've never even seen a photograph of her.

C.-C.: The house was full of them when she left. I think I told the butler to throw them in the dust-bin. She was very much photographed.

ELIZABETH: Won't you tell me what she was like?

C.-C.: She was very like you, Elizabeth, only she had dark hair instead of red.

ELIZABETH: Poor dear! It must be quite white now.

C.-C.: I daresay. She was a pretty little thing.

ELIZABETH: But she was one of the great beauties of her day. They say she was lovely.

C.-C.: She had the most adorable little nose, like yours. . . .

ELIZABETH: D'you like my nose?

C.-C.: And she was very dainty, with a beautiful little figure; very light on her feet. She was like a *marquise* in an old French comedy. Yes, she was lovely.

ELIZABETH: And I'm sure she's lovely still.

C.-C.: You're very romantic.

ELIZABETH: If everyone hadn't made such a mystery of it I daresay I shouldn't feel as I do. I know she did a great wrong to you and a great wrong to Arnold. I'm willing to acknowledge that.

C.-C.: I'm sure it's very kind of you.

ELIZABETH: But she loved and she dared. Romance is such an illusive thing. You read of it in books, but it's seldom you see it face to face. I can't help it if it thrills me.

C.-C.: I am painfully aware that the husband in these cases is not a romantic object.

Elizabeth: She had the world at her feet. You were rich. She was a figure in society. And she gave up every-thing for love.

C.-C. (*dryly*): I'm beginning to suspect it wasn't only for her sake and for Arnold's that you asked her to come here.

Elizabeth: I seem to know her already. I think her face is a little sad, for a love like that doesn't leave you gay, it leaves you grave, but I think her pale face is unlined. It's like a child's.

C.-C.: My dear, how you let your imagination run away with you!

Elizabeth: I imagine her slight and frail.

C.-C.: Frail, certainly.

Elizabeth: With beautiful thin hands and white hair. I've pictured her so often in that Renaissance palace that they live in, with old masters on the walls and lovely carved things all round, sitting in a black silk dress with old lace round her neck and old-fashioned diamonds. You see, I never knew my mother; she died when I was a baby. You can't confide in aunts with huge families of their own. I want Arnold's mother to be a mother to me. I've got so much to say to her.

C.-C.: Are you happy with Arnold?

Elizabeth: Why shouldn't I be?

C.-C.: Why haven't you got any babies?

Elizabeth: Give us a little time. We've only been married three years.

C.-C.: I wonder what Hughie is like now?

Elizabeth: Lord Porteous?

C.-C.: He wore his clothes better than any man in London. You know he'd have been Prime Minister if he'd remained in politics.

Elizabeth: What was he like then?

C.-C.: He was a nice-looking fellow. Fine horseman. I suppose there was something very fascinating about him.

Yellow hair and blue eyes, you know. He had a very
good figure. I liked him. I was his parliamentary secretary. He was Arnold's godfather.

ELIZABETH: I know.

C.-C.: I wonder if he ever regrets.

ELIZABETH: I wouldn't.

C.-C.: Well, I must be strolling back to my cottage.

ELIZABETH: You're not angry with me?

C.-C.: Not a bit.

(*She puts up her face for him to kiss. He kisses her on
both cheeks and then goes out. In a moment* TEDDIE
*is seen at the window.*)

TEDDIE: I saw the old blighter go.

ELIZABETH: Come in.

TEDDIE: Everything all right?

ELIZABETH: Oh, quite, as far as he's concerned. He's
going to keep out of the way.

TEDDIE: Was it beastly?

ELIZABETH: No, he made it very easy for me. He's a
nice old thing.

TEDDIE: You were rather scared.

ELIZABETH: A little. I am still. I don't know why.

TEDDIE: I guessed you were. I thought I'd come and
give you a little moral support. It's ripping here, isn't it?

ELIZABETH: It is rather nice.

TEDDIE: It'll be jolly to think of it when I'm back in the
F.M.S.

ELIZABETH: Aren't you homesick sometimes?

TEDDIE: Oh, everyone is now and then, you know.

ELIZABETH: You could have got a job in England if
you'd wanted to, couldn't you?

TEDDIE: Oh, but I love it out there. England's ripping
to come back to, but I couldn't live here now. It's like a
woman you're desperately in love with as long as you
don't see her, but when you're with her she maddens you
so that you can't bear her.

ELIZABETH (*smiling*): What's wrong with England?

TEDDIE: I don't think anything's wrong with England. I expect something's wrong with me. I've been away too long. England seems to me full of people doing things they don't want to because other people expect it of them.

ELIZABETH: Isn't that what you call a high degree of civilization?

TEDDIE: People seem to me so insincere. When you go to parties in London they're all babbling about art, and you feel that in their hearts they don't care twopence about it. They read the books that everybody is talking about because they don't want to be out of it. In the F.M.S. we don't get very many books, and we read those we have over and over again. They mean so much to us. I don't think the people over there are half so clever as the people at home, but one gets to know them better. You see, there are so few of us that we have to make the best of one another.

ELIZABETH: I imagine that frills are not much worn in the F.M.S. It must be a comfort.

TEDDIE: It's not much good being pretentious where everyone knows exactly who you are and what your income is.

ELIZABETH: I don't think you want too much sincerity in society. It would be like an iron girder in a house of cards.

TEDDIE: And then, you know, the place is ripping. You get used to a blue sky and you miss it in England.

ELIZABETH: What do you do with yourself all the time?

TEDDIE: Oh, one works like blazes. You have to be a pretty hefty fellow to be a planter. And then there's ripping bathing. You know, it's lovely, with palm trees all along the beach. And there's shooting. And now and then we have a little dance to a gramophone.

ELIZABETH (*pretending to tease him*): I think you've got a young woman out there, Teddie.

TEDDIE (*vehemently*): Oh, no!

*(She is a little taken aback by the earnestness of his
disclaimer. There is a moment's silence, then she
recovers herself.)*

ELIZABETH: But you'll have to marry and settle down
one of these days, you know.

TEDDIE: I want to, but it's not a thing you can do
lightly.

ELIZABETH: I don't know why there more than else-
where.

TEDDIE: In England if people don't get on they go
their own ways and jog along after a fashion. In a place
like that you're thrown a great deal on your own re-
sources.

ELIZABETH: Of course.

TEDDIE: Lots of girls come out because they think
they're going to have a good time. But if they're empty-
headed, then they're just faced with their own emptiness
and they're done. If their husbands can afford it they go
home and settle down as grass-widows.

ELIZABETH: I've met them. They seem to find it a very
pleasant occupation.

TEDDIE: It's rotten for their husbands, though.

ELIZABETH: And if the husbands can't afford it?

TEDDIE: Oh, then they tipple.

ELIZABETH: It's not a very alluring prospect.

TEDDIE: But if the woman's the right sort she wouldn't
exchange it for any life in the world. When all's said and
done, it's we who've made the Empire.

ELIZABETH: What sort is the right sort?

TEDDIE: A woman of courage and endurance and
sincerity. Of course, it's hopeless unless she's in love with
her husband.

*(He is looking at her earnestly and she, raising her
eyes, gives him a long look. There is silence between
them.)*

TEDDIE: My house stands on the side of a hill, and the coconut trees wind down to the shore. Azaleas grow in my garden, and camellias, and all sorts of ripping flowers. And in front of me is the winding coast line, and then the blue sea.

(*A pause.*)

Do you know that I'm awfully in love with you?
ELIZABETH (*gravely*): I wasn't quite sure. I wondered.
TEDDIE: And you?

(*She nods slowly.*)

I've never kissed you.
ELIZABETH: I don't want you to.

(*They look at one another steadily. They are both grave.* ARNOLD *comes in hurriedly.*)

ARNOLD: They're coming, Elizabeth.
ELIZABETH (*as though returning from a distant world*): Who?
ARNOLD (*impatiently*): My dear! My mother, of course. The car is just coming up the drive.
TEDDIE: Would you like me to clear out?
ARNOLD: No, no! For goodness' sake stay.
ELIZABETH: We'd better go meet them, Arnold.
ARNOLD: No, no; I think they'd much better be shown in. I feel simply sick with nervousness.

(ANNA *comes in from the garden.*)

ANNA: Your guests have arrived.
ELIZABETH: Yes, I know.
ARNOLD: I've given orders that luncheon should be served at once.
ELIZABETH: Why? It's not half-past one already, is it?

ARNOLD: I thought it would help. When you don't know exactly what to say you can always eat.

(*The* BUTLER *comes in and announces.*)

BUTLER: Lady Catherine Champion-Cheney. Lord Porteous.

(LADY KITTY *comes in, followed by* PORTEOUS, *and the* BUTLER *goes out.* LADY KITTY *is a gay little lady, with dyed red hair and painted cheeks. She is somewhat outrageously dressed. She never forgets that she has been a pretty woman and she still behaves as if she were twenty-five.* LORD PORTEOUS *is a very bald, elderly gentleman in loose, rather eccentric clothes. He is snappy and gruff. This is not at all the couple that* ELIZABETH *expected, and for a moment she stares at them with round, startled eyes.* LADY KITTY *goes up to her with outstretched hands.*)

LADY KITTY: Elizabeth! Elizabeth! (*She kisses her effusively.*) What an adorable creature! (*turning to* PORTEOUS) Hughie, isn't she adorable?
PORTEOUS (*with a grunt*): Ugh!

(ELIZABETH, *smiling now, turns to him and gives him her hand.*)

ELIZABETH: How d'you do?
PORTEOUS: Damnable road you've got down here. How d'you do, my dear? Why d'you have such damnable roads in England?

(LADY KITTY's *eyes fall on* TEDDIE *and she goes up to him with her arms thrown back, prepared to throw them round him.*)

LADY KITTY: My boy, my boy! I should have known you anywhere!

Elizabeth (*hastily*): That's Arnold.

Lady Kitty (*without a moment's hesitation*): The image of his father! I should have known him anywhere! (*She throws her arms round his neck.*) My boy, my boy!

Porteous (*with a grunt*): Ugh!

Lady Kitty: Tell me, would you have known me again? Have I changed?

Arnold: I was only five, you know, when—when you ...

Lady Kitty (*emotionally*): I remember as if it was yesterday. I went up into your room. (*with a sudden change of manner*) By the way, I always thought that nurse drank. Did you ever find out if she really did?

Porteous: How the devil can you expect him to know that, Kitty?

Lady Kitty: You've never had a child, Hughie; how can you tell what they know and what they don't?

Elizabeth (*coming to the rescue*): This is Arnold, Lord Porteous.

Porteous (*shaking hands with him*): How d'you do? I knew your father.

Arnold: Yes.

Porteous: Alive still?

Arnold: Yes.

Porteous: He must be getting on. Is he well?

Arnold: Very.

Porteous: Ugh! Takes care of himself, I suppose. I'm not at all well. This damned climate doesn't agree with me.

Elizabeth (*to* Lady Kitty): This is Mrs. Shenstone. And this is Mr. Luton. I hope you don't mind a very small party.

Lady Kitty (*shaking hands with* Anna *and* Teddie): Oh, no, I shall enjoy it. I used to give enormous parties here. Political, you know. How nice you've made this room!

Elizabeth: Oh, that's Arnold.

Arnold (*nervously*): D'you like this chair? I've just bought it. It's exactly my period.

Porteous (*bluntly*): It's a fake.

ARNOLD (*indignantly*): I don't think it is for a minute.

PORTEOUS: The legs are not right.

ARNOLD: I don't know how you can say that. If there is anything right about it, it's the legs.

LADY KITTY: I'm sure they're right.

PORTEOUS: You know nothing whatever about it, Kitty.

LADY KITTY: That's what you think. *I* think it's a beautiful chair. Hepplewhite?

ARNOLD: No, Sheraton.

LADY KITTY: Oh, I know. The School for Scandal.

PORTEOUS: Sheraton, my dear. Sheraton.

LADY KITTY: Yes, that's what I say. I acted the screen scene at some amateur theatricals in Florence, and Ermete Novelli, the great Italian tragedian, told me he'd never seen a Lady Teazle like me.

PORTEOUS: Ugh!

LADY KITTY (*to* ELIZABETH): Do you act?

ELIZABETH: Oh, I couldn't. I should be too nervous.

LADY KITTY: I'm never nervous. I'm a born actress. Of course, if I had my time over again I'd go on the stage. You know, it's extraordinary how they keep young. Actresses, I mean. I think it's because they're always playing different parts. Hughie, do you think Arnold takes after me or after his father? Of course I think he's the very image of me. Arnold, I think I ought to tell you that I was received into the Catholic Church last winter. I'd been thinking about it for years, and last time we were at Monte Carlo I met such a nice monsignore. I told him what my difficulties were and he was too wonderful. I knew Hughie wouldn't approve, so I kept it a secret. (*to* ELIZABETH) Are you interested in religion? I think it's too wonderful. We must have a long talk about it one of these days. (*pointing to her frock*) Callot?

ELIZABETH: No, Worth.

LADY KITTY: I knew it was either Worth or Callot. Of course, it's line that's the important thing. I go to Worth myself, and I always say to him, Line, my dear Worth, line. What *is* the matter, Hughie?

Porteous: These new teeth of mine are so damned uncomfortable.

Lady Kitty: Men are extraordinary. They can't stand the smallest discomfort. Why, a woman's life is uncomfortable from the moment she gets up in the morning till the moment she goes to bed at night. And d'you think it's comfortable to sleep with a mask on your face?

Porteous: They don't seem to hold up properly.

Lady Kitty: Well, that's not the fault of your teeth. That's the fault of your gums.

Porteous: Damned rotten dentist. That's what's the matter.

Lady Kitty: I thought he was a very nice dentist. He told me *my* teeth would last till I was fifty. He has a Chinese room. It's so interesting; while he scrapes your teeth he tells you all about the dear Empress Dowager. Are you interested in China? I think it's too wonderful. You know they've cut off their pigtails. I think it's such a pity. They were so picturesque.

(*The* Butler *comes in.*)

Butler: Luncheon is served, sir.

Elizabeth: Would you like to see your rooms?

Porteous: We can see our rooms after luncheon.

Lady Kitty: I must powder my nose, Hughie.

Porteous: Powder it down here.

Lady Kitty: I never saw any one so inconsiderate.

Porteous: You'll keep us all waiting half an hour. I know you.

Lady Kitty (*fumbling in her bag*): Oh, well, peace at any price, as Lord Beaconsfield said.

Porteous: He said a lot of damned silly things, Kitty, but he never said that.

(Lady Kitty's *face changes. Perplexity is followed by dismay, and dismay by consternation.*)

Lady Kitty: Oh!

ELIZABETH: What is the matter?

LADY KITTY (*with anguish*): My lip-stick!

ELIZABETH: Can't you find it?

LADY KITTY: I had it in the car. Hughie, you remember that I had it in the car.

PORTEOUS: I don't remember anything about it.

LADY KITTY: Don't be so stupid, Hughie. Why, when we came through the gates I said: My home, my home! and I took it out and put some on my lips.

ELIZABETH: Perhaps you dropped it in the car.

LADY KITTY: For heaven's sake send someone to look for it.

ARNOLD: I'll ring.

LADY KITTY: I'm absolutely lost without my lip-stick. Lend me yours, darling, will you?

ELIZABETH: I'm awfully sorry. I'm afraid I haven't got one.

LADY KITTY: Do you mean to say you don't use a lip-stick?

ELIZABETH: Never.

PORTEOUS: Look at her lips. What the devil d'you think she wants muck like that for?

LADY KITTY: Oh, my dear, what a mistake you make! You *must* use a lip-stick. It's so good for the lips. Men like it, you know. I couldn't *live* without a lip-stick.

(CHAMPION-CHENEY *appears at the window holding in his upstretched hand a little gold case.*)

C.-C. (*as he comes in*): Has any one here lost a diminutive utensil containing, unless I am mistaken, a favourite preparation for the toilet?

(ARNOLD *and* ELIZABETH *are thunderstruck at his appearance and even* TEDDIE *and* ANNA *are taken aback. But* LADY KITTY *is overjoyed.*

LADY KITTY: My lip-stick!

C.-C.: I found it in the drive and I ventured to bring it in.

Lady Kitty: It's Saint Anthony. I said a little prayer to him when I was hunting in my bag.

Porteous: Saint Anthony be blowed! It's Clive, by God!

Lady Kitty (*startled, her attention suddenly turning from the lip-stick.*): Clive!

C.-C.: You didn't recognize me. It's many years since we met.

Lady Kitty: My poor Clive, your hair has gone quite white!

C.-C. (*holding out his hand*): I hope you had a pleasant journey down from London.

Lady Kitty (*offering him her cheek*): You may kiss me, Clive.

C.-C. (*kissing her*): You don't mind, Hughie?

Porteous (*with a grunt*): Ugh!

C.-C. (*going up to him cordially*): And how are you, my dear Hughie?

Porteous: Damned rheumatic if you want to know. Filthy climate you have in this country.

C.-C.: Aren't you going to shake hands with me, Hughie?

Porteous: I have no objection to shaking hands with you.

C.-C.: You've aged, my poor Hughie.

Porteous: Someone was asking me how old you were the other day.

C.-C.: Were they surprised when you told them?

Porteous: Surprised! They wondered you weren't dead.

(*The* Butler *comes in.*)

Butler: Did you ring, sir?

Arnold: No. Oh, yes, I did. It doesn't matter now.

C.-C. (*as the* Butler *is going*): One moment. My dear Elizabeth, I've come to throw myself on your mercy. My servants are busy with their own affairs. There's not a thing for me to eat in my cottage.

ELIZABETH: Oh, but we shall be delighted if you'll lunch with us.

C.-C.: It either means that or my immediate death from starvation. You don't mind, Arnold?

ARNOLD: My dear father!

ELIZABETH (*to the* BUTLER): Mr. Cheney will lunch here.

BUTLER: Very good, ma'am.

C.-C. (*to* LADY KITTY): And what do you think of Arnold?

LADY KITTY: I adore him.

C.-C.: He's grown, hasn't he? But then you'd expect him to do that in thirty years.

ARNOLD: For God's sake let's go in to lunch, Elizabeth!

# ACT TWO

·•·◦·•·◦·•·◦·•·◦·•·◦·•·◦·•·◦·•·◦·•·◦·•·◦·•·◦·•·◦·•·◦·•·◦·•·◦·•·◦·•·◦·•·◦·•·◦·•·◦·•·◦·•·◦·•·◦·•·◦·•·

SCENE: *Same as in the preceding act.*

*It is afternoon. When the curtain rises* PORTEOUS *and* LADY KITTY, ANNA *and* TEDDIE *are playing bridge.* ELIZABETH *and* CHAMPION-CHENEY *are watching.* PORTEOUS *and* LADY KITTY *are partners.*

C.-C.: When will Arnold be back, Elizabeth?

ELIZABETH: Soon, I think.

C.-C.: Is he addressing a meeting?

ELIZABETH: No, it's only a conference with his agent and one or two constituents.

PORTEOUS (*irritably*): How any one can be expected to play bridge when people are shouting at the top of their voices all round them, I for one cannot understand.

ELIZABETH (*smiling*): I'm so sorry.

ANNA: I can see your hand, Lord Porteous.

PORTEOUS: It may help you.

LADY KITTY: I've told you over and over again to hold your cards up. It ruins one's game when one can't help seeing one's opponent's hand.

PORTEOUS: One isn't obliged to look.

LADY KITTY: What was Arnold's majority at the last election?

ELIZABETH: Seven hundred and something.

C.-C.: He'll have to fight for it if he wants to keep his seat next time.

30

PORTEOUS: Are we playing bridge, or talking politics?

LADY KITTY: I never find that conversation interferes with my game.

PORTEOUS: You certainly play no worse when you talk than when you hold your tongue.

LADY KITTY: I think that's a very offensive thing to say, Hughie. Just because I don't play the same game as you do you think I can't play.

PORTEOUS: I'm glad you acknowledge it's not the same game as I play. But why in God's name do you call it bridge?

C.-C.: I agree with Kitty. I hate people who play bridge as though they were at a funeral and knew their feet were getting wet.

PORTEOUS: Of course you take Kitty's part.

LADY KITTY: That's the least he can do.

C.-C.: I have a naturally cheerful disposition.

PORTEOUS: You've never had anything to sour it.

LADY KITTY: I don't know what you mean by that, Hughie.

PORTEOUS (*trying to contain himself*): Must you trump my ace?

LADY KITTY (*innocently*): Oh, was that your ace, darling?

PORTEOUS (*furiously*): Yes, it was my ace.

LADY KITTY: Oh, well, it was the only trump I had. I shouldn't have made it anyway.

PORTEOUS: You needn't have told them that. Now she knows exactly what I've got.

LADY KITTY: She knew before.

PORTEOUS: How could she know?

LADY KITTY: She said she'd seen your hand.

ANNA: Oh, I didn't. I said I could see it.

LADY KITTY: Well, I naturally supposed that if she could see it she did.

PORTEOUS: Really, Kitty, you have the most extraordinary ideas.

C.-C.: Not at all. If any one is such a fool as to show me his hand, of course I look at it.

PORTEOUS (*fuming*): If you study the etiquette of bridge, you'll discover that onlookers are expected not to interfere with the game.

C.-C.: My dear Hughie, this is a matter of ethics, not of bridge.

ANNA: Anyhow, I get the game. And rubber.

TEDDIE: I claim a revoke.

PORTEOUS: Who revoked?

TEDDIE: You did.

PORTEOUS: Nonsense. I've never revoked in my life.

TEDDIE: I'll show you. (*He turns over the tricks to show the faces of the cards.*) You threw away a club on the third heart trick and you had another heart.

PORTEOUS: I never had more than two hearts.

TEDDIE: Oh, yes, you had. Look here. That's the card you played on the last trick but one.

LADY KITTY (*delighted to catch him out*): There's no doubt about it, Hughie. You revoked.

PORTEOUS: I tell you I did not revoke. I never revoke.

C.-C.: You did, Hughie. I wondered what on earth you were doing.

PORTEOUS: I don't know how any one can be expected not to revoke when there's this confounded chatter going on all the time.

TEDDIE: Well, that's another hundred to us.

PORTEOUS (*to* CHAMPION-CHENEY): I wish you wouldn't breathe down my neck. I never can play bridge when there's somebody breathing down my neck.

(*The party have risen from the bridge-table, and they scatter about the room.*)

ANNA: Well, I'm going to take a book and lie down in the hammock till it's time to dress.

TEDDIE (*who has been adding up*): I'll put it down in the book, shall I?

PORTEOUS (*who has not moved, setting out the cards for a patience*): Yes, yes, put it down. I never revoke.

(ANNA *goes out.*)

LADY KITTY: Would you like to come for a little stroll, Hughie?

PORTEOUS: What for?

LADY KITTY: Exercise.

PORTEOUS: I hate exercise.

C.-C. (*looking at the patience*): The seven goes on the eight.

(PORTEOUS *takes no notice.*)

LADY KITTY: The seven goes on the eight, Hughie.

PORTEOUS: I don't choose to put the seven on the eight.

C.-C.: That knave goes on the queen.

PORTEOUS: I'm not blind, thank you.

LADY KITTY: The three goes on the four.

C.-C.: All these go over.

PORTEOUS (*furiously*): Am I playing this patience, or are you playing it?

LADY KITTY: But you're missing everything.

PORTEOUS: That's my business.

C.-C.: It's no good losing your temper over it, Hughie.

PORTEOUS: I don't want to be helped. I want to do it by myself.

LADY KITTY: I think your manners are perfectly deplorable, Hughie.

PORTEOUS: It's simply maddening when you're playing patience and people won't leave you alone.

C.-C.: We won't say another word.

PORTEOUS: That three goes. I believe it's coming out. If I'd been such a fool as to put that seven up I shouldn't have been able to bring these down.

(*He puts down several cards while they watch him silently.*)

LADY KITTY AND C.-C. (*together*): The four goes on the five.

Porteous (*throwing down the cards violently*): Damn you! Why don't you leave me alone? It's intolerable.

C.-C.: It was coming out, my dear fellow.

Porteous: I know it was coming out. Confound you!

Lady Kitty: How petty you are, Hughie!

Porteous: Petty, be damned! I've told you over and over again that I will not be interfered with when I'm playing patience.

Lady Kitty: Don't talk to me like that, Hughie.

Porteous: I shall talk to you as I please.

Lady Kitty (*beginning to cry*): Oh, you brute! You brute!

(*She flings out of the room.*)

Porteous: Oh, damn! Now she's going to cry.

(*He shambles out into the garden.* Champion-Cheney, Elizabeth *and* Teddie *are left alone. There is a moment's pause.* Champion-Cheney *looks from* Teddie *to* Elizabeth, *with an ironical smile.*)

C.-C.: Upon my soul, they might be married. They frip so much.

Elizabeth (*frigidly*): It's been nice of you to come here so often since they arrived. It's helped to make things easy.

C.-C.: Irony? It's a rhetorical form not much favoured in this blessed plot, this earth, this realm, this England.

Elizabeth: What exactly are you getting at?

C.-C.: How slangy the young women of the present day are! I suppose the fact that Arnold is a purist leads you to the contrary extravagance.

Elizabeth: Anyhow you know what I mean.

C.-C. (*with a smile*): I have a dim, groping suspicion.

Elizabeth: You promised to keep away. Why did you come back the moment they arrived?

C.-C.: Curiosity, my dear child. A surely pardonable curiosity.

ELIZABETH: And since then you've been here all the time. You don't generally favour us with so much of your company when you're down at your cottage.

C.-C.: I've been excessively amused.

ELIZABETH: It has struck me that whenever they started fripping you took a malicious pleasure in goading them on.

C.-C.: I don't think there's much love lost between them now, do you?

(TEDDIE *is making as though to leave the room.*)

ELIZABETH: Don't go, Teddie.

C.-C.: No, please don't. I'm only staying a minute. We were talking about Lady Kitty just before she arrived. (*to* ELIZABETH) Do you remember? The pale, frail lady in black satin and old lace.

ELIZABETH (*with a chuckle*): You are a devil, you know.

C.-C.: Ah, well, he's always had the reputation of being a humorist and a gentleman.

ELIZABETH: Did *you* expect her to be like that, poor dear?

C.-C.: My dear child, I hadn't the vaguest idea. You were asking me the other day what she was like when she ran away. I didn't tell you half. She was so gay and so natural. Who would have thought that animation would turn into such frivolity, and that charming impulsiveness lead to such a ridiculous affectation?

ELIZABETH: It rather sets my nerves on edge to hear the way you talk of her.

C.-C.: It's the truth that sets your nerves on edge, not I.

ELIZABETH: You loved her once. Have you no feeling for her at all?

C.-C.: None. Why should I?

ELIZABETH: She's the mother of your son.

C.-C.: My dear child, you have a charming nature, as

simple, frank and artless as hers was. Don't let pure humbug obscure your common sense.

ELIZABETH: We have no right to judge. She's only been here two days. We know nothing about her.

C.-C.: My dear, her soul is as thickly rouged as her face. She hasn't an emotion that's sincere. She's tinsel. You think I'm a cruel, cynical old man. Why, when I think of what she was, if I didn't laugh at what she has become I should cry.

ELIZABETH: How do you know she wouldn't be just the same now if she'd remained your wife? Do you think your influence would have had such a salutary effect on her?

C.-C. (*good-humouredly*): I like you when you're bitter and rather insolent.

ELIZABETH: D'you like me enough to answer my question?

C.-C.: She was only twenty-seven when she went away. She might have become anything. She might have become the woman you expected her to be. There are very few of us who are strong enough to make circumstances serve us. We are the creatures of our environment. She's a silly worthless woman because she's led a silly worthless life.

ELIZABETH (*disturbed*): You're horrible today.

C.-C.: I don't say it's I who could have prevented her from becoming this ridiculous caricature of a pretty woman grown old. But life could. Here she would have had the friends fit to her station, and a decent activity, and worthy interests. Ask her what her life has been all these years among divorced women and kept women and the men who consort with them. There is no more lamentable pursuit than a life of pleasure.

ELIZABETH: At all events she loved and she loved greatly. I have only pity and affection for her.

C.-C.: And if she loved what d'you think she felt when she saw that she had ruined Hughie? Look at him. He was tight last night after dinner and tight the night before.

ELIZABETH: I know.

C.-C.: And she took it as a matter of course. How long do you suppose he's been getting tight every night? Do you think he was like that thirty years ago? Can you imagine that that was a brilliant young man, whom every one expected to be Prime Minister? Look at him now. A grumpy sodden old fellow with false teeth.

ELIZABETH: You have false teeth, too.

C.-C.: Yes, but damn it all, they fit. She's ruined him and she knows she's ruined him.

ELIZABETH (*looking at him suspiciously*): Why are you saying all this to me?

C.-C.: Am I hurting your feelings?

ELIZABETH: I think I've had enough for the present.

C.-C.: I'll go and have a look at the gold-fish. I want to see Arnold when he comes in. (*politely*) I'm afraid we've been boring Mr. Luton.

TEDDIE: Not at all.

C.-C.: When are you going back to the F.M.S.?

TEDDIE: In about a month.

C.-C.: I see.

(*He goes out.*)

ELIZABETH: I wonder what he has at the back of his head.

TEDDIE: D'you think he was talking *at* you?

ELIZABETH: He's as clever as a bagful of monkeys.

(*There is a moment's pause.* TEDDIE *hesitates a little, and when he speaks it is in a different tone. He is grave and somewhat nervous.*)

TEDDIE: It seems very difficult to get a few minutes alone with you. I wonder if you've been making it difficult?

ELIZABETH: I wanted to think.

TEDDIE: I've made up my mind to go away tomorrow.

ELIZABETH: You're so arbitrary.

TEDDIE: You said you—you said you cared for me.

ELIZABETH: I do.

TEDDIE: Do you mind if we talk it over now?

ELIZABETH: No.

TEDDIE (*frowning*): It makes me feel rather shy and awkward. I've repeated to myself over and over again exactly what I want to say to you, and now all I'd prepared seems rather footling.

ELIZABETH: I'm so afraid I'm going to cry.

TEDDIE: I feel it's all so tremendously serious and I think we ought to keep emotion out of it. You're rather emotional, aren't you?

ELIZABETH (*half smiling and half in tears*): So are you for the matter of that.

TEDDIE: That's why I wanted to have everything I meant to say to you cut and dried. I think it would be awfully unfair if I made love to you and all that sort of thing, and you were carried away. I wrote it all down and thought I'd send it you as a letter.

ELIZABETH: Why didn't you?

TEDDIE: I got the wind up. A letter seems so—so cold. You see, I love you so awfully.

ELIZABETH: For goodness' sake don't say that.

TEDDIE: You mustn't cry. Please don't, or I shall go all to pieces.

ELIZABETH (*trying to smile*): I'm sorry. It doesn't mean anything really. It's only tears running out of my eyes.

TEDDIE: Our only chance is to be awfully matter-of-fact.

(*He stops for a moment. He finds it quite difficult to control himself. He clears his throat. He frowns with annoyance at himself.*)

ELIZABETH: What's the matter?

TEDDIE: I've got a sort of lump in my throat. It is idiotic. I think I'll have a cigarette.

(*She watches him in silence while he lights a ciga-rette.*)

You see, I've never been in love with anyone before, not really. It's knocked me endways. I don't know how I can live without you now.... Does that old fool know I'm in love with you?

ELIZABETH: I think so.

TEDDIE: When he was talking about Lady Kitty smash-ing up Lord Porteous' career I thought there was some-thing at the back of it.

ELIZABETH: I think he was trying to persuade me not to smash up yours.

TEDDIE: I'm sure that's very considerate of him, but I don't happen to have one to smash. I wish I had. It's the only time in my life I've wished I were a hell of a swell so that I could chuck it all and show you how much more you are to me than anything else in the world.

ELIZABETH (*affectionately*): You're a dear old thing, Teddie.

TEDDIE: You know, I don't really know how to make love, but if I did I couldn't do it now because I just want to be absolutely practical.

ELIZABETH (*chaffing him*): I'm glad you don't know how to make love. It would be almost more than I could bear.

TEDDIE: You see, I'm not at all romantic and that sort of thing. I'm just a common or garden business man. All this is so dreadfully serious and I think we ought to be sensible.

ELIZABETH (*with a break in her voice*): You owl!

TEDDIE: No, Elizabeth, don't say things like that to me. I want you to consider all the *pros* and *cons,* and my heart's thumping against my chest, and you know I love you, I love you, I love you.

ELIZABETH (*in a sigh of passion*): Oh, my precious.

TEDDIE (*impatiently, but with himself, rather than with* ELIZABETH): Don't be idiotic, Elizabeth. I'm not going to tell you that I can't live without you and a lot of muck like that. You know that you mean everything in the world to me. (*almost giving it up as a bad job*) Oh, my God!

ELIZABETH (*her voice faltering*): D'you think there's anything you can say to me that I don't know already?

TEDDIE (*desperately*): But I haven't said a single thing I wanted to. I'm a business man and I want to put it all in a business way, if you understand what I mean.

ELIZABETH (*smiling*): I don't believe you're a very good business man.

TEDDIE (*sharply*): You don't know what you're talking about. I'm a first-rate business man, but somehow this is different. (*hopelessly*) I don't know why it won't go right.

ELIZABETH: What are we going to do about it?

TEDDIE: You see, it's not just because you're awfully pretty that I love you. I'd love you just as much if you were old and ugly. It's you I love, not what you look like. And it's not only love; love be blowed! It's that I *like* you so tremendously. I think you're such a ripping good sort. I just want to be with you. I feel so jolly and happy just to think you're there. I'm so awfully *fond* of you.

ELIZABETH (*laughing through her tears*): I don't know if this is your idea of introducing a business proposition.

TEDDIE: Damn you, you won't let me.

ELIZABETH: You said, Damn you.

TEDDIE: I meant it.

ELIZABETH: Your voice sounded as if you meant, you perfect duck.

TEDDIE: Really, Elizabeth, you're intolerable.

ELIZABETH: I'm doing nothing.

TEDDIE: Yes, you are, you're putting me off my blow. What I want to say is perfectly simple. I'm a very ordinary business man.

ELIZABETH: You've said that before.

TEDDIE (*sharply*): Shut up. I haven't got a bob besides what I earn. I've got no position. I'm nothing. You're rich and you're a big pot and you've got everything that anyone can want. It's awful cheek my saying anything to you at all. But after all there's only one thing that really matters in the world, and that's love. I love you. Chuck all this, Elizabeth, and come to me.

ELIZABETH: Are you cross with me?

TEDDIE: Furious.

ELIZABETH: Darling!

TEDDIE: If you don't want me tell me so at once and let me get out quickly.

ELIZABETH: Teddie, nothing in the world matters anything to me but you. I'll go wherever you take me. I love you.

TEDDIE (*all to pieces*): Oh, my God!

ELIZABETH: Does it mean as much to you as that? Oh, Teddie!

TEDDIE (*trying to control himself*): Don't be a fool, Elizabeth.

ELIZABETH: It's you're the fool. You're making me cry.

TEDDIE: You're so damned emotional.

ELIZABETH: Damned emotional yourself. I'm sure you're a rotten business man.

TEDDIE: I don't care what you think. You've made me so awfully happy. I say, what a lark life's going to be.

ELIZABETH: Teddie, you are an angel.

TEDDIE: Let's get out quick. It's no good wasting time. Elizabeth.

ELIZABETH: What?

TEDDIE: Nothing. I just like to say Elizabeth.

ELIZABETH: You fool.

TEDDIE: I say, can you shoot?

ELIZABETH: No.

TEDDIE: I'll teach you. You don't know how ripping it is to start out from your camp at dawn and travel through the jungle. And you're so tired at night and the sky's all starry. It's a fair treat. Of course I didn't want to say anything about all that till you'd decided. I'd made up my mind to be absolutely practical.

ELIZABETH (*chaffing him*): The only practical thing you said was that love is the only thing that really matters.

TEDDIE (*happily*): Pull the other leg next time, will you? I should hate to have one longer than the other.

ELIZABETH: Isn't it fun being in love with someone who's in love with you?

TEDDIE: I say, I think I'd better clear out at once, don't you? It seems rather rotten to stay on in—in his house.

ELIZABETH: You can't go tonight. There's no train.

TEDDIE: I'll go tomorrow. I'll wait in London till you're ready to join me.

ELIZABETH: I'm not going to leave a note on the pincushion like Lady Kitty, you know. I'm going to tell Arnold.

TEDDIE: Are you? Don't you think there'll be an awful bother?

ELIZABETH: I must face it. I should hate to be sly and deceitful.

TEDDIE: Well, then, let's face it together.

ELIZABETH: No, I'll talk to Arnold by myself.

TEDDIE: You won't let anyone influence you?

ELIZABETH: No.

(*He holds out his hand and she takes it. They look into one another's eyes with grave, almost solemn affection. There is the sound outside of a car driving up.*)

ELIZABETH: There's the car. Arnold's come back. I must go and bathe my eyes. I don't want them to see I've been crying.

TEDDIE: All right. (*as she is going*) Elizabeth.

ELIZABETH (*stopping*): What?

TEDDIE: Bless you.

ELIZABETH (*affectionately*): Idiot!

(*She goes out of the door and* TEDDIE *through the French window into the garden. For an instant the room is empty.* ARNOLD *comes in. He sits down and takes some papers out of his dispatch-case.* LADY KITTY *enters. He gets up.*)

LADY KITTY: I saw you come in. Oh, my dear, don't get up. There's no reason why you should be so dreadfully polite to me.

ARNOLD: I've just rung for a cup of tea.

LADY KITTY: Perhaps we shall have the chance of a little talk. We don't seem to have had five minutes by ourselves. I want to make your acquaintance, you know.

ARNOLD: I should like you to know that it's not by my wish that my father is here.

LADY KITTY: But I'm so interested to see him.

ARNOLD: I was afraid that you and Lord Porteous must find it embarrassing.

LADY KITTY: Oh, no. Hughie was his greatest friend. They were at Eton and Oxford together. I think your father has improved so much since I saw him last. He wasn't goodlooking as a young man, but now he's quite handsome.

(*The* FOOTMAN *brings in a tray on which are tea-things.*)

LADY KITTY: Shall I pour it out for you?

ARNOLD: Thank you very much.

LADY KITTY: Do you take sugar?

ARNOLD: No. I gave it up during the war.

LADY KITTY: So wise of you. It's so bad for the figure. Besides being patriotic, of course. Isn't it absurd that I should ask my son if he takes sugar or not? Life is really very quaint. Sad, of course, but oh, so quaint! Often I lie in bed at night and have a good laugh to myself as I think how quaint life is.

ARNOLD: I'm afraid I'm a very serious person.

LADY KITTY: How old are you now, Arnold?

ARNOLD: Thirty-five.

LADY KITTY: Are you really? Of course, I was a child when I married your father.

ARNOLD: Really. He always told me you were twenty-two.

LADY KITTY: Oh, what nonsense! Why, I was married out of the nursery. I put my hair up for the first time on my wedding-day.

ARNOLD: Where is Lord Porteous?

LADY KITTY: My dear, it sounds too absurd to hear you call him Lord Porteous. Why don't you call him—Uncle Hughie?

ARNOLD: He doesn't happen to be my uncle.

LADY KITTY: No, but he's your godfather. You know, I'm sure you'll like him when you know him better. I'm so hoping that you and Elizabeth will come and stay with us in Florence. I simply adore Elizabeth. She's too beautiful.

ARNOLD: Her hair is very pretty.

LADY KITTY: It's not touched up, is it?

ARNOLD: Oh, no.

LADY KITTY: I just wondered. It's rather a coincidence that her hair should be the same colour as mine. I suppose it shows that your father and you are attracted by just the same thing. So interesting, heredity, isn't it?

ARNOLD: Very.

LADY KITTY: Of course, since I joined the Catholic Church I don't believe in it any more. Darwin and all that sort of thing. Too dreadful. Wicked, you know. Besides, it's not very good form, is it?

(CHAMPION-CHENEY *comes in from the garden.*)

C.-C.: Do I intrude?

LADY KITTY: Come in, Clive. Arnold and I have been having such a wonderful heart-to-heart talk.

C.-C.: Very nice.

ARNOLD: Father, I stepped in for a moment at the Harveys' on my way back. It's simply criminal what they're doing with that house.

C.-C.: What are they doing?

ARNOLD: It's an almost perfect Georgian house and they've got a lot of dreadful Victorian furniture. I gave them my ideas on the subject, but it's quite hopeless. They said they were attached to their furniture.

C.-C.: Arnold should have been an interior decorator.

LADY KITTY: He has wonderful taste. He gets that from me.

ARNOLD: I suppose I have a certain *flair*. I have a passion for decorating houses.

LADY KITTY: You've made this one charming.

C.-C.: D'you remember, we just had chintzes and comfortable chairs when we lived here, Kitty.

LADY KITTY: Perfectly hideous, wasn't it?

C.-C.: In those days gentlemen and ladies were not expected to have taste.

ARNOLD: You know, I've been looking at this chair again. Since Lord Porteous said the legs weren't right I've been very uneasy.

LADY KITTY: He only said that because he was in a bad temper.

C.-C.: His temper seems to me very short these days, Kitty.

LADY KITTY: Oh, it is.

ARNOLD: You feel he knows what he's talking about. I gave seventy-five pounds for that chair. I'm very seldom taken in. I always think if a thing's right you feel it.

C.-C.: Well, don't let it disturb your night's rest.

ARNOLD: But, my dear father, that's just what it does. I had a most horrible dream about it last night.

LADY KITTY: Here is Hughie.

ARNOLD: I'm going to fetch a book I have on Old English furniture. There's an illustration of a chair which is almost identical with this one.

(PORTEOUS *comes in*.)

PORTEOUS: Quite a family gathering, by George!

C.-C.: I was thinking just now we'd make a very pleasing picture of a typical English home.

ARNOLD: I'll be back in five minutes. There's something I want to show you, Lord Porteous.

*(He goes out.)*

C.-C.: Would you like to play piquet with me, Hughie?

Porteous: Not particularly.

C.-C.: You were never much of a piquet player, were you?

Porteous: My dear Clive, you people don't know what piquet is in England.

C.-C.: Let's have a game then. You may make money.

Porteous: I don't want to play with you.

Lady Kitty: I don't know why not, Hughie.

Porteous: Let me tell you that I don't like your manner.

C.-C.: I'm sorry for that. I'm afraid I can't offer to change it at my age.

Porteous: I don't know what you want to be hanging around here for.

C.-C.: A natural attachment to my home.

Porteous: If you'd had any tact you'd have kept out of the way while we were here.

C.-C.: My dear Hughie, I don't understand your attitude at all. If I'm willing to let bygones be bygones why should you object?

Porteous: Damn it all, they're not bygones.

C.-C.: After all, I am the injured party.

Porteous: How the devil are you the injured party?

C.-C.: Well, you did run away with my wife, didn't you?

Lady Kitty: Now, don't let's go into ancient history. I can't see why we shouldn't all be friends.

Porteous: I beg you not to interfere, Kitty.

Lady Kitty: I'm very fond of Clive.

Porteous: You never cared two straws for Clive. You only say that to irritate me.

Lady Kitty: Not at all. I don't see why he shouldn't come and stay with us.

C.-C.: I'd love to. I think Florence in spring-time is delightful. Have you central heating?

PORTEOUS: I never liked you, I don't like you now, and I never shall like you.

C.-C.: How very unfortunate! Because I liked you, I like you now, and I shall continue to like you.

LADY KITTY: There's something very nice about you, Clive.

PORTEOUS: If you think that, why the devil did you leave him?

LADY KITTY: Are you going to reproach me because I loved you? How utterly, utterly, utterly detestable you are!

C.-C.: Now, now, don't quarrel with one another.

LADY KITTY: It's all his fault. I'm the easiest person in the world to live with. But really he'd try the patience of a saint.

C.-C.: Come, come, don't get upset, Kitty. When two people live together there must be a certain amount of give and take.

PORTEOUS: I don't know what the devil you're talking about.

C.-C.: It hasn't escaped my observation that you are a little inclined to frip. Many couples are. I think it's a pity.

PORTEOUS: Would you have the very great kindness to mind your own business?

LADY KITTY: It is his business. He naturally wants me to be happy.

C.-C.: I have the very greatest affection for Kitty.

PORTEOUS: Then why the devil didn't you look after her properly?

C.-C.: My dear Hughie, you were my greatest friend. I trusted you. It may have been rash.

PORTEOUS: It was inexcusable.

LADY KITTY: I don't know what you mean by that, Hughie.

PORTEOUS: Don't, don't, don't try and bully me, Kitty.

LADY KITTY: Oh, I know what you mean.

PORTEOUS: Then why the devil did you say you didn't?

LADY KITTY: When I think that I sacrificed everything for that man! And for thirty years I've had to live in a filthy marble palace with no sanitary conveniences.

C.-C.: D'you mean to say you haven't got a bathroom?

LADY KITTY: I've had to wash in a tub.

C.-C.: My poor Kitty, how you've suffered!

PORTEOUS: Really, Kitty, I'm sick of hearing of the sacrifices you made. I suppose you think I sacrificed nothing. I should have been Prime Minister by now if it hadn't been for you.

LADY KITTY: Nonsense!

PORTEOUS: What do you mean by that? Every one said I should be Prime Minister. Shouldn't I have been Prime Minister, Clive?

C.-C.: It was certainly the general expectation.

PORTEOUS: I was the most promising young man of my day. I was bound to get a seat in the Cabinet at the next election.

LADY KITTY: They'd have found you out just as I've found you out. I'm sick of hearing that I ruined your career. You never had a career to ruin. Prime Minister! You haven't the brain. You haven't the character.

C.-C.: Cheek, push, and a gift of the gab will serve very well instead, you know.

LADY KITTY: Besides, in politics it's not the men that matter. It's the women at the back of them. I could have made Clive a Cabinet Minister if I'd wanted to.

PORTEOUS: Clive?

LADY KITTY: With my beauty, my charm, my force of character, my wit, I could have done anything.

PORTEOUS: Clive was nothing but my political secretary. When I was Prime Minister I might have made him Governor of some Colony or other. Western Australia, say. Out of pure kindliness.

LADY KITTY (*with flashing eyes*): D'you think I would have buried myself in Western Australia? With my beauty? My charm?

PORTEOUS: Or Barbadoes, perhaps.

LADY KITTY (*furiously*): Barbadoes! Barbadoes can go to—Barbadoes.

PORTEOUS: That's all you'd have got.

LADY KITTY: Nonsense! I'd have India.

PORTEOUS: I would never have given you India.

LADY KITTY: You would have given me India.

PORTEOUS: I tell you I wouldn't.

LADY KITTY: The King would have given me India. The nation would have insisted on my having India. I would have been a vice-reine or nothing.

PORTEOUS: I tell you that as long as the interests of the British Empire—Damn it all, my teeth are coming out!

(*He hurries from the room.*)

LADY KITTY: It's too much. I can't bear it any more. I've put up with him for thirty years and now I'm at the end of my tether.

C.-C.: Calm yourself, my dear Kitty.

LADY KITTY: I won't listen to a word. I've quite made up my mind. It's finished, finished, finished. (*with a change of tone*) I was so touched when I heard that you never lived in this house again after I left it.

C.-C.: The cuckoos have always been very plentiful. Their note has a personal application which, I must say, I have found extremely offensive.

LADY KITTY: When I saw that you didn't marry again I couldn't help thinking that you still loved me.

C.-C.: I am one of the few men I know who is able to profit by experience.

LADY KITTY: In the eyes of the Church I am still your wife. The Church is so wise. It knows that in the end a woman always comes back to her first love. Clive, I am willing to return to you.

C.-C.: My dear Kitty, I couldn't take advantage of your momentary vexation with Hughie to let you take a step which I know you would bitterly regret.

LADY KITTY: You've waited for me a long time. For Arnold's sake.

C.-C.: Do you think we really need bother about Arnold? In the last thirty years he's had time to grow used to the situation.

Lady Kitty (*with a little smile*): I think I've sown my wild oats, Clive.

C.-C.: I haven't. I was a good young man, Kitty.

Lady Kitty: I know.

C.-C.: And I'm very glad, because it has enabled me to be a wicked old one.

Lady Kitty: I beg your pardon.

(Arnold *comes in with a large book in his hand.*)

Arnold: I say, I've found the book I was hunting for. Oh, isn't Lord Porteous here?

Lady Kitty: One moment, Arnold. Your father and I are busy.

Arnold: I'm so sorry.

(*He goes out into the garden.*)

Lady Kitty: Explain yourself, Clive.

C.-C.: When you ran away from me, Kitty, I was sore and angry and miserable. But above all I felt a fool.

Lady Kitty: Men are so vain.

C.-C.: But I was a student of history, and presently I reflected that I shared my misfortune with very nearly all the greatest men.

Lady Kitty: I'm a great reader myself. It has always struck me as peculiar.

C.-C.: The explanation is very simple. Women dislike intelligence, and when they find it in their husbands they revenge themselves on them in the only way they can, by making them—well, what you made me.

Lady Kitty: It's ingenious. It may be true.

C.-C.: I felt I had done my duty by society and I determined to devote the rest of my life to my own entertainment. The House of Commons had always bored me excessively and the scandal of our divorce gave me an opportunity to resign my seat. I have been relieved to find that the country got on perfectly well without me.

LADY KITTY: But has love never entered your life?

C.-C.: Tell me frankly, Kitty, don't you think people make a lot of unnecessary fuss about love?

LADY KITTY: It's the most wonderful thing in the world.

C.-C.: You're incorrigible. Do you really think it was worth sacrificing so much for?

LADY KITTY: My dear Clive, I don't mind telling you that if I had my time over again I should be unfaithful to you, but I should not leave you.

C.-C.: For some years I was notoriously the prey of a secret sorrow. But I found so many charming creatures who were anxious to console that in the end it grew rather fatiguing. Out of regard to my health I ceased to frequent the drawing-rooms of Mayfair.

LADY KITTY: And since then?

C.-C.: Since then I have allowed myself the luxury of assisting financially a succession of dear little things, in a somewhat humble sphere, between the ages of twenty and twenty-five.

LADY KITTY: I cannot understand the infatuation of men for young girls. I think they're so dull.

C.-C.: It's a matter of taste. I love old wine, old friends and old books, but I like young women. On their twenty-fifth birthday I give them a diamond ring and tell them they must no longer waste their youth and beauty on an old fogey like me. We have a most affecting scene, my technique on these occasions is perfect, and then I start all over again.

LADY KITTY: You're a wicked old man, Clive.

C.-C.: That's what I told you. But, by George! I'm a happy one.

LADY KITTY: There's only one course open to me now.

C.-C.: What is that?

LADY KITTY (*with a flashing smile*): To go and dress for dinner.

C.-C.: Capital. I will follow your example.

(*As* Lady Kitty *goes out* Elizabeth *comes in.*)

Elizabeth: Where is Arnold?

C.-C.: He's on the terrace. I'll call him.

Elizabeth: Don't bother.

C.-C.: I was just strolling along to my cottage to put on a dinner jacket. (*as he goes out*) Arnold.

(*Exit C.-C.*)

Arnold: Hulloa! (*He comes in.*) Oh, Elizabeth, I've found an illustration here of a chair which is almost identical with mine. It's dated 1750. Look!

Elizabeth: That's very interesting.

Arnold: I want to show it to Porteous. (*moving a chair which has been misplaced*) You know, it does exasperate me the way people will not leave things alone. I no sooner put a thing in its place than somebody moves it.

Elizabeth: It must be maddening for you.

Arnold: It is. You are the worst offender. I can't think why you don't take the pride that I do in the house. After all, it's one of the show places in the county.

Elizabeth: I'm afraid you find me very unsatisfactory.

Arnold (*good-humouredly*): I don't know about that. But my two subjects are politics and decoration. I should be a perfect fool if I didn't see that you don't care two straws about either.

Elizabeth: We haven't very much in common, Arnold, have we?

Arnold: I don't think you can blame me for that.

Elizabeth: I don't. I blame you for nothing. I have no fault to find with you.

Arnold (*surprised at her significant tone*): Good gracious me, what's the meaning of all this?

Elizabeth: Well, I don't think there's any object in beating about the bush. I want you to let me go.

ARNOLD: Go where?

ELIZABETH: Away. For always.

ARNOLD: My dear child, what *are* you talking about?

ELIZABETH: I want to be free.

ARNOLD (*amused rather than disconcerted*): Don't be ridiculous, darling. I daresay you're run down and want a change. I'll take you over to Paris for a fortnight if you like.

ELIZABETH: I shouldn't have spoken to you if I hadn't quite made up my mind. We've been married for three years and I don't think it's been a great success. I'm frankly bored by the life you want me to lead.

ARNOLD: Well, if you'll allow me to say so, the fault is yours. We lead a very distinguished, useful life. We know a lot of extremely nice people.

ELIZABETH: I'm quite willing to allow that the fault is mine. But how does that make it any better? I'm only twenty-five. If I've made a mistake I have time to correct it.

ARNOLD: I can't bring myself to take you very seriously.

ELIZABETH: You see, I don't love you.

ARNOLD: Well, I'm awfully sorry. But you weren't obliged to marry me. You've made your bed and I'm afraid you must lie on it.

ELIZABETH: That's one of the falsest proverbs in the English language. Why should you lie on the bed you've made if you don't want to? There's always the floor.

ARNOLD: For goodness' sake don't be funny, Elizabeth.

ELIZABETH: I've quite made up my mind to leave you, Arnold.

ARNOLD: Come, come, Elizabeth, you must be sensible. You haven't any reason to leave me.

ELIZABETH: Why should you wish to keep a woman tied to you who wants to be free?

ARNOLD: I happen to be in love with you.

ELIZABETH: You might have said that before.

ARNOLD: I thought you'd take it for granted. You can't expect a man to go on making love to his wife after three

years. I'm very busy. I'm awfully keen on politics and
I've worked like a dog to make this house a thing of
beauty. After all, a man marries to have a home, but also
because he doesn't want to be bothered with sex and all
that sort of thing. I fell in love with you the first time I
saw you and I've been in love ever since.

Elizabeth: I'm sorry, but if you're not in love with a
man his love doesn't mean very much to you.

Arnold: It's so ungrateful. I've done everything in the
world for you.

Elizabeth: You've been very kind to me. But you've
asked me to lead a life I don't like and that I'm not
suited for. I'm awfully sorry to cause you pain, but now
you must let me go.

Arnold: Nonsense! I'm a good deal older than you are
and I think I have a little more sense. In your interest as
well as in mine I'm not going to do anything of the sort.

Elizabeth (*with a smile*): How can you prevent me?
You can't keep me under lock and key.

Arnold: Please don't talk to me as if I were a foolish
child. You're my wife and you're going to remain my
wife.

Elizabeth: What sort of a life do you think we should
lead? Do you think there'd be any more happiness for
you than for me?

Arnold: But what is it precisely that you suggest?

Elizabeth: Well, I want you to let me divorce you.

Arnold (*astounded*): Me? Thank you very much. Are
you under the impression I'm going to sacrifice my
career for a whim of yours?

Elizabeth: How will it do that?

Arnold: My seat's wobbly enough as it is. Do you
think I'd be able to hold it if I were in a divorce case?
Even if it were a put-up job, as most divorces are
nowadays, it would damn me.

Elizabeth: It's rather hard on a woman to be divorced.

Arnold (*with sudden suspicion*): What do you mean
by that? Are you in love with someone?

ELIZABETH: Yes.
ARNOLD: Who?
ELIZABETH: Teddie Luton.

(*He is astonished for a moment, then bursts into a laugh.*)

ARNOLD: My poor child, how can you be so ridiculous? Why, he hasn't a bob. He's a perfectly commonplace young man. It's so absurd I can't even be angry with you.

ELIZABETH: I've fallen desperately in love with him, Arnold.

ARNOLD: Well, you'd better fall desperately out.

ELIZABETH: He wants to marry me.

ARNOLD: I daresay he does. He can go to hell.

ELIZABETH: It's no good talking like that.

ARNOLD: Is he your lover?

ELIZABETH: No, certainly not.

ARNOLD: It shows that he's a mean skunk to take advantage of my hospitality to make love to you.

ELIZABETH: He's never even kissed me.

ARNOLD: I'd try telling that to the horse marines if I were you.

ELIZABETH: It's because I wanted to do nothing shabby that I told you straight out how things were.

ARNOLD: How long have you been thinking of this?

ELIZABETH: I've been in love with Teddie ever since I knew him.

ARNOLD: And you never thought of me at all, I suppose.

ELIZABETH: Oh, yes, I did. I was miserable. But I can't help myself. I wish I loved you, but I don't.

ARNOLD: I recommend you to think very carefully before you do anything foolish.

ELIZABETH: I have thought very carefully.

ARNOLD: By God, I don't know why I don't give you a sound hiding. I'm not sure if that wouldn't be the best thing to bring you to your senses.

ELIZABETH: Oh, Arnold, don't take it like that.

ARNOLD: How do you expect me to take it? You come to me quite calmly and say: "I've had enough of you. We've been married three years and I think I'd like to marry somebody else now. Shall I break up your home? What a bore for you! Do you mind my divorcing you? It'll smash up your career, will it? What a pity!" Oh, no, my girl, I may be a fool, but I'm not a damned fool.

ELIZABETH: Teddie is leaving here by the first train tomorrow. I warn you that I mean to join him as soon as he can make the necessary arrangements.

ARNOLD: Where is he?

ELIZABETH: I don't know. I suppose he's in his room.

(ARNOLD *goes to the door and calls.*)

ARNOLD: George!

(*For a moment he walks up and down the room impatiently.* ELIZABETH *watches him. The* FOOTMAN *comes in.*)

FOOTMAN: Yes, sir.

ARNOLD: Tell Mr. Luton to come here at once.

ELIZABETH: Ask Mr. Luton if he wouldn't mind coming here for a moment.

(*Exit* FOOTMAN.)

ELIZABETH: What are you going to say to him?

ARNOLD: That's my business.

ELIZABETH: I wouldn't make a scene if I were you.

ARNOLD: I'm not going to make a scene.

(*They wait in silence.*)

Why did you insist on my mother coming here?

ELIZABETH: It seemed to me rather absurd to take up

the attitude that I should be contaminated by her when . . .

ARNOLD (*interrupting*): When you were proposing to do exactly the same thing. Well, now you've seen her what do you think of her? Do you think it's been a success? Is that the sort of woman a man would like his mother to be?

ELIZABETH: I've been ashamed. I've been so sorry. It all seemed dreadful and horrible. This morning I happened to notice a rose in the garden. It was all overblown and bedraggled. It looked like a painted old woman. And I remembered that I'd looked at it a day or two ago. It was lovely then, fresh and blooming and fragrant. It may be hideous now, but that doesn't take away from the beauty it had once. That was real.

ARNOLD: Poetry, by God! As if this were the moment for poetry!

(TEDDIE *comes in. He has changed into a dinner jacket.*)

TEDDIE (*to* ELIZABETH): Did you want me?
ARNOLD: *I* sent for you.

(TEDDIE *looks from* ARNOLD *to* ELIZABETH. *He sees that something has happened.*)

When would it be convenient for you to leave this house?

TEDDIE: I was proposing to go tomorrow morning. But I can very well go at once if you like.

ARNOLD: I do like.

TEDDIE: Very well. Is there anything else you wish to say to me?

ARNOLD: Do you think it was a very honourable thing to come down here and make love to my wife?

TEDDIE: No, I don't. I haven't been very happy about it. That's why I wanted to go away.

ARNOLD: Upon my word you're cool.

TEDDIE: I'm afraid it's no good saying I'm sorry and that sort of thing. You know what the situation is.

ARNOLD: Is it true that you want to marry Elizabeth?

TEDDIE: Yes. I should like to marry her as soon as ever I can.

ARNOLD: Have you thought of me at all? Has it struck you that you're destroying my home and breaking up my happiness?

TEDDIE: I don't see how there could be much happiness for you if Elizabeth doesn't care for you.

ARNOLD: Let me tell you that I refuse to have my home broken up by a twopenny-halfpenny adventurer who takes advantage of a foolish woman. I refuse to allow myself to be divorced. I can't prevent my wife from going off with you if she's determined to make a damned fool of herself, but this I tell you: nothing will induce me to divorce her.

ELIZABETH: Arnold, that would be monstrous.

TEDDIE: We could force you.

ARNOLD: How?

TEDDIE: If we went away together openly you'd have to bring an action.

ARNOLD: Twenty-four hours after you leave this house I shall go down to Brighton with a chorus-girl. And neither you nor I will be able to get a divorce. We've had enough divorces in our family. And now get out, get out, get out!

(TEDDIE *looks uncertainly at* ELIZABETH.)

ELIZABETH (*with a little smile*): Don't bother about me. I shall be all right.

ARNOLD: Get out! Get out!

# ACT THREE

SCENE: *The same.*

*It is the night of the same day as that on which takes place the action of the second act.*

CHAMPION-CHENEY *and* ARNOLD, *both in dinner jackets, are discovered.* CHAMPION-CHENEY *is seated.* ARNOLD *walks restlessly up and down the room.*

C.-C.: I think, if you'll follow my advice to the letter, you'll probably work the trick.

ARNOLD: I don't like it, you know. It's against all my principles.

C.-C.: My dear Arnold, we all hope that you have before you a distinguished political career. You can't learn too soon that the most useful thing about a principle is that it can always be sacrificed to expediency.

ARNOLD: But supposing it doesn't come off? Women are incalculable.

C.-C.: Nonsense! Men are romantic. A woman will always sacrifice herself if you give her the opportunity. It is her favourite form of self-indulgence.

ARNOLD: I never know whether you're a humorist or a cynic, father.

C.-C.: I'm neither, my dear boy; I'm merely a very truthful man. But people are so unused to the truth that they're apt to mistake it for a joke or a sneer.

59

Arnold (*irritably*): It seems so unfair that this should happen to me.

C.-C.: Keep your head, my boy, and do what I tell you.

(Lady Kitty *and* Elizabeth *come in.* Lady Kitty *is in a gorgeous evening gown.*)

Elizabeth: Where is Lord Porteous?

C.-C.: He's on the terrace. He's smoking a cigar. (*going to window*) Hughie!

(Porteous *comes in.*)

Porteous (*with a grunt*): Yes? Where's Mrs. Shenstone?

Elizabeth: Oh, she had a headache. She's gone to bed.

(*When* Porteous *comes in* Lady Kitty *with a very haughty air purses her lips and takes up an illustrated paper.* Porteous *gives her an irritated look, takes another illustrated paper and sits himself down at the other end of the room. They are not on speaking terms.*)

C.-C.: Arnold and I have just been down to my cottage.

Elizabeth: I wondered where you'd gone.

C.-C.: I came across an old photograph album this afternoon. I meant to bring it along before dinner, but I forgot, so we went and fetched it.

Elizabeth: Oh, do let me see it. I love old photographs.

(*He gives her the album, and she, sitting down, puts it on her knees and begins to turn over the pages. He stands over her.* Lady Kitty *and* Porteous *take surreptitious glances at one another.*)

C.-C.: I thought it might amuse you to see what pretty women looked like five-and-thirty years ago. That was the day of beautiful women.

ELIZABETH: Do you think they were more beautiful then than they are now?

C.-C.: Oh, much. Now you see lots of pretty little things, but very few beautiful women.

ELIZABETH: Aren't their clothes funny?

C.-C. (*pointing to a photograph*): That's Mrs. Langtry.

ELIZABETH: She has a lovely nose.

C.-C.: She was the most wonderful thing you ever saw. Dowagers used to jump on chairs in order to get a good look at her when she came into a drawing-room. I was riding with her once, and we had to have the gates of the livery stable closed when she was getting on her horse because the crowd was so great.

ELIZABETH: And who's that?

C.-C.: Lady Lonsdale. That's Lady Dudley.

ELIZABETH: This is an actress, isn't it?

C.-C.: It is, indeed. Ellen Terry. By George, how I loved that woman!

ELIZABETH (*with a smile*): Dear Ellen Terry!

C.-C.: That's Bwabs. I never saw a smarter man in my life. And Oliver Montagu. Henry Manners with his eyeglass.

ELIZABETH: Nice-looking, isn't he? And this?

C.-C.: That's Mary Anderson. I wish you could have seen her in A Winter's Tale. Her beauty just took your breath away. And look! There's Lady Randolph. Bernal Osborne—the wittiest man I ever knew.

ELIZABETH: I think it's too sweet. I love their absurd bustles and those tight sleeves.

C.-C.: What figures they had! In those days a woman wasn't supposed to be as thin as a rail and as flat as a pancake.

ELIZABETH: Oh, but aren't they laced in? How could they bear it?

C.-C.: They didn't play golf then, and nonsense like

that, you know. They hunted, in a tall hat and a long black habit, and they were very gracious and charitable to the poor in the village.

ELIZABETH: Did the poor like it?

C.-C.: They had a very thin time if they didn't. When they were in London they drove in the Park every afternoon, and they went to ten-course dinners, where they never met anybody they didn't know. And they had their box at the opera when Patti was singing or Madame Albani.

ELIZABETH: Oh, what a lovely little thing! Who on earth is that?

C.-C.: That?

ELIZABETH: She looks so fragile, like a piece of exquisite china, with all those furs on and her face up against her muff, and the snow falling.

C.-C.: Yes, there was quite a rage at that time for being taken in an artificial snowstorm.

ELIZABETH: What a sweet smile, so roguish and frank, and debonair! Oh, I wish I looked like that. Do tell me who it is.

C.-C.: Don't you know?

ELIZABETH: No.

C.-C.: Why—it's Kitty.

ELIZABETH: Lady Kitty! (*to* LADY KITTY) Oh, my dear, do look. It's too ravishing. (*She takes the album over to her impulsively.*) Why didn't you tell me you looked like that? Everybody must have been in love with you.

(LADY KITTY *takes the album and looks at it. Then she lets it slip from her hands and covers her face with her hands. She is crying.*)

(*in consternation*) My dear, what's the matter? Oh, what have I done? I'm so sorry.

LADY KITTY: Don't, don't talk to me. Leave me alone. It's stupid of me.

(ELIZABETH *looks at her for a moment perplexed,*

*then, turning round, slips her arm in* CHAMPION-CHENEY'S *and leads him out on to the terrace.*)

ELIZABETH (*as they are going, in a whisper*): Did you do that on purpose?

(PORTEOUS *gets up and goes over to* LADY KITTY. *He puts his hand on her shoulder. They remain thus for a little while.*)

PORTEOUS: I'm afraid I was very rude to you before dinner, Kitty.

LADY KITTY (*taking his hand which is on her shoulder*): It doesn't matter. I'm sure I was very exasperating.

PORTEOUS: I didn't mean what I said, you know.

LADY KITTY: Neither did I.

PORTEOUS: Of course I know that I'd never have been Prime Minister.

LADY KITTY: How can you talk such nonsense, Hughie? No one would have had a chance if you'd remained in politics.

PORTEOUS: I haven't the character.

LADY KITTY: You have more character than anyone I've ever met.

PORTEOUS: Besides, I don't know that I much wanted to be Prime Minister.

LADY KITTY: Oh, but I should have been so proud of you. Of course you'd have been Prime Minister.

PORTEOUS: I'd have given you India, you know. I think it would have been a very popular appointment.

LADY KITTY: I don't care twopence about India. I'd have been quite content with Western Australia.

PORTEOUS: My dear, you don't think I'd have let you bury yourself in Western Australia?

LADY KITTY: Or Barbadoes.

PORTEOUS: Never. It sounds like a cure for flat feet. I'd have kept you in London.

(*He picks up the album and is about to look at the photograph of* Lady Kitty. *She puts her hand over it.*)

Lady Kitty: No, don't look.

(*He takes her hand away.*)

Porteous: Don't be so silly.

Lady Kitty: Isn't it hateful to grow old?

Porteous: You know, you haven't changed much.

Lady Kitty (*enchanted*): Oh, Hughie, how can you talk such nonsense?

Porteous: Of course you're a little more mature, but that's all. A woman's all the better for being rather mature.

Lady Kitty: Do you really think that?

Porteous: Upon my soul I do.

Lady Kitty: You're not saying it just to please me?

Porteous: No, no.

Lady Kitty: Let me look at the photograph again.

(*She takes the album and looks at the photograph complacently.*)

The fact is, if your bones are good, age doesn't really matter. You'll always be beautiful.

Porteous (*with a little smile, almost as if he were talking to a child*): It was silly of you to cry.

Lady Kitty: It hasn't made my eyelashes run, has it?

Porteous: Not a bit.

Lady Kitty: It's very good stuff I use now. They don't stick together either.

Porteous: Look here, Kitty, how much longer do you want to stay here?

Lady Kitty: Oh, I'm quite ready to go whenever you like.

Porteous: Clive gets on my nerves. I don't like the way he keeps hanging about you.

LADY KITTY (*surprised, rather amused, and delighted*):
Hughie, you don't mean to say you're jealous of poor
Clive?

PORTEOUS: Of course I'm not jealous of him, but he
does look at you in a way that I can't help thinking
rather objectionable.

LADY KITTY: Hughie, you may throw me downstairs
like Amy Robsart; you may drag me about the floor by
the hair of my head; I don't care, you're jealous. I shall
never grow old.

PORTEOUS: Damn it all, the man was your husband.

LADY KITTY: My dear Hughie, he never had your style.
Why, the moment you come into a room everyone looks
and says, Who the devil is that?

PORTEOUS: What? You think that, do you? Well, I
daresay there's something in what you say. These
damned Radicals can say what they like, but, by God,
Kitty, when a man's a gentleman—well, damn it all, you
know what I mean.

LADY KITTY: I think Clive has degenerated dreadfully
since we left him.

PORTEOUS: What do you say to making a bee line for
Italy and going to San Michele?

LADY KITTY: Oh, Hughie! It's years since we were
there.

PORTEOUS: Wouldn't you like to see it again—just once
more?

LADY KITTY: Do you remember the first time we went?
It was the most heavenly place I'd ever seen. We'd only
left England a month, and I said I'd like to spend all my
life there.

PORTEOUS: Of course, I remember. And in a fortnight it
was yours, lock, stock and barrel.

LADY KITTY: We were very happy there, Hughie.

PORTEOUS: Let's go back once more.

LADY KITTY: I daren't. It must be all peopled with the
ghosts of our past. One should never go again to a place
where one has been happy. It would break my heart.

PORTEOUS: Do you remember how we used to sit on

the terrace of the old castle and look at the Adriatic? We
might have been the only people in the world, you and I,
Kitty.

LADY KITTY (*tragically*): And we thought our love
would last for ever.

(*Enter* CHAMPION-CHENEY.)

PORTEOUS: Is there any chance of bridge this evening?

C.-C.: I don't think we can make up a four.

PORTEOUS: What a nuisance that boy went away like
that! He wasn't a bad player.

C.-C.: Teddie Luton?

LADY KITTY: I think it was very funny his going
without saying good-bye to anyone.

C.-C.: The young men of the present day are very
casual.

PORTEOUS: I thought there was no train in the evening.

C.-C.: There isn't. The last train leaves at 5:45.

PORTEOUS: How did he go then?

C.-C.: He went.

PORTEOUS: Damned selfish I call it.

LADY KITTY (*intrigued*): Why did he go, Clive?

(CHAMPION-CHENEY *looks at her for a moment reflectively.*)

C.-C.: I have something very grave to say to you.
Elizabeth wants to leave Arnold.

LADY KITTY: Clive! What on earth for?

C.-C.: She's in love with Teddie Luton. That's why he
went. The men of my family are really very unfortunate.

PORTEOUS: Does she want to run away with him?

LADY KITTY (*with consternation*): My dear, what's to
be done?

C.-C.: I think you can do a great deal.

LADY KITTY: I? What?

C.-C.: Tell her, tell her what it means.

(*He looks at her fixedly. She stares at him.*)

LADY KITTY: Oh, no, no!

C.-C.: She's a child. Not for Arnold's sake. For her sake. You must.

LADY KITTY: You don't know what you're asking.

C.-C.: Yes, I do.

LADY KITTY: Hughie, what shall I do?

PORTEOUS: Do what you like. I shall never blame you for anything.

(*The* FOOTMAN *comes in with a letter on a salver. He hesitates on seeing that* ELIZABETH *is not in the room.*)

C.-C.: What is it?

FOOTMAN: I was looking for Mrs. Champion-Cheney, sir.

C.-C.: She's not here. Is that a letter?

FOOTMAN: Yes, sir. It's just been sent up from The Champion Arms.

C.-C.: Leave it. I'll give it to Mrs. Cheney.

FOOTMAN: Very good, sir.

(*He brings the tray to* CLIVE, *who takes the letter. The* FOOTMAN *goes out.*)

PORTEOUS: Is The Champion Arms the local pub?

C.-C. (*looking at the letter*): It's by way of being a hotel, but I never heard of anyone staying there.

LADY KITTY: If there was no train I suppose he had to go there.

C.-C.: Great minds. I wonder what he has to write about. (*He goes to the door leading on to the garden.*) Elizabeth.

ELIZABETH (*outside*): Yes.

C.-C.: Here's a note for you.

(*There is silence. They wait for* Elizabeth *to come.
She enters.*)

Elizabeth: It's lovely in the garden tonight.
C.-C.: They've just sent this up from The Champion
Arms.
Elizabeth: Thank you.

(*Without embarrassment she opens the letter. They
watch her while she reads it. It covers three pages.
She puts it away in her bag.*)

Lady Kitty: Hughie, I wish you'd fetch me a cloak. I'd
like to take a little stroll in the garden, but after thirty
years in Italy I find these English summers rather chilly.

(*Without a word* Porteous *goes out.* Elizabeth *is
lost in thought.*)

I want to talk to Elizabeth, Clive.
C.-C.: I'll leave you.

(*He goes out.*)

Lady Kitty: What does he say?
Elizabeth: Who?
Lady Kitty: Mr. Luton.
Elizabeth (*gives a little start. Then she looks at* Lady
Kitty.): They've told you?
Lady Kitty: Yes. And now they have I think I knew it
all along.
Elizabeth: I don't expect you to have much sympathy
for me. Arnold is your son.
Lady Kitty: So pitifully little.
Elizabeth: I'm not suited for this sort of existence.
Arnold wants me to take what he calls my place in
Society. Oh, I get so bored with those parties in London.
All those middle-aged painted women, in beautiful
clothes, lolloping round ball-rooms with rather old young

men. And the endless luncheons where they gossip about so-and-so's love affairs.

LADY KITTY: Are you very much in love with Mr. Luton?

ELIZABETH: I love him with all my heart.

LADY KITTY: And he?

ELIZABETH: He's never cared for anyone but me. He never will.

LADY KITTY: Will Arnold let you divorce him?

ELIZABETH: No, he won't hear of it. He refuses even to divorce me.

LADY KITTY: Why?

ELIZABETH: He thinks a scandal will revive all the old gossip.

LADY KITTY: Oh, my poor child.

ELIZABETH: It can't be helped. I'm quite willing to accept the consequences.

LADY KITTY: You don't know what it is to have a man tied to you only by his honour. When married people don't get on they can separate, but if they're not married it's impossible. It's a tie that only death can sever.

ELIZABETH: If Teddie stopped caring for me I shouldn't want him to stay with me for five minutes.

LADY KITTY: One says that when one's sure of a man's love, but when one isn't any more—oh, it's so different. In those circumstances one's got to keep a man's love. It's the only thing one has.

ELIZABETH: I'm a human being. I can stand on my own feet.

LADY KITTY: Have you any money of your own?

ELIZABETH: None.

LADY KITTY: Then how can you stand on your own feet? You think I'm a silly, frivolous woman, but I've learnt something in a bitter school. They can make what laws they like, they can give us the suffrage, but when you come down to bedrock it's the man who pays the piper who calls the tune. Women will only be the equal of man when she earns her living in the same way that he does.

ELIZABETH (*smiling*): It sounds rather funny to hear you talk like that.

LADY KITTY: A cook who marries a butler can snap her fingers in his face because she can earn just as much as he can. But a woman in your position and a woman in mine will always be dependent on the men who keep them.

ELIZABETH: I don't want luxury. You don't know how sick I am of all this beautiful furniture. These over-decorated houses are like a prison in which I can't breathe. When I drive about in a Callot frock and a Rolls-Royce I envy the shop-girl in a coat and skirt whom I see jumping on the tailboard of a bus.

LADY KITTY: You mean that if need be you could earn your own living?

ELIZABETH: Yes.

LADY KITTY: What could you be? A nurse or a typist. It's nonsense. Luxury saps a woman's nerve. And when she's known it once it becomes a necessity.

ELIZABETH: That depends on the woman.

LADY KITTY: When we're young we think we're different from everyone else, but when we grow a little older we discover we're all very much of a muchness.

ELIZABETH: You're very kind to take so much trouble about me.

LADY KITTY: It breaks my heart to think that you're going to make the same pitiful mistake that I made.

ELIZABETH: Oh, don't say it was that, don't, don't.

LADY KITTY: Look at me, Elizabeth, and look at Hughie. Do you think it's been a success? If I had my time over again do you think I'd do it again? Do you think he would?

ELIZABETH: You see, you don't know how much I love Teddie.

LADY KITTY: And do you think I didn't love Hughie? Do you think he didn't love me?

ELIZABETH: I'm sure he did.

LADY KITTY: Oh, of course in the beginning it was heavenly. We felt so brave and adventurous and we were so much in love. The first two years were wonderful. People cut me, you know, but I didn't mind. I thought love was everything. It *is* a little uncomfortable when you come upon an old friend and go towards her eagerly, so glad to see her, and are met with an icy stare.

ELIZABETH: Do you think friends like that are worth having?

LADY KITTY: Perhaps they're not very sure of themselves. Perhaps they're honestly shocked. It's a test one had better not put one's friends to if one can help it. It's rather bitter to find how few one has.

ELIZABETH: But one has some.

LADY KITTY: Yes, they ask you to come and see them when they're quite certain no one will be there who might object to meeting you. Or else they say to you, My dear, you know I'm devoted to you, and I wouldn't mind at all, but my girl's growing up—I'm sure you understand; you won't think it unkind of me if I don't ask you to the house?

ELIZABETH (*smiling*): That doesn't seem to me very serious.

LADY KITTY: At first I thought it rather a relief, because it threw Hughie and me together more. But you know, men are very funny. Even when they are in love they're not in love all day long. They want change and recreation.

ELIZABETH: I'm not inclined to blame them for that, poor dears.

LADY KITTY: Then we settled in Florence. And because we couldn't get the society we'd been used to, we became used to the society we could get. Loose women and vicious men. Snobs who liked to patronize people with a handle to their names. Vague Italian princes who were glad to borrow a few francs from Hughie and seedy countesses who liked to drive with me in the Cascine. And then Hughie began to hanker after his old life. He wanted to go big game shooting, but I dared not let him go. I was afraid he'd never come back.

ELIZABETH: But you knew he loved you.

Lady Kitty: Oh, my dear, what a blessed institution marriage is—for women, and what fools they are to meddle with it! The Church is so wise to take its stand on the indi—indi—

Elizabeth: Solu—

Lady Kitty: Bility of marriage. Believe me, it's no joke when you have to rely only on yourself to keep a man. I could never afford to grow old. My dear, I'll tell you a secret that I've never told a living soul.

Elizabeth: What is that?

Lady Kitty: My hair is not naturally this colour.

Elizabeth: Really.

Lady Kitty: I touch it up. You would never have guessed, would you?

Elizabeth: Never.

Lady Kitty: Nobody does. My dear, it's white, prematurely of course, but white. I always think it's a symbol of my life. Are you interested in symbolism? I think it's too wonderful.

Elizabeth: I don't think I know very much about it.

Lady Kitty: However tired I've been I've had to be brilliant and gay. I've never let Hughie see the aching heart behind my smiling eyes.

Elizabeth (*amused and touched*): You poor dear.

Lady Kitty: And when I saw he was attracted by someone else the fear and the jealousy that seized me! You see, I didn't dare make a scene as I should have done if I'd been married. I had to pretend not to notice.

Elizabeth (*taken aback*): But do you mean to say he fell in love with anyone else?

Lady Kitty: Of course he did eventually.

Elizabeth (*hardly knowing what to say*): You must have been very unhappy.

Lady Kitty: Oh, I was, dreadfully. Night after night I sobbed my heart out when Hughie told me he was going to play cards at the club and I knew he was with that odious woman. Of course, it wasn't as if there weren't plenty of men who were only too anxious to console me. Men have always been attracted by me, you know.

ELIZABETH: Oh, of course, I can quite understand it.

LADY KITTY: But I had my self-respect to think of. I felt that whatever Hughie did I would do nothing that I should regret.

ELIZABETH: You must be very glad now.

LADY KITTY: Oh, yes. Notwithstanding all my temptations I've been absolutely faithful to Hughie in spirit.

ELIZABETH: I don't think I quite understand what you mean.

LADY KITTY: Well, there was a poor Italian boy, young Count Castel Giovanni, who was so desperately in love with me that his mother begged me not to be too cruel. She was afraid he'd go into a consumption. What could I do? And then, oh, years later, there was Antonio Melita. He said he'd shoot himself unless I—well, you understand I couldn't let the poor boy shoot himself.

ELIZABETH: D'you think he really would have shot himself?

LADY KITTY: Oh, one never knows, you know. Those Italians are so passionate. He was really rather a lamb. He had such beautiful eyes.

(ELIZABETH *looks at her for a long time and a certain horror seizes her of this dissolute, painted old woman.*)

ELIZABETH (*hoarsely*): Oh, but I think that's—dreadful.

LADY KITTY: Are you shocked? One sacrifices one's life for love and then one finds that love doesn't last. The tragedy of love isn't death or separation. One gets over them. The tragedy of love is indifference.

(ARNOLD *comes in.*)

ARNOLD: Can I have a little talk with you, Elizabeth?

ELIZABETH: Of course.

ARNOLD: Shall we go for a stroll in the garden?

ELIZABETH: If you like.

LADY KITTY: No, stay here. I'm going out anyway.

(*Exit* LADY KITTY).

ARNOLD: I want you to listen to me for a few minutes, Elizabeth. I was so taken aback by what you told me just now that I lost my head. I was rather absurd and I beg your pardon. I said things I regret.

ELIZABETH: Oh, don't blame yourself. I'm sorry that I should have given you occasion to say them.

ARNOLD: I want to ask you if you've quite made up your mind to go.

ELIZABETH: Quite.

ARNOLD: Just now I seem to have said all that I didn't want to say and nothing that I did. I'm stupid and tongue-tied. I never told you how deeply I loved you.

ELIZABETH: Oh, Arnold.

ARNOLD: Please let me speak now. It's so very difficult. If I seemed absorbed in politics and the house, and so on, to the exclusion of my interest in you, I'm dreadfully sorry. I suppose it was absurd of me to think you would take my great love for granted.

ELIZABETH: But, Arnold, I'm not reproaching you.

ARNOLD: I'm reproaching myself. I've been tactless and neglectful. But I do ask you to believe that it hasn't been because I didn't love you. Can you forgive me?

ELIZABETH: I don't think that there's anything to forgive.

ARNOLD: I'm so proud of you. I admire you so much. When I see you at a party, so fresh and lovely, and everybody wondering at you, I have a sort of little thrill because you're mine, and afterwards I shall take you home.

ELIZABETH: Oh, Arnold, you're exaggerating.

ARNOLD: I can't imagine this house without you. Life seems on a sudden all empty and meaningless. Oh, Elizabeth, don't you love me at all?

ELIZABETH: It's much better to be honest. No.

ARNOLD: Doesn't my love mean anything to you?

ELIZABETH: I'm very grateful to you. I'm sorry to cause you pain. What would be the good of my staying with you when I should be wretched all the time?

ARNOLD: Do you love that man as much as all that? Does my unhappiness mean nothing to you?

ELIZABETH: Of course it does. It breaks my heart. You see, I never knew I meant so much to you. I'm so touched. And I'm so sorry, Arnold, really sorry. But I can't help myself.

ARNOLD: Poor child, it's cruel of me to torture you.

ELIZABETH: Oh, Arnold, believe me, I have tried to make the best of it. I've tried to love you, but I can't. After all, one either loves or one doesn't. Trying is no help. And now I'm at the end of my tether. I can't help the consequences—I must do what my whole self yearns for.

ARNOLD: My poor child, I'm so afraid you'll be unhappy. I'm so afraid you'll regret.

ELIZABETH: You must leave me to my fate. I hope you'll forget me and all the unhappiness I've caused you.

ARNOLD (*There is a pause. Arnold walks up and down the room reflectively. He stops and faces her.*): If you love this man and want to go to him I'll do nothing to prevent you. My only wish is to do what is best for you.

ELIZABETH: Arnold, that's awfully kind of you. If I'm treating you badly at least I want you to know that I'm grateful for all your kindness to me.

ARNOLD: But there's one favour I should like you to do me. Will you?

ELIZABETH: Oh, Arnold, of course I'll do anything I can.

ARNOLD: Teddie hasn't very much money. You've been used to a certain amount of luxury, and I can't bear to think that you should do without anything you've had. It would kill me to think that you were suffering any hardship or privation.

ELIZABETH: Oh, but Teddie can earn enough for our needs. After all, we don't want much money.

ARNOLD: I'm afraid my mother's life hasn't been very

easy, but it's obvious that the only thing that's made it possible is that Porteous was rich. I want you to let me make you an allowance of two thousand a year.

Elizabeth: Oh, no, I couldn't think of it. It's absurd.

Arnold: I beg you to accept it. You don't know what a difference it will make.

Elizabeth: It's awfully kind of you, Arnold. It humiliates me to speak about it. Nothing would induce me to take a penny from you.

Arnold: Well, you can't prevent me from opening an account at my bank in your name. The money shall be paid in every quarter whether you touch it or not, and if you happen to want it, it will be there waiting for you.

Elizabeth: You overwhelm me, Arnold. There's only one thing I want you to do for me. I should be very grateful if you would divorce me as soon as you possibly can.

Arnold: No, I won't do that. But I'll give you cause to divorce me.

Elizabeth: You!

Arnold: Yes. But of course you'll have to be very careful for a bit. I'll put it through as quickly as possible, but I'm afraid you can't hope to be free for over six months.

Elizabeth: But, Arnold, your seat and your political career!

Arnold: Oh, well, my father gave up his seat under similar circumstances. He's got along very comfortably without politics.

Elizabeth: But they're your whole life.

Arnold: After all one can't have it both ways. You can't serve God and Mammon. If you want to do the decent thing you have to be prepared to suffer for it.

Elizabeth: But I don't want you to suffer for it.

Arnold: At first I rather hesitated at the scandal. But I daresay that was only weakness on my part. In the circumstances I should have liked to keep out of the Divorce Court if I could.

ELIZABETH: Arnold, you're making me absolutely miserable.

ARNOLD: What you said before dinner was quite right. It's nothing for a man, but it makes so much difference to a woman. Naturally I must think of you first.

ELIZABETH: That's absurd. It's out of the question. Whatever there's to pay I must pay it.

ARNOLD: It's not very much I'm asking for, Elizabeth.

ELIZABETH: I'm taking everything from you.

ARNOLD: It's the only condition I make. My mind is absolutely made up. I will never divorce you, but I will enable you to divorce me.

ELIZABETH: Oh, Arnold, it's cruel to be so generous.

ARNOLD: It's not generous at all. It's the only way I have of showing you how deep and passionate and sincere my love is for you.

(*There is silence. He holds out his hand.*)

Good-night. I have a great deal of work to do before I go to bed.

ELIZABETH: Good-night.

ARNOLD: Do you mind if I kiss you?

ELIZABETH (*with agony*): Oh, Arnold!

(*He gravely kisses her on the forehead and then goes out. ELIZABETH stands lost in thought. She is shattered. LADY KITTY and PORTEOUS come in. LADY KITTY wears a cloak.*)

LADY KITTY: You're alone, Elizabeth?

ELIZABETH: That note you asked me about, Lady Kitty, from Teddie ...

LADY KITTY: Yes?

ELIZABETH: He wanted to have a talk with me before he went away. He's waiting for me in the summer house by the tennis court. Would Lord Porteous mind going down and asking him to come here?

PORTEOUS: No trouble at all.

(*He goes out.*)

LADY KITTY: Hughie and I will leave you alone.

ELIZABETH: But I don't want to be left alone. I want you to stay.

LADY KITTY: What are you going to say to him?

ELIZABETH (*desperately*): Please don't ask me questions. I'm so frightfully unhappy.

LADY KITTY: My poor child.

ELIZABETH: Oh, isn't life rotten? Why can't one be happy without making other people unhappy?

LADY KITTY: I wish I knew how to help you. I'm simply devoted to you. (*She hunts about in her mind for something to do or say.*) Would you like my lip-stick?

ELIZABETH (*smiling through her tears*): Thanks. I never use one.

LADY KITTY: Oh, but just try. It's such a comfort when you're in trouble.

(*Enter* PORTEOUS *and* TEDDIE.)

PORTEOUS: I brought him. He said he'd be damned if he'd come.

LADY KITTY: When a lady sent for him? Are these the manners of the young men today?

TEDDIE: When you've been solemnly kicked out of a house once I think it seems rather pushing to come back again as though nothing had happened.

ELIZABETH: Teddie, I want you to be serious.

TEDDIE: Darling, I had such a rotten dinner at that pub. If you ask me to be serious on the top of that I shall cry.

ELIZABETH: Don't be idiotic, Teddie. (*her voice faltering*) I'm so utterly wretched.

(*He looks at her for a moment gravely.*)

TEDDIE: What is it?

ELIZABETH: I can't come away with you, Teddie.

TEDDIE: Why not?

ELIZABETH (*looking away in embarrassment*): I don't love you enough.

TEDDIE: Fiddle!

ELIZABETH (*with a flash of anger*): Don't say Fiddle to me.

TEDDIE: I shall say exactly what I like to you.

ELIZABETH: I won't be bullied.

TEDDIE: Now look here, Elizabeth, you know perfectly well that I'm in love with you, and I know perfectly well that you're in love with me. So what are you talking nonsense for?

ELIZABETH (*her voice breaking*): I can't say it if you're cross with me.

TEDDIE (*smiling very tenderly*): I'm not cross with you, silly.

ELIZABETH: It's harder still when you're being rather an owl.

TEDDIE (*with a chuckle*): Am I mistaken in thinking you're not very easy to please?

ELIZABETH: Oh, it's monstrous. I was all wrought up and ready to do anything, and now you've thoroughly put me out. I feel like a great big fat balloon that some one has put a long pin into. (*with a sudden look at him*) Have you done it on purpose?

TEDDIE: Upon my soul I don't know what you're talking about.

ELIZABETH: I wonder if you're really much cleverer than I think you are.

TEDDIE (*taking her hands and making her sit down*): Now tell me exactly what you want to say. By the way, do you want Lady Kitty and Lord Porteous to be here?

ELIZABETH: Yes.

LADY KITTY: Elizabeth asked us to stay.

TEDDIE: Oh, I don't mind, bless you. I only thought you might feel rather in the way.

LADY KITTY (*frigidly*): A gentlewoman never feels in the way, Mr. Luton.

TEDDIE: Won't you call me Teddie? Everybody does, you know.

(LADY KITTY *tries to give him a withering look, but she finds it very difficult to prevent herself from smiling.* TEDDIE *strokes* ELIZABETH's *hands. She draws them away.*)

ELIZABETH: No, don't do that. Teddie, it wasn't true when I said I didn't love you. Of course I love you. But Arnold loves me, too. I didn't know how much.

TEDDIE: What has he been saying to you?

ELIZABETH: He's been very good to me, and so kind. I didn't know he could be so kind. He offered to let me divorce him.

TEDDIE: That's very decent of him.

ELIZABETH: But don't you see, it ties my hands. How can I accept such a sacrifice? I should never forgive myself if I profited by his generosity.

TEDDIE: If another man and I were devilish hungry and there was only one mutton chop between us, and he said, You eat it, I wouldn't waste a lot of time arguing. I'd wolf it before he changed his mind.

ELIZABETH: Don't talk like that. It maddens me. I'm trying to do the right thing.

TEDDIE: You're not in love with Arnold; you're in love with me. It's idiotic to sacrifice your life for a slushy sentiment.

ELIZABETH: After all, I did marry him.

TEDDIE: Well, you made a mistake. A marriage without love is no marriage at all.

ELIZABETH: *I* made the mistake. Why should he suffer for it? If anyone has to suffer it's only right that I should.

TEDDIE: What sort of a life do you think it would be with him? When two people are married it's very difficult for one of them to be unhappy without making the other unhappy too.

ELIZABETH: I can't take advantage of his generosity.

TEDDIE: I daresay he'll get a lot of satisfaction out of it.

ELIZABETH: You're being beastly, Teddie. He was simply wonderful. I never knew he had it in him. He was really noble.

TEDDIE: You are talking rot, Elizabeth.

ELIZABETH: I wonder if you'd be capable of acting like that.

TEDDIE: Acting like what?

ELIZABETH: What would you do if I were married to you and came and told you I loved somebody else and wanted to leave you?

TEDDIE: You have very pretty blue eyes, Elizabeth. I'd black first one and then the other. And after that we'd see.

ELIZABETH: You damned brute!

TEDDIE: I've often thought I wasn't quite a gentleman. Had it never struck you?

(*They look at one another for a while.*)

ELIZABETH: You know, you are taking an unfair advantage of me. I feel as if I came to you quite unsuspectingly and when I wasn't looking you kicked me on the shins.

TEDDIE: Don't you think we'd get on rather well together?

PORTEOUS: Elizabeth's a fool if she don't stick to her husband. It's bad enough for the man, but for the woman—it's damnable. I hold no brief for Arnold. He plays bridge like a foot. Saving your presence, Kitty, I think he's a prig.

LADY KITTY: Poor dear, his father was at his age. I daresay he'll grow out of it.

PORTEOUS: But you stick to him, Elizabeth, stick to him. Man is a gregarious animal. We're members of a herd. If we break the herd's laws we suffer for it. And we suffer damnably.

LADY KITTY: Oh, Elizabeth, my dear child, don't go.

It's not worth it. It's not worth it. I tell you that, and I've sacrificed everything to love.

(*A pause.*)

ELIZABETH: I'm afraid.
TEDDIE (*in a whisper*): Elizabeth.
ELIZABETH: I can't face it. It's asking too much of me. Let's say good-bye to one another, Teddie. It's the only thing to do. And have pity on me. I'm giving up all my hope of happiness.

(*He goes up to her and looks into her eyes.*)

TEDDIE: But I wasn't offering you happiness. I don't think my sort of love tends to happiness. I'm jealous. I'm not a very easy man to get on with. I'm often out of temper and irritable. I should be fed to the teeth with you sometimes, and so would you be with me. I daresay we'd fight like cat and dog, and sometimes we'd hate each other. Often you'd be wretched and bored stiff and lonely, and often you'd be frightfully homesick, and then you'd regret all you'd lost. Stupid women would be rude to you because we'd run away together. And some of them would cut you. I don't offer you peace and quietness. I offer you unrest and anxiety. I don't offer you happiness. I offer you love.
ELIZABETH (*stretching out her arms*): You hateful creature, I absolutely adore you.

(*He throws his arms round her and kisses her passionately on the lips.*)

LADY KITTY: Of course the moment he said he'd give her a black eye I knew it was finished.
PORTEOUS (*good-humouredly*): You are a fool, Kitty.
LADY KITTY: I know I am, but I can't help it.
TEDDIE: Let's make a bolt for it now.
ELIZABETH: Shall we?

TEDDIE: This minute.

PORTEOUS: You're damned fools, both of you, damned fools. If you like you can have my car.

TEDDIE: That's awfully kind of you. As a matter of fact, I got it out of the garage. It's just along the drive.

PORTEOUS (*indignantly*): How do you mean, you got it out of the garage?

TEDDIE: Well, I thought there'd be a lot of bother, and it seemed to me the best thing would be for Elizabeth and me not to stand upon the order of our going, you know. Do it now. An excellent motto for a business man.

PORTEOUS: Do you mean to say you were going to steal my car.

TEDDIE: Not exactly. I was only going to bolshevise it, so to speak.

PORTEOUS: I'm speechless. I'm absolutely speechless.

TEDDIE: Hang it all, I couldn't carry Elizabeth all the way to London. She's so damned plump.

ELIZABETH: You dirty dog!

PORTEOUS (*spluttering*): Well, well, well! . . . (*helplessly*) I like him, Kitty, it's no good pretending I don't. I like him.

TEDDIE: The moon's shining, Elizabeth. We'll drive all through the night.

PORTEOUS: They'd better go to San Michele. I'll wire to have it got ready for them.

LADY KITTY: That's where we went when Hughie and I . . . (*faltering*) Oh, you dear things, how I envy you.

PORTEOUS (*mopping his eyes*): Now don't cry, Kitty, Confound you, don't cry.

TEDDIE: Come, darling.

ELIZABETH: But I can't go like this.

TEDDIE: Nonsense! Lady Kitty will lend you her cloak. Won't you?

LADY KITTY (*taking it off*): You're capable of tearing it off my back if I don't.

TEDDIE (*putting the cloak on* ELIZABETH): And we'll buy you a tooth-brush in London in the morning.

LADY KITTY: She must write a note for Arnold. I'll put it on her pincushion.

TEDDIE: Pincushion be blowed. Come, darling. We'll drive through the dawn and through the sunrise.

ELIZABETH (*kissing* LADY KITTY *and* PORTEOUS): Goodbye. Good-bye.

(TEDDIE *stretches out his hand and she takes it. Hand in hand they go out into the night.*)

LADY KITTY: Oh, Hughie, how it all comes back to me. Will they suffer all we suffered? And have we suffered all in vain?

PORTEOUS: My dear, I don't know that in life it matters so much what you do as what you are. No one can learn by the experience of another because no circumstances are quite the same. If we made rather a hash of things perhaps it was because we were rather trivial people. You can do anything in this world if you're prepared to take the consequences, and consequences depend on character.

(*Enter* CHAMPION-CHENEY, *rubbing his hands. He is as pleased as Punch.*)

C.-C.: Well, I think I've settled the hash of that young man.

LADY KITTY: Oh?

C.-C.: You have to get up very early in the morning to get the better of your humble servant.

(*There is the sound of a car starting.*)

LADY KITTY: What is that?

C.-C.: It sounds like a car. I expect it's your chauffeur taking one of the maids for a joy-ride.

PORTEOUS: Whose hash are you talking about?

C.-C.: Mr. Edward Luton's, my dear Hughie. I told Arnold exactly what to do and he's done it. What makes a prison? Why, bars and bolts. Remove them and a prisoner won't want to escape. Clever, I flatter myself.

PORTEOUS: You were always that, Clive, but at the moment you're obscure.

C.-C.: I told Arnold to go to Elizabeth and tell her she could have her freedom. I told him to sacrifice himself all along the line. I know what women are. The moment every obstacle was removed to her marriage with Teddie Luton, half the allurement was gone.

LADY KITTY: Arnold did that?

C.-C.: He followed my instructions to the letter. I've just seen him. She's shaken. I'm willing to bet five hundred pounds to a penny that she won't bolt. A downy old bird, eh? Downy's the word. Downy.

(*He begins to laugh. They laugh too. Presently they are all three in fits of laughter.*)

# OUR

# BETTERS

〜

# CHARACTERS

LADY GRAYSTON

DUCHESSE DE SURENNES

PRINCIPESSA DELLA CERCOLA

ELIZABETH SAUNDERS

ARTHUR FENWICK

THORNTON CLAY

FLEMING HARVEY

ANTHONY PAXTON

LORD BLEANE

POLE

ERNEST

———

*The action of the play takes place at* LADY
GRAYSTON's *house in Grosvenor Street, Mayfair, and
at her husband's place in Suffolk, Abbots Kenton.*

# ACT ONE

SCENE: *The drawing-room at* LADY GRAYSTON'S *house in Grosvenor Street, Mayfair. It is a sumptuous double room, of the period of George II, decorated in green and gold, with a coromandel screen and lacquer cabinets; but the coverings of the chairs, the sofas and cushions, show the influence of Bakst and the Russian Ballet; they offer an agreeable mixture of rich plum, emerald green, canary and ultramarine. On the floor is a Chinese carpet, and here and there are pieces of Ming pottery.*

*It is about half-past four, early in the season, and a fine day. When the curtain rises, from the street below is heard the melancholy chant of the lavender man.*

> Won't you buy my sweet lavender?
> Sixteen blue branches for a penny.
> If you buy it once,
> You'll buy it twice,
> For it makes your clothes
> Smell very nice—
> Sweet-scented lavender.

BESSIE SAUNDERS *comes in. She is a very pretty American girl, of twenty-two, with fair hair and blue eyes. She is dressed in the latest mode. She wears a hat and gloves, and carries a bag. She has just come in from the street. She has in her hand a telephone message, and going over to the telephone she takes up the receiver.*

BESSIE: Gerrard 4321. Is that the Berkeley? Put me through to Mr. Harvey, please. Fleming Harvey, that's right. (*She listens and smiles.*) Yes. Who d'you think it is? (*She laughs.*) I've just got your telephone message. Where have you sprung from? That's fine. How long are you staying in London? I see. I want to see you at once. Nonsense. This very minute. Now just jump into a taxi and come right away. Pearl will be in presently. Ring off, Fleming. No, I will not ring off first. (*a pause*) Are you there? How tiresome you are. You might be half-way here by now. Well, hustle.

(*She puts down the receiver and begins to take off her gloves.* POLE, *the butler, comes in with a bunch of roses.*)

POLE: These flowers have just come for you, miss.

BESSIE: Oh! Thank you. Aren't they lovely? You must give me something to put them in, Pole.

POLE: I'll bring a vase, miss.

(*He goes out. She buries her face in the flowers and inhales their fragrance. The* BUTLER *enters with a bowl filled with water.*)

BESSIE: Thank you. You're sure they *are* for me? There's no label.

POLE: Yes, miss. The person who brought them said

they was for you, miss. I asked if there wasn't a card, and he said no, miss.

BESSIE (*with a faint smile*): I think I know who they're from. (*She begins to arrange the flowers.*) Her ladyship hasn't come in yet, has she?

POLE: Not yet, miss.

BESSIE: D'you know if anyone is coming in to tea?

POLE: Her ladyship didn't say, miss.

BESSIE: You'd better prepare for fifteen, then.

POLE: Very good, miss.

BESSIE: I was being funny, Pole.

POLE: Yes, miss? Shall I take the paper away, miss?

BESSIE (*with a slight sigh of resignation*): Yes, do, will you? (*The telephone bell rings.*) Oh, I forgot, I switched the telephone on here. See who it is.

   (POLE *takes up the receiver and listens, then puts his hand over its mouth.*)

POLE: Will you speak to Lord Bleane, miss?

BESSIE: Say I'm not at home.

POLE: Miss Saunders hasn't come in yet. I beg pardon, my lord. I didn't recognize your lordship's voice. (*a pause*) Well, my lord, I did hear them say there was a private view they thought of going to at the Grosvenor. You might find Miss Saunders there.

BESSIE: You needn't elaborate, Pole.

POLE: I was only making it more convincing, miss. (*listening*) I think so, my lord. Of course, I couldn't say for certain, my lord; they might have gone out to Rane-lagh.

BESSIE: Really, Pole!

POLE: Very good, my lord. (*He puts down the receiver.*) His lordship asked if you was expected in to tea, miss.

BESSIE: I see.

POLE: Is there anything else, miss?

BESSIE: No, Pole, thank you.

*(He goes out. She finishes arranging the flowers. The
door is flung open and LADY GRAYSTON comes in,
followed by FLEMING HARVEY. PEARL—LADY GRAY-
STON—is a handsome, dashing creature, a woman of thirty-four, with red hair, and a face outrageously painted. She is dressed in a Paris frock, but
of greater daring both in colour and cut than a
Frenchwoman would wear. FLEMING is a nice-looking young American in clothes that were obviously
made in New York.)*

PEARL: My dear Bessie, I've found an entirely strange
young man on the doorstep who says he is a cousin.

BESSIE (*giving him her hands enthusiastically*): Fleming.

FLEMING: I introduced myself to Lady Grayston. She
drove up just as they were opening the door. Please
reassure your sister, Bessie. She looks upon me with
suspicion.

BESSIE: You must remember Fleming Harvey, Pearl.

PEARL: I've never set eyes on him in my life. But he
looks quite nice.

BESSIE: He is.

PEARL: He's apparently come to see you.

FLEMING: I rang up five minutes ago and Bessie
ordered me to come round right away.

PEARL: Well, make him stop to tea. I've got to telephone. I've suddenly remembered that I've asked twelve
people to dinner.

BESSIE: Does George know?

PEARL: Who is George?

BESSIE: Don't be absurd, Pearl. George—your husband.

PEARL: Oh! I couldn't make out who you meant. No, he
doesn't know. But what's much more important, the cook
doesn't know either. I'd forgotten George was in London.

*(She goes out.)*

BESSIE: George generally dines out when Pearl is giving a party, because he doesn't like people he doesn't know, and he seldom dines at home when we're alone, because it bores him.

FLEMING: It doesn't sound as if Sir George enjoyed many of the benefits of home life.

BESSIE: Now let's sit down and make ourselves comfortable. You are going to stay to tea, aren't you?

FLEMING: It's not a beverage that I'm in the habit of imbibing.

BESSIE: When you've been in England a month you won't be able to do without it. When did you land?

FLEMING: This morning. You see, I've lost no time in coming to see you.

BESSIE: I should think not. It *is* good to see someone straight from home.

FLEMING: Have you been having a good time, Bessie?

BESSIE: Wonderful! Since the beginning of the season, except when Pearl has had people here, I've been out to lunch and dinner every day, and I've been to a ball every night, generally two and sometimes three.

FLEMING: Gee!

BESSIE: If I stopped now I'd drop down dead.

FLEMING: D'you like England?

BESSIE: I adore it. I think it's too bad of dad never to have let me come over to London before. Rome and Paris are nothing. We're just trippers there, but here we're at home.

FLEMING: Don't get too much at home, Bessie.

BESSIE: Oh, Fleming, I never thanked you for sending me the roses. It was perfectly sweet of you.

FLEMING (*with a smile*): I didn't send you any roses.

BESSIE: Didn't you? Well, why didn't you?

FLEMING: I hadn't time. But I will.

BESSIE: It's too late now. I naturally thought they were from you, because Englishmen don't send flowers in the same way as American boys do.

FLEMING: Is that so?

*(There is a slight pause. BESSIE gives him a quick look.)*

BESSIE: Fleming, I want to thank you for that charming letter you wrote me.

FLEMING: There's no occasion to do that, Bessie.

BESSIE: I was afraid you might feel badly about it. But we'll always be the greatest friends, won't we?

FLEMING: Always.

BESSIE: After all, you were eighteen when you asked me to marry you, and I was sixteen. It wasn't a very serious engagement. I don't know why we didn't break it off before.

FLEMING: I suppose it never occurred to us.

BESSIE: I'd almost forgotten it, but when I came over here I thought I'd better make everything quite clear.

FLEMING *(with a smile)*: Bessie, I believe you're in love.

BESSIE: No, I'm not. I tell you I'm having a wonderful time.

FLEMING: Well, who sent you the roses?

BESSIE: I don't know. Lord Bleane.

FLEMING: You're not going to marry a lord, Bessie?

BESSIE: Have you any objection?

FLEMING: Well, on first principles, I think American girls had better marry American men, but then I happen to be an American man.

*(BESSIE looks at him for a moment.)*

BESSIE: Pearl gave a dinner party last night. I was taken in by a cabinet minister, and on the other side of me I had an ambassador. Just opposite was a man who'd been Viceroy in India. Madame Angelotti dined with us, and she sang afterwards, and a lot of people came on from an official dinner in their stars and ribands. Pearl looked superb. She's a wonderful hostess, you know. Several people told me they would rather come here than to any house in London. Before Pearl married

George Grayston she was engaged to a boy who was in business in Portland, Oregon.

FLEMING (*smiling*): I see you're quite determined to marry a lord.

BESSIE: No, I'm not. I'm keeping an open mind on the subject.

FLEMING: What d'you mean by that?

BESSIE: Well, Fleming, it hasn't escaped my notice that a certain noble lord is not unwilling to lay his beautiful coronet at my feet.

FLEMING: Don't talk like a novelette, Bessie.

BESSIE: But it feels just like a novelette. The poor dear is trying to propose to me every time he sees me, and I'm doing all I can to prevent him.

FLEMING: Why?

BESSIE: I don't want to refuse him, and then wish I hadn't.

FLEMING: You could easily make him ask you again. Women find that so simple.

BESSIE: Ah, but supposing he went right away to shoot big game in Africa. It's what they do, you know, in novelettes.

FLEMING: I'm reassured about one thing. You're not in the least in love with him.

BESSIE: I told you I wasn't. You don't mind my saying all this to you, Fleming?

FLEMING: Gracious, no; why should I?

BESSIE: You're sure you don't feel sore at my throwing you over?

FLEMING (*cheerfully*): Not a bit.

BESSIE: I am glad, because then I can tell you all about the noble lord.

FLEMING: Has it occurred to you that he wants to marry you for your money?

BESSIE: You can put it more prettily. You can say that he wants to marry me with my money.

FLEMING: And is that a prospect that allures you?

BESSIE: Poor dear, what else can he do? He's got a large place to keep up, and he simply hasn't a cent.

FLEMING: Really, Bessie, you amaze me.

BESSIE: I shan't when you've been here a month.

(PEARL *comes in.*)

PEARL: Now, Bessie, tell me all about this strange young man.

BESSIE: He's quite capable of telling you about himself.

PEARL (*to* FLEMING): How long are you staying?

FLEMING: A couple of months. I want to see something of English life.

PEARL: I see. D'you want to improve your mind or d'you want to go into society?

FLEMING: I suppose I couldn't combine the two.

PEARL: Are you rich?

FLEMING: Not at all.

PEARL: It doesn't matter, you're good-looking. If one wants to be a success in London one must either have looks, wit, or a bank-balance. You know Arthur Fenwick, don't you?

FLEMING: Only by reputation.

PEARL: How superciliously you say that!

FLEMING: He provides bad food to the working classes of the United States at an exorbitant price. I have no doubt he makes a lot of money.

BESSIE: He's a great friend of Pearl's.

PEARL: When he first came over because they turned up their noses at him in New York, I said to him: My dear Mr. Fenwick, you're not good-looking, you're not amusing, you're not well-bred, you're only rich. If you want to get into society you must spend money.

FLEMING: It was evidently in the nature of a straight talk.

BESSIE: We must do what we can for Fleming, Pearl.

PEARL (*with a chuckle*): We'll introduce him to Minnie Surennes.

FLEMING: Who in the world is she?

PEARL: The Duchesse de Surennes. Don't you remember? She was a Miss Hodgson. Chicago people. Of course, they're nobody in America, but that doesn't matter over here. She adores good-looking boys, and I daresay she's getting rather tired of Tony. (*to* BESSIE) By the way, they're coming in this afternoon.

BESSIE: I don't like Tony.

PEARL: Why not? I think he's charming. He's the most unprincipled ruffian I ever met.

FLEMING: Is Tony the duke?

PEARL: What duke? Her husband? Oh no, she divorced him years ago.

BESSIE: I think Fleming would like the Princess much better.

PEARL: Oh, well, he'll meet her here today, too.

BESSIE: She was a Miss van Hoog, Fleming.

FLEMING: Is she divorced too?

PEARL: Oh no, her husband's an Italian. It's very difficult to get a divorce in Italy. She's only separated. She's quite nice. She's one of my greatest friends. She bores me a little.

(POLE *comes in to announce* THORNTON CLAY *and then goes out.* THORNTON CLAY *is a stout American with a bald head and an effusive manner. He is somewhat overdressed. He speaks with a marked American accent.*)

POLE: Mr. Thornton Clay.

CLAY: How d'you do?

PEARL: You're the very person we want, Thornton. An entirely strange young man has suddenly appeared on my doorstep, and says he's my cousin.

CLAY: My dear Pearl, that is a calamity which we Americans must always be prepared for.

BESSIE: I won't have you say such things, Mr. Clay. Fleming is not only our cousin, but he's my very oldest friend. Aren't you, Fleming?

PEARL: Bessie has a charming nature. She really thinks that friendship puts one under an obligation.

Fleming: Since you're talking of me, won't you introduce me to Mr. Clay?

Pearl: How American you are!

Fleming (*smiling*): It's not unnatural, is it?

Pearl: Over here we haven't the passion that you have in America for introducing people. My dear Thornton, allow me to present to you my long-lost cousin, Mr. Fleming Harvey.

Clay: It's so long since I was in America that I almost forget, but I believe the proper answer to that is: Mr. Fleming Harvey, I'm pleased to make your acquaintance.

Fleming: Aren't you an American, Mr. Clay?

Clay: I won't deny that I was born in Virginia.

Fleming: I beg your pardon, I thought from the way you spoke . . .

Clay (*interrupting*): But, of course, my home is London.

Pearl: Nonsense, Thornton, your home is wherever there's a first-class hotel.

Clay: I went to America seven years ago. My father died and I had to go and settle up his affairs. Everyone took me for an Englishman.

Fleming: That must have gratified you very much, Mr. Clay.

Clay: Of course, I haven't a trace of an American accent. I suppose that was the reason. And then my clothes.

(*He looks down at them with satisfaction.*)

Pearl: Fleming wants to see life in London, Thornton. He can't do better than put himself under your wing.

Clay: I know everyone who's worth knowing. I can't deny that.

Pearl: Thornton calls more countesses by their Christian names than any man in town.

Clay: I'll get him cards for some good balls, and I'll see that he's asked to one or two of the right parties.

PEARL: He's good-looking, and I'm sure he dances well. He'll be a credit to you, Thornton.

CLAY (*to* FLEMING): But, of course, there's really nothing I *can* do for you. At Lady Grayston's you are in the very hub of society. I don't mean the stuffy, old-fashioned society, that goes about in barouches and bores itself stiff, but the society that counts, the society that figures in the newspapers. Pearl is the most wonderful hostess in London.

PEARL: What *do* you want, Thornton?

CLAY: In this house, sooner or later, you'll meet every remarkable man in England except one. That is George Grayston. And he's only remarkable because he's her husband.

PEARL (*with a chuckle*): I might have known you were only saying a pleasant thing in order to make the next one more disagreeable.

CLAY: Of course, I can't make out why you never ask George to your parties. Personally I like him.

PEARL: That's all the nicer of you, Thornton, since he always speaks of you as that damned snob.

CLAY (*with a shrug of the shoulders*): Poor George, he has such a limited vocabulary. I met Flora della Cercola at luncheon today. She told me she was coming to tea with you.

PEARL: She's getting up a concert in aid of something or other, and she wants me to help her.

CLAY: Poor Flora, with her good works! She takes philanthropy as a drug to allay the pangs of unrequited love.

PEARL: I always tell her she'd do much better to take a lover.

CLAY: You'll shock Mr. Harvey.

PEARL: It won't hurt him. It'll do him good.

CLAY: Did you ever know her husband?

PEARL: Oh, yes, I met him. Just the ordinary little Dago. I cannot imagine why she should ever have been in love with him. She's an extraordinary creature. D'you know, I'm convinced that she's never had an affair.

CLAY: Some of these American women are strangely sexless.

FLEMING: I have an idea that some of them are even virtuous.

PEARL (*with a smile*): It takes all sorts to make a world.

(POLE *enters to announce the* DUCHESSE DE SURENNES *and then goes out.*)

POLE: The Duchesse de Surennes.

(*The* DUCHESSE *is a large, dark woman of forty-five with scarlet lips and painted cheeks, a woman of opulent form, bold, self-assured and outrageously sensual. She suggests a drawing of a Roman Emperor by Aubrey Beardsley. She is gowned with a certain dashing magnificence, and wears a long string of large pearls round her neck. During the conversation* POLE *and two footmen bring in tea, and place it in the back drawing-room.*)

PEARL: My dear, how nice of you to come.

DUCHESSE: Isn't Tony here?

PEARL: No.

DUCHESSE: He said he was coming straight here.

PEARL: I daresay he's been delayed.

DUCHESSE: I can't understand it. He telephoned a quarter of an hour ago that he was starting at once.

PEARL (*reassuringly*): He'll be here presently.

DUCHESSE (*with an effort over herself*): How pretty you're looking, Bessie. No wonder all the men I meet rave about you.

BESSIE: Englishmen are so shy. Why don't they rave *to* me?

DUCHESSE: They'll never let you go back to America.

PEARL: Of course, she's never going back. I'm determined that she shall marry an Englishman.

CLAY: She'll make a charming addition to our American peeresses.

PEARL: And there'll be another that you can call by her Christian name, Thornton.

BESSIE: I wish you wouldn't talk as if I hadn't a word to say in the matter.

CLAY: Of course, you've got a word to say, Bessie—a very important one.

BESSIE: Yes, I suppose?

CLAY: Exactly.

PEARL: Pour out the tea, darling, will you?

BESSIE: Surely. (*to* CLAY) I know you don't share Fleming's contempt for tea, Mr. Clay.

CLAY: I couldn't live a day without it. Why, I never travel without a tea basket.

FLEMING (*ironically*): Is that so?

CLAY: You Americans who live in America . . .

FLEMING (*under his breath*): So queer of us.

CLAY: Despise the delectable habit of drinking tea because you are still partly barbarous. The hour that we spend over it is the most delightful of the day. We do not make a business of eating as at luncheon or dinner. We are at ease with ourselves. We toy with pretty cakes as an excuse for conversation. We discuss the abstract, our souls, our morals; we play delicately with the concrete, our neighbour's new bonnet or her latest lover. We drink tea because we are a highly civilized nation.

FLEMING: I must be very stupid, but I don't follow.

CLAY: My dear fellow, the degree of a nation's civilization is marked by its disregard for the necessities of existence. You have gone so far as to waste money, but we have gone farther; we waste what is infinitely more precious, more transitory, more irreparable—we waste time.

DUCHESSE: My dear Thornton, you fill me with despair. Compton Edwardes has cut me off my tea. I thought he was only depriving me of a luxury, now I see he's depriving me also of a religious rite.

FLEMING: Who in heaven's name is Compton Edwardes, that he should have such influence?

PEARL: My dear Fleming, he's the most powerful man in London. He's the great reducer.

FLEMING: Gracious! What does he reduce?

PEARL: Fat.

DUCHESSE: He's a perfect marvel, that man. Do you know, the Duchess of Arlington told me he'd taken nine pounds off her.

PEARL: My dear, that's nothing. Why, Clara Hollington gave me her word of honour she'd lost over a stone.

BESSIE (*from the tea-table*): Anyone who wants tea must come and fetch it.

(*The men saunter over to the next room, while* PEARL *and the* DUCHESSE *go on with their conversation.*)

DUCHESSE: Who is that nice-looking young man, Pearl?

PEARL: Oh, he's a young American. He pretends to be a cousin of mine. He's come to see Bessie.

DUCHESSE: Does he want to marry her?

PEARL: Good heavens, I hope not. He's only an old friend. You know the funny ways they have in America.

DUCHESSE: I suppose nothing is really settled about Harry Bleane?

PEARL: No. But I shouldn't be surprised if you saw an announcement in the Morning Post one day.

DUCHESSE: Has she enough money for him?

PEARL: She has a million.

DUCHESSE: Not pounds?

PEARL: Oh no, dollars.

DUCHESSE: That's only eight thousand a year. I shouldn't have thought he'd be satisfied with that.

PEARL: People can't expect so much nowadays. There won't be any more enormous heiresses as there were in your time. Besides, Harry Bleane isn't such a catch as all that. Of course, it's better to be an English baron than an Italian count, but that's about all you can say for it.

DUCHESSE: Of course she'll accept him?

PEARL: Oh yes, she's crazy to live in England. And as I tell her, it's quite pleasant to be a peeress even now.

DUCHESSE: What on earth can have happened to Tony?

PEARL: My dear, he's not likely to have been run over by a motor-bus.

DUCHESSE: I'm not afraid of motor-buses running over him; I'm afraid of him running after Gaiety girls.

PEARL (*drily*): I should have thought you kept a very sharp eye on him.

DUCHESSE: You see, he hasn't got anything to do from morning till night.

PEARL: Why doesn't he get a job?

DUCHESSE: I've been trying to get him something, but it's so difficult. You've got such a lot of influence, Pearl. Can't you do something? I should be so grateful.

PEARL: What can he do?

DUCHESSE: Anything. And as you know he's very good-looking.

PEARL: Does he know French and German?

DUCHESSE: No, he has no gift for languages.

PEARL: Can he type and write shorthand?

DUCHESSE: Oh, no. Poor dear, you can hardly expect that.

PEARL: Can he do accounts?

DUCHESSE: No, he has no head for figures.

PEARL (*reflecting*): Well, the only thing I can see that he'd do for is a government office.

DUCHESSE: Oh, my dear, if you only could manage that. You can't think what a comfort it would be for me to know that he couldn't get into mischief at least from ten to four every day.

(POLE *announces* TONY PAXTON. TONY *is a handsome youth of twenty-five, in beautiful clothes, with engaging manners and a charming smile.*)

POLE: Mr. Paxton.

PEARL: Well, Tony, how is life?

TONY: Rotten. I haven't backed a winner or won a rubber this week.

PEARL: Ah well, that's the advantage of not having money, you can afford to lose it.

DUCHESSE (*bursting in*): Where have you been, Tony?

TONY: I? Nowhere.

DUCHESSE: You said you were coming straight here. It doesn't take twenty-five minutes to get here from Dover Street.

TONY: I thought there wasn't any hurry. I was just hanging about the club.

DUCHESSE: I rang up the club again, and they said you'd gone.

TONY (*after a very slight pause*): I was downstairs having a shave, and I suppose they never thought of looking for me in the barber's shop.

DUCHESSE: What on earth did you want to be shaved for at half-past four in the afternoon?

TONY: I thought you'd like me to look nice and clean.

PEARL: Go and get Bessie to give you some tea, Tony; I'm sure you want it after the strenuous day you've had.

(*He nods and walks into the inner room.*)

PEARL: Minnie, how can you be so silly? You can't expect to keep a man if you treat him like that.

DUCHESSE: I know he's lying to me, there's not a word of truth in anything he says, but he's so slim I can never catch him out. Oh, I'm so jealous.

PEARL: Are you really in love with him?

DUCHESSE: I'm not cold-blooded like you.

PEARL: You seem to have a passion for rotters, and they always treat you badly.

DUCHESSE: Oh, I don't care about the others. Tony is the only one I've ever really loved.

PEARL: Nonsense! You were just as much in love with Jack Harris. You did everything in the world for him. You taught him to wear his clothes. You got him into society. And the moment he could do without you he chucked you. Tony will do just the same.

DUCHESSE: I'm not going to be such a fool this time. I'm going to take care he can't do without me.

PEARL: I can't imagine what you see in him. You must know that . . .

DUCHESSE (*interrupting*): There's very little I don't know. He's a liar, a gambler, an idler, a spendthrift, but in his way he is fond of me. (*appealingly*) You can see he's fond of me, can't you?

PEARL: He's so much younger than you, Minnie.

DUCHESSE: I can't help it. I love him.

PEARL: Oh, well, I suppose it's no good talking. As long as he makes you happy.

DUCHESSE: He doesn't. He makes me miserable. But I love him. . . . He wants me to marry him, Pearl.

PEARL: You're not going to?

DUCHESSE: No, I won't be such a fool as that. If I married him I'd have no hold over him at all.

> (*Enter* POLE *to announce the* PRINCESS DELLA CERCOLA. *She is a tall, thin woman of thirty-five, with a pale, haggard face and great dark eyes. She is a gentle, kind creature, but there is something pathetic, almost tragic, in her appearance. She is dressed, though very well, and obviously by a Paris dressmaker, more quietly than the* DUCHESSE *or* PEARL. *She has not only wealth, but distinction.*)

POLE: Princess della Cercola.

> (*Exit.* PEARL *gets up to receive her. They kiss.*)

PEARL: Darling!

PRINCESS: D'you hate me for coming to bother you? I ran up because I know how difficult you are to catch. (*kissing the* DUCHESSE) How are you, Minnie?

DUCHESSE: Don't ask me for a subscription, Flora. I'm so poor.

PRINCESS (*smiling*): Wait till I tell you what it's for,

and then you'll remember that you had a father called
Spencer Hodgson.

DUCHESSE (*with a little groan*): As if I wanted to be
reminded of it!

PEARL: You're so absurd, Minnie. You should make a
joke of the pork. I always tell people about father's hardware store, and when I haven't got a funny story to tell
about it, I invent one.

PRINCESS: You've made your father quite a character
in London.

PEARL: That's why I never let him come over. He
couldn't possibly live up to his reputation.

(FLEMING HARVEY *comes forward from the inner
room.*)

FLEMING: I'm going to say good-bye to you.

PEARL: You mustn't go before I've introduced you to
Flora. Flora, this is Mr. Fleming Harvey. He's just come
from America. He probably carries a six-shooter in his
hip-pocket.

FLEMING: I'm told I mayn't say I'm pleased to make
your acquaintance, Princess.

PRINCESS: When did you land?

FLEMING: This morning.

PRINCESS: I envy you.

FLEMING: Because I landed this morning?

PRINCESS: No, because a week ago you were in
America.

DUCHESSE: Flora!

FLEMING: I was beginning to think it was something
to be rather ashamed of.

PRINCESS: Oh, you mustn't pay any attention to Pearl
and the Duchesse. They're so much more English than
the English.

PEARL: I notice you show your devotion to the country
of your birth by staying away from it, Flora.

PRINCESS: Last time I was in America it made me so
unhappy that I vowed I'd never go there again.

DUCHESSE: I was there ten years ago, when I was divorcing Gaston. I hadn't been in America since my marriage, and I'd forgotten what it was like. Oh, it was so crude. Oh, it was so provincial. You don't mind my saying so, Mr. Harvey?

FLEMING: Not at all. You're just as American as I am, and there's no reason why among ourselves we shouldn't abuse the mother that bore us.

DUCHESSE: Oh, but I don't look upon myself as American. I'm French. After all, I haven't a trace of an American accent. To show you how it got on my nerves, I almost didn't divorce Gaston because I thought I couldn't bring myself to stay in America long enough.

PRINCESS: It's not because it was crude and provincial that I was unhappy in America. I was unhappy because after all it was home, the only real home I've ever had, and I was a stranger.

PEARL: My dear Flora, you're being very sentimental.

PRINCESS (smiling): I'm sorry; I apologize. You're a New Yorker, Mr. Harvey?

FLEMING: I'm proud of it, madam.

PRINCESS: New York's wonderful, isn't it? It has something that no other city in the world has got. I like to think of Fifth Avenue on a spring day. The pretty girls in their smart frocks and neat shoes, who trip along so gaily, and all the good-looking boys.

DUCHESSE: I grant you that; some of the boys are too lovely for words.

PRINCESS: Everyone is so strong and confident. There's such an exaltation in the air. You feel in the passers-by a serene and unshakable belief in the future. Oh, it's very good to be alive in Fifth Avenue on a sunny day in April.

FLEMING: It's good for an American to hear another American say such pleasant things about his country.

PRINCESS: You must come and see me, and you shall tell me all the news of home.

PEARL: How high the newest building is, and how much money the latest millionaire has got.

FLEMING: Good-bye.

PEARL: Have you made friends with Thornton Clay?

FLEMING: I hope so.

PEARL: You must get him to give you the address of his tailor.

FLEMING: Aren't you pleased with my clothes?

PEARL: They're very American, you know.

FLEMING: So am I.

(THORNTON CLAY *comes forward. The* DUCHESSE *strolls over to the inner room and is seen talking with* BESSIE *and* TONY PAXTON.)

PEARL: Thornton, I was just telling Mr. Harvey that you'd take him to your tailor.

CLAY: I was going to suggest it.

FLEMING: My clothes are not at all a success.

PEARL: Who d'you go to? Stultz?

CLAY: Of course. He's the only tailor in London. (*to* FLEMING) Of course he's a German, but art has no nationality.

FLEMING: I'm pleased at all events to think that it's a German tailor who's going to make me look like an Englishman.

(*He goes out.* THORNTON *makes his farewells.*)

CLAY: Good-bye, Pearl.

PEARL: Are you going? Don't forget you're coming down to Kenton on Saturday.

CLAY: I won't, indeed. I adore your week-end parties, Pearl. I'm so exhausted by Monday morning that I'm fit for nothing the rest of the week. Good-bye.

(*He shakes hands and goes out. As he is going,* POLE *opens the door to announce* LORD BLEANE. *He is a young man, very English in appearance, pleasant, clean and well-groomed.*)

POLE: Lord Bleane.

(*Exit.*)

PEARL: Dear Harry, how nice of you to come.

BLEANE: I'm in absolute despair.

PEARL: Good heavens, why?

BLEANE: They're sending a mission to Rumania to hand the Garter to some bigwig and I've got to go with it.

PEARL: Oh, but that'll be very interesting.

BLEANE: Yes, but we start tomorrow, and I shan't be able to come down to Kenton on Saturday.

PEARL: When do you come back?

BLEANE: In four weeks.

PEARL: Then come down to Kenton the Saturday after that.

BLEANE: May I?

PEARL: You must go and break the news to Bessie. She was so looking forward to your visit.

BLEANE: D'you think she'll give me some tea?

PEARL: I have no doubt, if you ask her nicely.

(*He goes over to the inner room.*)

PRINCESS: Now I've got you to myself for two minutes. You will help me with my concert, won't you?

PEARL: Of course. What do you want me to do? I'll make Arthur Fenwick take any number of tickets. You know how charitable he is.

PRINCESS: It's for a very good cause.

PEARL: I'm sure it is. But don't harrow me with revolting stories of starving children. I'm not interested in the poor.

PRINCESS (*smiling*): How can you say that?

PEARL: Are you? I often wonder if your philanthropy isn't an elaborate pose. You don't mind my saying that, do you?

PRINCESS (*good-humouredly*): Not at all. You have no

heart, and you can't imagine that anyone else should have.

PEARL: I have plenty of heart, but it beats for people of my own class.

PRINCESS: I've only found one thing really worth doing with all this money I have, and that is to help a little those who need help.

PEARL (*with a shrug*): So long as it makes you happy.

PRINCESS: It doesn't, but it prevents me from being utterly miserable.

PEARL: You make me so impatient, Flora. You've got more money than you know what to do with. You're a princess. You've practically got rid of your husband. I cannot imagine what more you want. I wish I could get rid of mine.

PRINCESS (*smiling*): I don't know what you've got to complain of in George.

PEARL: That's just it. I shouldn't mind if he beat me or made love to chorus girls. I could divorce him then. Oh, my dear, thank your stars that you had a husband who was grossly unfaithful to you. Mine wants me to live nine months of the year in the country and have a baby every five minutes. I didn't marry an Englishman for that.

PRINCESS: Why *did* you marry him?

PEARL: I made a mistake. I'd lived all my life in New York. I was very ignorant. I thought if you were a baronet you must be in society.

PRINCESS: I often wonder if you're happy, Pearl.

PEARL: Do you? Of course I'm happy.

PRINCESS: An ambassador told me the other day that you were the most powerful woman in London. It's very wonderful how you've made your way. You had nothing very much to help you.

PEARL: Shall I tell you how it was done? By force of character, wit, unscrupulousness and push.

PRINCESS (*smiling*): You're very frank.

PEARL: That has always been my pose.

PRINCESS: I sometimes think there's positive genius in the way you've ignored the snubs of the great.

PEARL (*with a chuckle*): You're being very unpleasant, Flora.

PRINCESS: And there's something very like heroism in the callousness with which you've dropped people when they've served your turn.

PEARL: You're driving me to the conclusion that you don't altogether approve of me.

PRINCESS: On the other hand I can't help admiring you. You've brought all the determination, insight, vigour, strength, which have made our countrymen turn America into what it is, to get what you wanted. In a way your life has been a work of art. And what makes it more complete is that what you've aimed at is trivial, transitory and worthless.

PEARL: My dear Flora, people don't hunt in order to catch a fox.

PRINCESS: Sometimes, doesn't it make you rather nervous, when you're sitting on the top of your ladder, in case anyone sould give it a kick as he passes?

PEARL: It'll want more than a kick to topple my ladder over. D'you remember when that silly woman made such a fuss because her husband was in love with me? It wasn't till I only just escaped the divorce court that the duchesses really took me up.

(*The* DUCHESSE *comes forward with* TONY PAXTON.)

DUCHESSE: We really must be going, Pearl. I expect my masseur at six. Compton Edwards told me about him. He's wonderful, but he's so run after, if you keep him waiting a moment he goes away.

PEARL: My dear, do be careful. Fanny Hallam got herself down to a mere nothing, but it made her look a hundred.

DUCHESSE: Oh, I know, but Compton Edwardes has recommended to me a wonderful woman who comes every morning to do my face.

PEARL: You are coming to my ball, aren't you?

DUCHESSE: Of course we're coming. Yours are almost

the only parties in London where one amuses oneself as much as at a night club.

PEARL: I'm having Ernest to come in and dance.

DUCHESSE: I thought of having him one evening. How much does he charge for coming in socially?

PEARL: Twenty guineas.

DUCHESSE: Good heavens, I could never afford that.

PEARL: What nonsense! You're far richer than I am.

DUCHESSE: I'm not so clever, darling. I can't think how you do so much on your income.

PEARL (*amused*): I'm a very good manager.

DUCHESSE: One would never think it. Good-bye, dear. Are you coming, Tony?

TONY: Yes.

(*She goes out.*)

TONY (*shaking hands with* PEARL): I've not had a word with you today.

PEARL (*chaffing him*): What are we to do about it?

PRINCESS: I *must* get Minnie to go to my concert. Minnie.

(*She goes out.* TONY *is left face to face with* PEARL).

TONY: You're looking perfectly divine today. I don't know what there is about you.

PEARL (*amused, but not disconcerted*): It is nice of you to say so.

TONY: I simply haven't been able to take my eyes off you.

PEARL: Are you making love to me?

TONY: That's nothing new, is it?

PEARL: You'll get into trouble.

TONY: Don't be disagreeable, Pearl.

PEARL: I don't remember that I ever told you you might call me Pearl.

TONY: It's how I think of you. You can't prevent me from doing that.

PEARL: Well, I think it's very familiar.

TONY: I don't know what you've done to me. I think of you all day long.

PEARL: I don't believe it for a minute. You're an unprincipled ruffian, Tony.

TONY: Do you mind?

PEARL (*with a chuckle*): Shameless creature. I wonder what it is that Minnie sees in you.

TONY: I have all sorts of merits.

PEARL: I'm glad you think so. I can only discover one.

TONY: What is that?

PEARL: You're somebody else's property.

TONY: Oh!

PEARL (*holding out her hand*): Good-bye.

(*He kisses her wrist. His lips linger. She looks at him from under her eyelashes.*)

PEARL: It doesn't make you irresistible, you know.

TONY: There's always the future.

PEARL: The future's everybody's property.

TONY (*in an undertone*): Pearl.

PEARL: Be quick and go. Minnie will be wondering why you don't come.

(*He goes out.* PEARL *turns away with a smile.* BESSIE *and* LORD BLEANE *advance into the room.*)

PEARL: Has Harry broken the news to you that he can't come down to us on Saturday?

(*The* PRINCESS *comes in.*)

PRINCESS: I've got my subscription.

PEARL: I kept Tony up here as long as I could so as to give you a chance.

PRINCESS (*with a laugh*): That was really tactful.

PEARL: Poor Minnie, she's as mean as cat's meat. (*with a glance at* BESSIE *and* LORD BLEANE) If you'd like to

come down to the morning-room we can go through my
visitors' book and see who'll be useful to you.

PRINCESS: Oh, that would be kind of you.

PEARL (*to* BLEANE): Don't go till I come back, will you?
I haven't had a word with you yet.

BLEANE: All right.

(PEARL *and the* PRINCESS *go out.*)

BESSIE: I wonder if you sent me those flowers, Lord
Bleane?

BLEANE: I did. I thought you wouldn't mind.

BESSIE: It was very kind of you.

(*She takes two of the roses and puts them in her
dress.* BLEANE *is overcome with shyness. He does
not know how to begin.*)

BLEANE: D'you mind if I light a cigarette?

BESSIE: Not at all.

BLEANE (*as he lights it*): D'you know, this is the first
time I've ever been alone with you. It was very tactful of
Lady Grayston to leave us.

BESSIE: I'm not sure if it wasn't a trifle too tactful.

BLEANE: I was hoping most awfully to have the chance
of getting a talk with you.

(*The song of the lavender is heard again in the street.*
BESSIE *welcomes the diversion.*)

BESSIE: Oh, listen, there's the lavender man come back
again. (*She goes to the window and listens.*) Throw him
down a shilling, will you?

BLEANE: All right. (*He takes a coin from his pocket
and throws it into the street.*)

BESSIE: I seem to feel all the charm of England in that
funny little tune. It suggests cottage gardens, and
hedges, and winding roads.

BLEANE: My mother grows lavender at home. When

we were kids we were made to pick it, and my mother used to put it in little muslin bags and tie them up with pink ribbon. And she used to put them under the pillows of one's bed and in all the drawers. Shall I ask her to send you some?

BESSIE: Oh, that would be such a bother for her.

BLEANE: It wouldn't. She'd like to. And you know, it's not like the lavender you buy. It knocks spots off anything you can get in shops.

BESSIE: You must hate leaving London at this time of year.

BLEANE: Oh, I'm not very keen on London. (*making a dash for it*) I hate leaving you.

BESSIE (*with comic desperation*): Let's not talk about me, Lord Bleane.

BLEANE: But that's the only topic that occurs to me.

BESSIE: There's always the weather in England.

BLEANE: You see, I'm off tomorrow.

BESSIE: I never saw anyone so obstinate.

BLEANE: I shan't see you again for nearly a month. We haven't known one another very long, and if I hadn't been going away I expect I'd have thought it better to wait a bit.

BESSIE (*clasping her hands*): Lord Bleane, don't propose to me.

BLEANE: Why not?

BESSIE: Because I shall refuse you.

BLEANE: Oh!

BESSIE: Tell me about the part of the country you live in. I don't know Kent at all. Is it pretty?

BLEANE: I don't know. It's home.

BESSIE: I love those old Elizabethan houses that you have in England with all their chimneys.

BLEANE: Oh, ours isn't a show place, you know. It's just a rather ugly yellow brick house that looks like a box, and it's got a great big stucco portico in front of it. I think the garden's rather jolly.

BESSIE: Pearl hates Abbots Kenton. She'd sell it if George would. She's only really happy in London.

BLEANE: I don't know that I was so particularly struck on Bleane till I was over in France. When I was in hospital at Boulogne there didn't seem much to do but to think about things. . . . It didn't seem as if I *could* get well. I knew I should if they'd only let me come home, but they wouldn't; they said I couldn't be moved. . . . It's rather bleak in our part of the country. We've got an east wind that people find a bit trying, but if you've been used to it all your life it bucks you up wonderful. In summer it can be awfully hot down there, but there's always something fresh and salt in the air. You see, we're so near the marshes. . . . It was only just across the water, and it seemed such an awful long way off. I ain't boring you, am I?

BESSIE: No. I want you to tell me.

BLEANE: It's a funny sort of country. There are a lot of green fields and elm trees, and the roads wind about— it's rotten for motoring; and then you have the marshes, with dykes in them—we used to jump them when we were boys, and fall in mostly; and then there's the sea. It doesn't sound much, but I felt it was the most ripping thing I knew. And then there are hop-fields—I forgot them—and the oast-houses. They're rather picturesque, I suppose. I expect it's like the lavender to you. To me it's just England.

(BESSIE *gets up and walks towards the window. In the distance is heard the melancholy cry of the lavender man.*)

BLEANE: What are you thinking about?

BESSIE: It must be very wonderful to feel like that about one's home. I've never known anything but a red stone house in Nineteenth Street. As soon as dad can get a decent offer for it we're going to move further up town. Mother has a fancy for Seventy-Second Street, I don't know why.

BLEANE: Of course, I know it couldn't mean the same

to a girl that it means to me. I shouldn't expect anyone to live there always. I can be quite happy in London.

BESSIE (*with a smile*): You're determined to do it?

BLEANE: If you *could* bring yourself to marry me, I'd try and give you a good time.

BESSIE: Well, I suppose that's a proposal.

BLEANE: I've never made one before, and it makes me a bit nervous.

BESSIE: You haven't said anything that I can answer yes or no to.

BLEANE: I don't want to say anything that you *can* answer no to.

BESSIE (*with a chuckle*): Let me say that I'll think it over, may I?

BLEANE: I'm going away tomorrow.

BESSIE: I'll give you an answer when you come back.

BLEANE: But that won't be for four weeks.

BESSIE: It'll give us both a chance to make up our minds. After all, it *is* rather a serious step. You may come to the conclusion that you don't really want to marry me.

BLEANE: There's no fear of that.

BESSIE: You're coming down to Kenton for the week-end after you get back. If you change your mind send Pearl a wire putting yourself off. I shall understand, and I shan't be in the least hurt or offended.

BLEANE: Then it's good-bye till then.

BESSIE: Yes. And . . . thank you very much for wishing to marry me.

BLEANE: Thank you very much for not refusing me outright.

(*They shake hands and he goes out. She walks over to the window to look at him, glances at the watch on her wrist, and then leaves the room. In a moment* POLE *shows in* ARTHUR FENWICK. *He is a tall, elderly man with a red face and grey hair.*)

POLE: I'll tell her ladyship you're here, sir.

FENWICK: That'll be very good of you.

(Pole *goes out.* Fenwick *takes a cigar from his case, and the evening paper from a table, and settles himself down comfortably to read and smoke. He makes himself very much at home.* Pearl *comes in.*)

Pearl: Aren't Bessie and Harry Bleane here?

Fenwick: No.

Pearl: That's very strange. I wonder what can have happened.

Fenwick: Never mind about Bessie and Harry Bleane. Give me your attention now.

Pearl: You're very late.

Fenwick: I like to come when I stand a chance of finding you alone, girlie.

Pearl: I wish you wouldn't call me girlie, Arthur. I do hate it.

Fenwick: That's how I think of you. When I'm present at one of your big set-outs, and watch you like a queen among all those lords and ambassadors and bigwigs, I just say to myself, She's my girlie, and I feel warm all over. I'm so proud of you then. You've got there, girlie, you've got there.

Pearl (*smiling*): You've been very kind to me, Arthur.

Fenwick: You've got brains, girlie, that's how you've done it. It's brains. Underneath your flighty ways and that casual air of yours, so that one might think you were just enjoying yourself and nothing more, I see you thinking it all out, pulling a string here and a string there; you've got them in the hollow of your hand all the time. You leave nothing to chance, Pearl, you're a great woman.

Pearl: Not great enough to make you obey your doctor's orders.

Fenwick (*taking the cigar out of his mouth*): You're not going to ask me to throw away the first cigar I've had today?

Pearl: To please me, Arthur. They're so bad for you.

Fenwick: If you put it like that I must give in.

Pearl: I don't want you to be ill.

FENWICK: You've got a great heart, girlie. The world just thinks you're a smart, fashionable woman, clever, brilliant, beautiful, a leader of fashion, but I know different. I know you've got a heart of gold.

PEARL: You're a romantic old thing, Arthur.

FENWICK: My love for you is the most precious thing I have in the world. You're my guiding star, you're my ideal. You stand to me for all that's pure and noble and clean in womanhood. God bless you, girlie. I don't know what I should do if you failed me. I don't believe I could live if I ever found out that you weren't what I think you.

PEARL (*with her tongue in her cheek*): You shan't, if I can help it.

FENWICK: You do care for me a little, girlie?

PEARL: Of course I do.

FENWICK: I'm an old man, girlie.

PEARL: What nonsense! I look upon you as a mere boy.

FENWICK (*flattered*): Well, I expect a good many young men would be glad to have my physique. I can work fourteen hours on end and feel as fresh as a daisy at the end of it.

PEARL: Your vitality is wonderful.

FENWICK: I sometimes wonder what it is that first drew you to me, girlie.

PEARL: I don't know. I suppose it was the impression of strength you give.

FENWICK: Yes, I've often been told that. It's very difficult for people to be with me long without realizing that—well, that I'm not just the man in the street.

PEARL: I always feel I can rely on you.

FENWICK: You couldn't have said anything to please me better. I want you to rely on me. I know you. I'm the only man who's ever understood you. I know that, deep down in that big, beating, human heart of yours, you're a timid, helpless little thing, with the innocence of a child, and you want a man like me to stand between you and the world. My God, how I love you, girlie!

PEARL: Take care, there's the butler.

FENWICK: Oh, damn it, there's always the butler.

(POLE *comes in with a telegram and a parcel of books.*)

PEARL (*taking the telegram and glancing at the parcel*):
What's that, Pole?

POLE: They're books, my lady. They've just come from Hatchard's.

PEARL: Oh, I know. Undo them, will you? (POLE *cuts open the parcel and takes out a bundle of four or five books.* PEARL *opens the telegram.*) Oh, bother! There's no answer, Pole.

POLE: Very good, my lady.

(*Exit.*)

FENWICK: Is anything the matter?

PEARL: That fool Sturrey was dining here tonight, and he's just wired to say he can't come. I do hate having my parties upset. I'd asked ten people to meet him.

FENWICK: That's too bad.

PEARL: Pompous owl. He's refused invitation after invitation. I asked him six weeks ago this time, and he hadn't the face to say he was engaged.

FENWICK: Well, I'm afraid you must give him up. I daresay you can do without him.

PEARL: Don't be a fool, Arthur. I'll get hold of him somehow. He may be Prime Minister one of these days. (*She reflects for a moment.*) I wonder what his telephone number is. (*She gets up and looks in a book, then sits down at the telephone.*) Gerrard 7035. If he comes once because I force him to he'll come again because he likes it. This house is like the kingdom of heaven: I have to compel them to come in.... Is Lord Sturrey in? Lady Grayston. I'll hold the line. (*making her voice sweet and charming*) Is that you, Lord Sturrey? It's Pearl Grayston speaking. I just rang up to say it doesn't matter a bit about tonight. Of course, I'm disappointed you can't come. But you must come another day, will you? That's very nice of you. How about this day week? Oh, I'm sorry. Would Thursday suit you? Oh! Well, how about Friday? You're engaged every evening next week? You are in demand. Well, I'll tell you what, get your book and tell me what day you are free.

FENWICK: You're the goods, girlie. You'll get there.

PEARL: Tuesday fortnight. Yes, that'll suit me beautiful-ly. 8:30. I'm so glad you chose that day, because I'm having Kreisler in to play. I shall look forward to seeing you. Good-bye. (*She puts down the receiver.*) This time I've got him. The ape thinks he understands music.

FENWICK: Have you got Kreisler for Tuesday fort-night?

PEARL: No.

FENWICK: Are you sure you can get him?

PEARL: No, but I'm sure you can.

FENWICK: You shall have him, girlie. (*She takes the books that* POLE *brought in and puts them about the room. One she places face downwards, open.*) What are you doing that for?

PEARL: They're Richard Twining's books. He's coming to dinner tonight.

FENWICK: Why d'you trouble about authors, girlie?

PEARL: London isn't like New York, you know. People like to meet them over here.

FENWICK: I should have thought your position was quite strong enough to do without them.

PEARL: We live in a democratic age. They take the place in society of the fools whom kings kept about their courts in the Middle Ages. They have the advantage that they don't presume on their position to tell one home truths. They're cheap. A dinner and a little flattery is all they want. And they provide their own clothes.

FENWICK: You litter up your house with their rotten books.

PEARL: Oh, but I don't keep them. These are on approval. I shall send them all back to the bookseller tomorrow morning.

Fenwick: Pearl, you're a little wonder. When you want to go into business you come to me and I'll take you into partnership.

Pearl: How is business?

Fenwick: Fine! I'm opening two new branches next week. They laughed at me when I first came over here. They said I'd go bankrupt. I've turned their silly old methods upside down. He laughs longest who laughs last.

Pearl (*reflectively*): Ah, I can't help thinking that's what my dressmaker said when she sent me in my bill.

(*He gives a slight start and looks at her shrewdly. He sees her blandly smiling.*)

Fenwick: Girlie, you promised me you wouldn't run up any more bills.

Pearl: That's like promising to love, honour, and obey one's husband, the kind of undertaking no one is really expected to carry out.

Fenwick: You naughty little thing.

Pearl: It's Suzanne—you know, the dressmaker in the Place Vendôme. The war has dislocated her business and she wants to get her money in. It isn't very convenient for me to pay just at present. It's rather a large sum. (*She gives him a sheaf of typewritten documents.*)

Fenwick: This looks more like a five-act play than a bill.

Pearl: Clothes are expensive, aren't they? I wish I could dress in fig-leaves. It would be cheap, and I believe it would suit me.

Fenwick (*putting the bill in his pocket*): Well, I'll see what I can do about it.

Pearl: You are a duck, Arthur. . . . Would you like me to come and lunch with you tomorrow?

Fenwick: Why, sure.

Pearl: All right. Now you must go, as I want to lie down before I dress for dinner.

FENWICK: That's right. Take care of yourself, girlie, you're very precious to me.

PEARL: Good-bye, dear old thing.

FENWICK: Good-bye, girlie.

(*He goes out. As he goes to the door the telephone rings.* PEARL *takes up the receiver.*)

PEARL: You're speaking to Lady Grayston. Tony! Of course I knew your voice. Well, what is it? I'm not at all stern. I'm making my voice as pleasant as I can. I'm sorry you find it disagreeable. (*She gives a chuckle.*) No, I'm afraid I couldn't come to tea tomorrow. I shall be engaged all the afternoon. What is the day after tomorrow? (*smiling*) Well, I must ask Bessie. I don't know if she's free. Of course I'm not coming alone. It would be most compromising. A nice-looking young man like you. What would Minnie say? Oh, I know all about that. . . . I didn't promise anything. I merely said the future was everybody's property. A sleepless night. Fancy! Well, good-bye. . . . Tony, do you know the most enchanting word in the English language? Perhaps.

(*She puts down the telephone quickly, and the curtain falls.*)

# ACT TWO

SCENE: *The scene is a morning-room at Abbots Kenton, the Graystons' place in the country. It has an old-fashioned, comfortable look; nothing is very new; the chintzes are faded. Three long French windows lead on to a terrace.*

*It is after dinner, a fine night, and the windows are open.*

*The women of the party are sitting down, waiting for the men; they are* PEARL *and* BESSIE, *the* DUCHESSE DE SURENNES *and the* PRINCESS DELLA CERCOLA.

PRINCESS: You must be exhausted after all the tennis you played this afternoon, Minnie.

DUCHESSE: Not a bit. I only played four sets.

PRINCESS: You played so vigorously. It made me quite hot to look at you.

DUCHESSE: If I didn't take exercise I should be enormous. Oh, Flora, how I envy you! You can eat anything you choose and it has no effect on you. And what makes it so unfair is that you don't care about food. I am a lazy and a greedy woman. I never eat any of the things I like, and I never miss a day without taking at least an hour's exercise.

126

PRINCESS (*smiling*): If mortification is the first step in sanctity, I'm sure you must be on the high road to it.

PEARL: One of these days you'll give up the struggle, Minnie, and, like Flora, take to good works.

DUCHESSE (*with immense decision*): Never! I shall lie on my death-bed with my hair waved and a little rouge on my cheeks and with my last breath murmur: Not gruel, it's so fattening.

PEARL: Well, you'll have more serious tennis tomorrow. Harry Bleane plays much better than Thornton.

DUCHESSE: It was very tiresome of him not to come till it was just time to dress.

PEARL: He only got back from Rumania yesterday, and he had to go down to see his mother. (*with an amused glance at her sister*) Bessie asked me not to put him next her at dinner.

BESSIE: Pearl, you are a cat! I do think it's hateful the way you discuss my private affairs with all and sundry.

DUCHESSE: My dear Bessie, they've long ceased to be your private affairs.

PEARL: I'm afraid Bessie misses her opportunities. Just before he went to Rumania I left them alone together, and nothing happened. All my tact was wasted.

BESSIE: Your tact was too obvious, Pearl.

DUCHESSE: Well, do be quick and bring him to the scratch, my dear. I'm growing tired of people asking me, Is he going to propose or is he not?

BESSIE: Don't they ever ask, Is she going to accept him or is she not?

DUCHESSE: Of course, you'll accept him.

BESSIE: I'm not so sure.

PRINCESS (*smiling*): Perhaps it depends on the way he asks.

PEARL: For heaven's sake, don't expect too much romance. Englishmen aren't romantic. It makes them feel absurd. George proposed to me when he was in New York for the Horse Show. I wasn't very well that day, and I was lying down. I was looking a perfect fright. He told me all about a mare he had, and he told me all about her father and her mother and her uncles and her aunts, and then he said: (*imitating him*) Look here, you'd better marry me.

PRINCESS: How very sudden.

PEARL: Oh, I said, why didn't you tell me you were going to propose? I'd have had my hair waved. Poor George, he asked *why?*

DUCHESSE: The French are the only nation who know how to make love. When Gaston proposed to me he went down on his knees, and he took my hand, and he said he couldn't live without me. Of course I knew that, because he hadn't a cent, but still it thrilled me. He said I was his guiding star and his guardian angel —oh, I don't know what! It was beautiful! I knew he'd been haggling with papa for a fortnight about having his debts paid; but it was beautiful.

PRINCESS: Were you quite indifferent to him?

DUCHESSE: Oh, quite. I'd made up my mind to marry a foreigner. People weren't very nice to us in Chicago. My cousin Mary had married the Count de Moret, and mother couldn't bear Aunt Alice. She said, If Alice has got hold of a Count for Mary, I'm determined that you shall have a Duke.

PEARL: And you did.

DUCHESSE: I wish you could have seen the fuss those Chicago people made of me when I went over last. It was hard to realize that I used to cry my eyes out because I wasn't asked to the balls I wanted to go to.

PRINCESS: Still, I hope Bessie won't marry any man she doesn't care for.

PEARL: My dear, don't put ideas in the child's head. The French are a much more civilized nation than we are, and they've come to the conclusion long ago that marriage is an affair of convenience rather than of sentiment. Think of the people you know who've married for love. After five years do they care for one another any more than the people who've married for money?

PRINCESS: They have the recollection.

PEARL: Nonsense! As if anyone remembered an emotion when he no longer felt it!

DUCHESSE: It's true. I've been in love a dozen times, desperately, and when I've got over it and look back, though I remember I was in love, I can't for the life of me remember my love. It always seems to me so odd.

PEARL: Believe me, Bessie, the flourishing state of father's hardware store is a much sounder basis for matrimonial happiness than any amount of passion.

BESSIE: Oh, Pearl, what is this you've been telling people about dad selling bananas?

PEARL: Bananas? Oh, I remember. They were saying that Mrs. Hanley used to wash the miners' clothes in California. That and her pearls are taking her everywhere. I wasn't going to be outdone, so I said father used to sell bananas in the streets of New York.

BESSIE: He never did anything of the kind.

PEARL: I know he didn't, but I thought people were getting rather tired of the hardware store, and I made a perfectly killing story out of it. I had a new Callot frock on and I thought I could manage the bananas.

DUCHESSE: A most unpleasant vegetable. So fattening.

(*The men come in.* THORNTON CLAY, ARTHUR FENWICK, *and* FLEMING. PEARL *and* BESSIE *get up.*)

BESSIE: You've been a long time.

DUCHESSE: Where is Tony?

CLAY: He and Bleane are finishing their cigars.

DUCHESSE: Well, Mr. Harvey, are you still enjoying life in London?

CLAY: He should be. I've got him invitations to all the nicest parties. But he will waste his time in sightseeing. The other day—Thursday, wasn't it?—I wanted to take him to Hurlingham, and he insisted on going to the National Gallery instead.

PEARL (*smiling*): What an outrageous proceeding!

FLEMING: I don't see that it was any more outrageous for me than for you. I saw you coming in just as I was going out.

PEARL: I had a reason to go. Arthur Fenwick has just bought a Bronzino, and I wanted to see those in the National Gallery.

DUCHESSE: I think it's much more likely that you had an assignation. I've always heard it's a wonderful place for that. You never meet any of your friends, and if you do they're there for the same purpose, and pretend not to see you.

FLEMING: I certainly only went to see the pictures.

CLAY: But, good heavens, if you want to do that there's Christie's, and there you *will* meet your friends.

FLEMING: I'm afraid you'll never make a man of fashion out of me, Thornton.

CLAY: I'm beginning to despair. You have a natural instinct for doing the wrong thing. D'you know, the other day I caught him in the act of delivering half a bagful of letters of introduction? I implored him to put them in the wastepaper basket.

FLEMING: I thought as people had taken the trouble to give them to me, it was only polite to make use of them.

CLAY: Americans give letters so carelessly. Before you know where you are you'll know all the wrong people. And, believe me, the wrong people are very difficult to shake off.

FLEMING (*amused*): Perhaps some of my letters are to the right people.

CLAY: Then they'll take no notice of them.

FLEMING: It looks as though the wrong people had better manners than the right ones.

CLAY: The right people *are* rude. They can afford to be. I was a very young man when I first came to London, and I made mistakes. All of us Americans make mistakes. It wanted a good deal of character to cut people who'd taken me about, asked me to dine, stay with them in the country, and heaven knows what, when I found they weren't the sort of people one ought to know.

PEARL: Of course, one has to do it.

DUCHESSE: Of course. It shows that you have a nice nature, Thornton, to worry yourself about it.

CLAY: I'm curiously sentimental. Another of our American faults. I remember when I'd been in London two or three years, I knew pretty well everyone that was worth knowing, but I'd never been asked to Hereford House. The Duchess doesn't like Americans anyway, and she'd been very disagreeable about me in particular. But I was determined to go to her ball. I felt it wasn't the sort of function I could afford to be left out of.

PEARL: They're very dull balls.

CLAY: I know, but they're almost the only ones you can't go to without an invitation. Well, I found out that the Duchess had a widowed sister who lived in the country with her two daughters. Lady Helen Blair. My dear, she was a very stuffy, dowdy woman of fifty-five, and her two daughters were stuffier and dowdier still, and if possible, older. They were in the habit of coming up to London for the season. I got introduced to them, and I laid myself out. I took them to the play, I showed them round the Academy, I stood them luncheons, I gave them cards for private views, for a month I worked like a Trojan. Then the Duchess sent out her invitations, and the Blair girls had half a dozen cards for their young men. I received one, and, by George, I'd earned it. Of course, as soon as I got my invitation I dropped them, but you know I felt quite badly about it.

DUCHESSE: I expect they're used to that.

CLAY: A strangely tactless woman, Lady Helen Blair. She wrote and asked me if I was offended about anything because I never went near them.

PEARL: I wish those men would come, and then we could dance.

DUCHESSE: Oh, that'll be charming! It's such good exercise, isn't it? I'm told that you dance divinely, Mr. Harvey.

FLEMING: I don't know about that. I dance.

DUCHESSE (*to the* PRINCESS): Oh, my dear, who d'you think I danced with the other night? (*impressively*) Ernest.

PRINCESS: Oh!

DUCHESSE: My dear, don't say, Oh! like that. Don't you know who Ernest is?

PEARL: Ernest is the most sought after man in London.

PRINCESS: You don't mean the dancing master?

DUCHESSE: Oh, my dear, you mustn't call him that. He'd be furious. He isn't a professional. He gives lessons at ten guineas an hour, but only to oblige. He's invited to all the best dances.

FLEMING: One of the things that rather surprised me at balls was to see all these dancing-masters. Do English girls like to be pawed about by Greeks, Dagos and Bowery toughs?

CLAY: You Americans who live in America, you're so prudish.

DUCHESSE: Believe me, I would go to *any* dance where there was the remotest chance of meeting Ernest. It's a perfect dream to dance with him. He showed me a new step, and I can't get it quite right. I don't know what I shall do if I don't run across him again very soon.

PRINCESS: But why don't you let him give you a lesson?

DUCHESSE: My dear, ten guineas an hour! I couldn't possibly afford that. I'm sure to meet him at a dance in a day or two, and I shall get a lesson for nothing.

PEARL: You ought to make him fall in love with you.

DUCHESSE: Oh, my dear, if he only would! But he's so run after.

(BLEANE *and* TONY PAXTON *come in from the terrace.*)

DUCHESSE: At last!

TONY: We've been taking a stroll in the garden.

PEARL: I hope you showed him my tea-house.

BESSIE: It's Pearl's new toy. You must be sure to admire it.

PEARL: I'm very proud of it. You know, George won't let me do anything here. He says it's his house, and he isn't going to have any of my muck. He won't even have new chintzes. Well, there was an old summer-house just over there, and it was all worm-eaten and horrid and tumbledown, what they call picturesque, but it was rather a nice place to go and have tea in as it had a really charming view; I wanted to pull it down and put up a smart Japanese tea-house instead, but George wouldn't hear of it, because, if you please, his mother—a peculiarly plain woman—used to sit and sew there. Well, I bided my time, and the other day, when George was in London, I pulled down the old summer-house, got my Japanese tea-house down from town, put it up, and had everything finished by the time George came back twenty-four hours later. He very nearly had an apoplectic stroke. If he had I should have killed two birds with one stone.

BESSIE: Pearl!

PRINCESS: I don't know why you've furnished it so elaborately.

PEARL: Well, I thought in the hot weather I'd sleep there sometimes. It'll be just like sleeping in the open air.

FENWICK: These young people want to start dancing, Pearl.

PEARL: Where would you like to dance, in here with the gramophone, or in the drawing-room with the pianola?

BESSIE: Oh, in the drawing-room.

PEARL: Let's go there then.

Bessie (*to* Clay): Come and help me get the rolls out.

Clay: Right you are.

(*They go out, followed by the* Duchesse *and* Pearl, Tony, Fenwick, *and* Bleane.)

Fleming (*to the* Princess): Aren't you coming?

Princess: No, I think I'll stay here for the present. But don't bother about me. You must go and dance.

Fleming: There are enough men without me. I'm sure Thornton Clay is a host in himself.

Princess: You don't like Thornton?

Fleming: He's been very kind to me since I came to London.

Princess: I was watching your face when he told that story about the Hereford ball. You must learn to conceal your feelings better.

Fleming: Didn't you think it was horrible?

Princess: I've known Thornton for ten years. I'm used to him. And as you say yourself, he's very kind.

Fleming: That's what makes life so difficult. People don't seem to be good or bad as the squares on a chessboard are black or white. Even the worthless ones have got good traits, and it makes it so hard to know how to deal with them.

Princess (*smiling a little*): You don't approve of poor Thornton?

Fleming: What do you expect me to think of a man who's proud of having forced his way into a house where he knew he wasn't wanted? He reckons success by the number of invitations he receives. He holds himself up to me as an example. He tells me that if I want to get into society, I must work for it. What do they think of a man like Thornton Clay in England? Don't they despise him?

Princess: Everywhere, in New York just as much as in London, there are masses of people struggling to get into society. It's so common a sight that one loses the sense of there being anything disgraceful in it. Pearl would tell you that English society is a little pompous; they welcome a man who can make them laugh. Thornton is very useful. He has high spirits, he's amusing, he makes a party go.

FLEMING: I should have thought a man could find some better use for his life than that.

PRINCESS: Thornton has plenty of money. Do you think there is any point in his spending his life making more? I sometimes think there's too much money in America already.

FLEMING: There are things a man can do besides making money.

PRINCESS: You know, American wealth has reached a pitch when it was bound to give rise to a leisured class. Thornton is one of the first members of it. Perhaps he doesn't play the part very well, but remember he hasn't had the time to learn it that they've had in Europe.

FLEMING (*smiling*): I'm afraid you don't think me very charitable.

PRINCESS: You're young. It's a real pleasure to me to know a nice clean American boy. And I'm so glad that you're not going to be dazzled by this English life that dazzles so many of our countrymen. Amuse yourself, learn what you can from it, take all the good it offers you, and go back to America.

FLEMING: I shall be glad to go back. Perhaps I ought never to have come.

PRINCESS: I'm afraid you're not very happy.

FLEMING: I don't know what makes you think that.

PRINCESS: It's not very hard to see that you're in love with Bessie.

FLEMING: Did you know that I was engaged to her?

PRINCESS (*surprised*): No.

FLEMING: I was engaged to her before I went to Harvard. I was eighteen then, and she was sixteen.

PRINCESS: How very early in life you young people settle things in America!

FLEMING: Perhaps it was rather silly and childish. But

when she wrote and told me that she thought we'd better break it off, I discovered I cared more than I thought.

Princess: What did you say to her?

Fleming: I couldn't try to hold her to a promise she gave when she was a schoolgirl. I answered that I sympathized and understood.

Princess: When did this happen?

Fleming: A couple of months ago. Then I got the chance to go over to Europe and I thought I'd come to see what was going on. It didn't take me long to tumble.

Princess: You're bearing it very well.

Fleming: Oh, the only thing I could do was to be pleasant. I should only have bored her if I'd made love to her. She took our engagement as an amusing joke, and there wasn't anything for me to do but accept her view of it. She was having the time of her life. At first I thought perhaps she'd grow tired of all these balls and parties, and then if I was on the spot I might persuade her to come back to America with me.

Princess: You may still.

Fleming: No, I haven't a chance. The first day I arrived she told me how wonderful she thought this English life. She thinks it full and varied. She thinks it has beauty.

Princess: That sounds rather satirical.

Fleming: Pearl has been very nice to me. She's taken me about, I've driven with her constantly, I've sat in her box at the opera, I'm her guest at the moment. If I had any decency I'd hold my tongue.

Princess: Well?

Fleming (*bursting out impetuously*): There's something in these surroundings that makes me feel terribly uncomfortable. Under the brilliant surface I suspect all kinds of ugly and shameful secrets that everyone knows and pretends not to. This is a strange house in which the husband is never seen and Arthur Fenwick, a vulgar sensualist, acts as host; and it's an attractive spectacle, this painted duchess devouring with her eyes a boy young enough to be her son. And the conversation—I don't want to seem a prude, I daresay people over here talk more freely than the people I've known; but surely there are women who don't have lovers, there are such things as honour and decency and self-restraint. If Bessie is going to remain over here I wish to God she'd marry her lord at once and get out of it quickly.

PRINCESS: D'you think she'll be happy?

FLEMING: Are they any of them happy? How can they expect to be happy when they marry for ... (*The* PRINCESS *gives a sudden start, and* FLEMING *stops short.*) I beg your pardon. I was forgetting. Please forgive me. You see, you're so different.

PRINCESS: I'm sorry I interrupted you. What were you going to say?

FLEMING: It wasn't of any importance. You see, I've been thinking it over so much that it's rather got on my nerves. And I haven't been able to tell anyone what I was thinking about. I'm dreadfully sorry.

PRINCESS: You were going to say, how can they expect to be happy when they marry for a trumpery title? You thought, they're snobs, vulgar snobs, and the misery of their lives is the proper punishment for their ignoble desires.

FLEMING (*very apologetically*): Princess.

PRINCESS (*ironically*): Princess.

FLEMING: Believe me, I hadn't the smallest intention of saying anything to wound you.

PRINCESS: You haven't. It's too true. Most of us who marry foreigners are merely snobs. But I wonder if it's all our fault. We're not shown a better way of life. No one has even hinted to us that we have any duty towards our own country. We're blamed because we marry foreigners, but columns are written about us in the papers, and our photographs are in all the magazines. Our friends are excited and envious. After all, we are human. At first, when people addressed me as Princess, I couldn't help feeling thrilled. Of course it was snobbishness.

FLEMING: You make me feel a terrible cad.

Princess: But sometimes there've been other motives, too. Has it ever occurred to you that snobbishness is the spirit of romance in a reach-me-down? I was only twenty when I married Marino. I didn't see him as a fortune-hunting Dago, but as the successor of a long line of statesmen and warriors. There'd been a pope in his family, and a dozen cardinals, one of his ancestors had been painted by Titian; for centuries they'd been men of war, with power of life and death; I'd seen the great feudal castle, with its hundred rooms, where they had ruled as independent sovereigns. When Marino came and asked me to marry him it was romance that stood in his shoes and beckoned to me. I thought of the palace in Rome, which I had visited as a tripper, and where I might reign as mistress. I thought it was splendid to take my place after all those great ladies, Orsinis, Colonnas, Gaetanis, Aldobrandinis. I loved him.

Fleming: But there's no need to tell me that you could never do anything from an unworthy motive.

Princess: My husband's family had been ruined by speculation. He was obliged to sell himself. He sold himself for five million dollars. And I loved him. You can imagine the rest. First he was indifferent to me, then I bored him, and at last he hated me. Oh, the humiliation I endured. When my child died I couldn't bear it any longer; I left him. I went back to America. I found myself a stranger. I was out of place, the life had become foreign to me; I couldn't live at home. I settled in England; and here we're strangers too. I've paid very heavily for being a romantic girl.

(Bessie *comes in.*)

Bessie: Really, Fleming, it's too bad of you to sit in here and flirt with the Princess. We want you to come and dance.

(*The* Princess, *agitated, gets up and goes out into the garden.*)

BESSIE (*looking after her*): Is anything the matter?

FLEMING: No.

BESSIE: Are you coming to dance, or are you not?

FLEMING: I had quite a talk with Lord Bleane after dinner, Bessie.

BESSIE (*smiling*): Well?

FLEMING: Are you going to accept the coronet that he's dangling before your eyes?

BESSIE: It would be more to the point if you asked whether I'm going to accept the coronet that he's laying at my feet.

FLEMING: He's a very nice fellow, Bessie.

BESSIE: I know that.

FLEMING: I wanted to dislike him.

BESSIE: Why?

FLEMING: Well, I don't think much of these English lords who run after American girls for their money. I expected him to be a brainless loafer, with just enough cunning to know his market value, but he's a modest, unassuming fellow. To tell you the truth, I'm puzzled.

BESSIE (*chaffing him*): Fancy that!

FLEMING: I think it's a low-down thing that he's doing, and yet he doesn't seem to be a low-down fellow.

BESSIE: He might be in love with me, you know.

FLEMING: Is he?

BESSIE: No.

FLEMING: Are you going to marry him?

BESSIE: I don't know.

FLEMING: I suppose he's come here to ask you?

BESSIE (*after a short pause*): He asked me a month ago. I promised to give him an answer when he came back from Rumania. . . . I'm in a panic. He's waiting to get me alone. I was able to be quite flippant about it when I had a month before me, but now, when I've got to say yes or no, I'm so jumpy I don't know what to do with myself.

FLEMING: Don't marry him, Bessie.

BESSIE: Why not?

FLEMING: Well, first, you're no more in love with him than he is with you.

BESSIE: And then?

FLEMING: Isn't that enough?

BESSIE: I wonder if you realize what he offers me. Do you know what the position of an English peeress is?

FLEMING: Does it mean so much to be called Your Ladyship by tradesmen?

BESSIE: You donkey, Fleming. If I marry an American boy my life will be over; if I marry Harry Bleane it will be only just beginning. Look at Pearl. I could do what she's done; I could do more, because George Grayston isn't ambitious. I could make Harry do anything I liked. He would go into politics, and I should have a salon. Why, I could do anything.

FLEMING (*dryly*): I don't know why you should be in a panic. You've evidently made up your mind. You'll have a brilliant marriage with crowds outside the church, your photograph will be in all the papers, you'll go away for your honeymoon, and you'll come back. What will you do then?

BESSIE: Why, settle down.

FLEMING: Will you break your heart like the Princess because your husband has taken a mistress, or will you take lovers like the Duchesse de Surennes, or will you bore yourself to death like Pearl because your husband is virtuous, and wants you to do your duty?

BESSIE: Fleming, you've got no right to say things like that to me.

FLEMING: I'm sorry if I've made you angry. I had to say it.

BESSIE: Are you quite sure that it's for my sake you don't want me to marry Lord Bleane?

FLEMING: Yes, I think it is. When you broke off our engagement I didn't blame you. You wouldn't have done it if you'd cared for me, and it wasn't your fault if you didn't. When I came over I saw that I could expect nothing but friendship from you. You must do me the justice to acknowledge that during this month I haven't given the smallest sign that I wanted anything else.

BESSIE: Oh, you've been charming. You always were the best friend I've had.

FLEMING: If in a corner of my heart I kept my love for you, that is entirely my affair. I don't know that it puts you to any inconvenience, and it pleases me. I'm quite sure that I'm only thinking now of your happiness. Go back to America, and fall in love with some nice fellow, and marry him. You'll have all my best wishes. Perhaps your life won't be so brilliant or so exciting, but it will be simpler and wholesomer, and more becoming.

BESSIE: You're a dear, Fleming, and if I said anything disagreeable just now, forgive me. I didn't mean it. I shall always want you to be my dearest friend.

(LORD BLEANE *enters from the terrace.*)

BLEANE: I was looking for you everywhere. I wondered where you'd got to.

(*There is a moment's pause.* FLEMING HARVEY *looks from* BESSIE *to* BLEANE.)

FLEMING: I really must go and dance with the Duchesse or she'll never forgive me.

BLEANE: I've just been dancing with her. My dear fellow, it's the most violent form of exercise I've ever taken.

FLEMING: I'm in very good condition.

(*He goes out.*)

BLEANE: Blessings on him.
BESSIE: Why?
BLEANE: Because he's left us alone. Ask me another.
BESSIE: I don't think I will.
BLEANE: Then I'll ask you one.
BESSIE: Please don't. Tell me all about Rumania.

Bleane: Rumania is a Balkan State. Its capital is Bucharest. It has long been known for its mineral springs.

Bessie: You're in very high spirits tonight.

Bleane: You may well wonder. Everything has conspired to depress them.

Bessie: Oh, what nonsense!

Bleane: First I was in England thirty-six hours before I had a chance of seeing you; secondly, when I arrived you'd already gone up to dress; then, when I was expecting to sit next you at dinner, I was put between Lady Grayston and the Princess; and, lastly, you made me pound away at that beastly pianola when I wanted to dance with you.

Bessie: Well, you've survived it all.

Bleane: What I want to point out to you is that if notwithstanding I'm in high spirits, I must have a most engaging nature.

Bessie: I never dreamt of denying it.

Bleane: So much to the good.

Bessie: The man's going to propose to me.

Bleane: No, I'm not.

Bessie: I beg your pardon. My mistake.

Bleane: I did that a month ago.

Bessie: There's been a change of moon since then, and no proposal holds good after the new moon.

Bleane: I never knew that.

Bessie: You've been down to see your mother.

Bleane: She sends you her love.

Bessie: Have you told her?

Bleane: I told her a month ago.

(Bessie *does not speak for a moment; when she answers it is more gravely.*)

Bessie: You know, I want to be frank with you. You won't think it disagreeable of me, will you? I'm not in love with you.

Bleane: I know. But you don't positively dislike me?

BESSIE: No. I like you very much.

BLEANE: Won't you risk it then?

BESSIE (*almost tragically*): I can't make up my mind.

BLEANE: I'll do all I can to make you happy. I'll try not to make a nuisance of myself.

BESSIE: I know quite well that I wouldn't marry you if you weren't who you are, and I'm afraid I know that you wouldn't marry me if I hadn't a certain amount of money.

BLEANE: Oh, yes, I would.

BESSIE: It's nice of you to say so.

BLEANE: Don't you believe it?

BESSIE: I suppose I'm a perfect fool. I ought to play the game prettily. You see, I know that you can't afford to marry a girl who isn't well-to-do. Everyone knows what I have. Pearl has taken good care that they should. You wouldn't ever have thought of me otherwise. We're arranging a deal. You give your title and your position, and I give my money. It's a commonplace thing enough, but somehow it sticks in my throat.

(BLEANE *hesitates a moment, and walks up and down thinking.*)

BLEANE: You make me feel an awful swine. The worst of it is that some part of what you say is true. I'm not such a fool that I didn't see your sister was throwing us together. I don't want to seem a conceited ass, but a fellow in my sort of position can't help knowing that many people think him rather a catch. Mothers of marriageable daughters are very transparent sometimes, you know, and if they don't marry their daughters they're determined it shan't be for want of trying.

BESSIE: Oh, I can quite believe that. I have noticed it in American mothers, too.

BLEANE: I knew it would be a good thing if I married you. I don't suppose I should have thought about you if I hadn't been told you were pretty well off. It's beastly now, saying all that.

BESSIE: I don't see why.

BLEANE: Because after a bit I found out I'd fallen in love with you. And then I didn't care if you hadn't got a bob. I wanted to marry you because—because I didn't know what to do without you.

BESSIE: Harry!

BLEANE: Do believe me. I swear it's true. I don't care a hang about the money. After all, we could get along without it. And I love you.

BESSIE: It's very good to hear you say that. I'm so absurdly pleased and flattered.

BLEANE: You do believe it, don't you?

BESSIE: Yes.

BLEANE: And will you marry me?

BESSIE: If you like.

BLEANE: Of course I like. (*He takes her in his arms and kisses her.*)

BESSIE: Take care, someone might come in.

BLEANE (*smiling and happy*): Come into the garden with me.

(*He stretches out his hand, she hesitates a moment, smiles, takes it, and together they go out on to the terrace.*

*For a moment the music of a one-step is heard more loudly, and then the* DUCHESSE *and* TONY PAXTON *come in. She sinks into a chair, fanning herself, and he goes over to a table, takes a cigarette, and lights it.*)

DUCHESSE: Did you see? That was Harry Bleane and Bessie. I wondered where they were.

TONY: You've got eyes like a lynx.

DUCHESSE: I'm positive they were hand in hand.

TONY: It looks as if she'd worked it at last.

DUCHESSE: I don't know about that. It looks as if he'd worked it.

TONY: She's not such a catch as all that. If I were a

peer I'd sell myself for a damned sight more than eight thousand a year.

DUCHESSE: Don't stand so far away, Tony. Come and sit on the sofa by me.

TONY (*going over to her*): I say, I've been talking to Bleane about two-seaters.

DUCHESSE (*very coldly*): Oh!

TONY (*giving her a look out of the corner of his eye*): He says I can't do better than get a Talbot.

DUCHESSE: I don't see why you want a car of your own. You can always use one of mine.

TONY: That's not the same thing. After all, it won't cost much. I can get a ripper for just over twelve hundred pounds, with a really smart body.

DUCHESSE: You talk as though twelve hundred pounds were nothing at all.

TONY: Hang it all, it isn't anything to you.

DUCHESSE: What with the income tax and one thing and another, I'm not so terribly flush just now. No one knows the claims I have on me. Because one has a certain amount of money one's supposed to be made of it. They don't realize that if one spends it in one way one can't spend it in another. It cost me seven thousand pounds to have my house redecorated.

TONY (*sulkily*): You said I could buy myself a car.

DUCHESSE: I said I'd think about it. I wasn't under the impression that you'd go and order one right away.

TONY: I've practically committed myself now.

DUCHESSE: You only want a car so that you can be independent of me.

TONY: Well, hang it all, you can't expect me to be tied to your apron-strings always. It's a bit thick if whenever I want to take a man down to play golf I have to ring up and ask if I can have one of your cars. It makes me look such an ass.

DUCHESSE: If it's only to play golf you want it, I'm sure anyone would rather go down to the links in a comfortable Rolls-Royce than in a two-seater.

(*A silence.*)

TONY: If you don't want to give me a car, why on earth did you say you would?

DUCHESSE (*putting her hand on him*): Tony.

TONY: For goodness' sake don't touch me.

DUCHESSE (*hurt and mortified*): Tony!

TONY: I don't want to force you to make me presents. I can quite well do without a two-seater. I can go about in omnibuses if it comes to that.

DUCHESSE: Don't you love me?

TONY: I wish you wouldn't constantly ask me if I love you. It is maddening.

DUCHESSE: Oh, how can you be so cruel to me!

TONY (*exasperated*): D'you think this is quite the best place to choose to make a scene?

DUCHESSE: I love you with all my heart. I've never loved anybody as much as I love you.

TONY: No man could stand being loved so much. D'you think it's jolly for me to feel that your eyes are glued on me whatever I'm doing? I can never put my hand out without finding yours there ready to press it.

DUCHESSE: I can't help it if I love you. That's my temperament.

TONY: Yes, but you needn't show it so much. Why don't you leave me to do the love-making?

DUCHESSE: If I did that there wouldn't be any love-making.

TONY: You make me look such a fool.

DUCHESSE: Don't you know there's nothing in the world I wouldn't do for you?

TONY (*quickly*): Well, why don't you marry me?

DUCHESSE (*with a gasp*): I can't do that. You know that I can't do that.

TONY: Why not? You could still call yourself Duchesse de Surennes.

DUCHESSE: No; I've always told you nothing would induce me to marry.

TONY: That shows how much you love me.

DUCHESSE: Marriage is so middle-class. It takes away all the romance of love.

TONY: You simply want to have your freedom and keep me bound hand and foot. D'you think it's jolly for me to know what people say about me? After all, I have got some pride.

DUCHESSE: I'm sure we shall be able to get you a job soon, and then no one will be able to say anything.

TONY: I'm getting fed up with the whole business; I tell you that straight. I'd just as soon chuck it.

DUCHESSE: Tony, you don't mean to say you want to leave me. I'll kill myself if you do. I couldn't bear it, I couldn't bear it. I'll kill myself.

TONY: For God's sake, don't make such a row.

DUCHESSE: Say you don't mean it, Tony. I shall scream.

TONY: After all, I've got my self-respect to think of. It seems to me the best thing would be if we put a stop to the whole thing now.

DUCHESSE: Oh, I can't lose you. I can't.

TONY: No one can say I'm mercenary, but hang it all, one has to think of one's future. I shan't be twenty-five for ever. I ought to be settling down.

DUCHESSE: Don't you care for me any more?

TONY: Of course I care for you. If I didn't, d'you think I'd have let you do all you have for me?

DUCHESSE: Then why d'you make me so unhappy?

TONY: I don't want to make you unhappy, but really sometimes you are unreasonable.

DUCHESSE: You mean about the car?

TONY: I wasn't thinking about the car then.

DUCHESSE: You can have it if you like.

TONY: I don't want it now.

DUCHESSE: Tony, don't be unkind.

TONY: I'm not going to take any more presents from you.

DUCHESSE: I didn't mean to be unreasonable. I'd like you to have the car, Tony. I'll give you a cheque for it tomorrow. (*coaxingly*) Tell me what the body's like.

Tony (*sulkily*): Oh, it's a torpedo body.

Duchess: You'll take me for drives in it sometimes?

(*He turns round and looks at her, she puts out her
hand, he thaws, and smiles engagingly.*)

Tony: I say, you are awfully kind to me.

Duchesse: You do like me a little, don't you?

Tony: Of course I do.

Duchesse: You have a good heart, Tony. Kiss me.

Tony (*kissing her, pleased and excited*): I saw an
awfully jolly body in a shop in Trafalgar Square the day
before yesterday. I've got half a mind to get the people
who made your body to copy it.

Duchesse: Why don't you get it at the shop you saw it
at? My people are terribly expensive, and they aren't any
better than anybody else.

Tony: Well, you see, I don't know anything about the
firm. I just happened to catch sight of it as I was passing.

Duchesse: What on earth were you doing in Trafalgar
Square on Thursday? I thought you were going to Ranelagh.

Tony: I was put off. I hadn't got anything to do, so I
thought I'd just slope round the National Gallery for half
an hour.

Duchesse: That's the last place I should have expected
you to go.

Tony: I don't mind having a look at pictures now and
then.

(*A sudden suspicion comes to the* Duchesse *that he
was there with* Pearl, *but she makes no sign that he
can see.*)

Duchesse (*blandly*): Did you look at the Bronzinos?

Tony (*falling into the trap*): Yes. Arthur Fenwick
bought one the other day at Christie's. He paid a devil of
a price for it too.

DUCHESSE (*clenching her hands in the effort to hide her agitation*): Oh?

TONY: I do think it's rot, the prices people pay for old masters. I'm blowed if I'd give ten thousand pounds for a picture.

DUCHESSE: We'll go to the National Gallery together one of these days, shall we?

TONY: I don't know that I want to make a habit of it, you know.

> (PEARL *and* THORNTON CLAY *come in. During the conversation the* DUCHESSE *surreptitiously watches* PEARL *and* TONY *for signs of an intelligence between them.*)

PEARL: I've got great news for you. Bessie and Harry Bleane are engaged.

DUCHESSE: Oh, my dear, I'm so glad. How gratified you must be!

PEARL: Yes, I'm delighted. You must come and congratulate them.

CLAY: Above all we must congratulate one another. We've all worked for it, Pearl.

TONY: He hadn't much chance, poor blighter, had he?

PEARL: We're going to have one more dance, and then Arthur wants to play poker. You must come.

CLAY (*to the* DUCHESSE): Will you dance this with me, Minnie?

DUCHESSE: I'd like to.

> (CLAY *gives her his arm. She throws* TONY *and* PEARL *a glance, and purses her lips. She goes out with* CLAY.)

PEARL: You haven't danced with me yet, Tony. You should really pay some attention to your hostess.

TONY: I say, don't go.

PEARL: Why not?

TONY: Because I want to talk to you.

PEARL (*flippantly*): If you want to whisper sweet nothings in my ear, you'll find the one-step exceedingly convenient.

TONY: You're a little beast, Pearl.

PEARL: You've been having a long talk with Minnie.

TONY: Oh, she's been making a hell of a scene.

PEARL: Poor thing, she can't help it. She adores you.

TONY: I wish she didn't, and you did.

PEARL (*with a chuckle*): My dear, it's your only attraction for me that she adores you. Come and dance with me.

TONY: You've got a piece of hair out of place.

PEARL: Have I? (*She takes a small glass out of her bag and looks at herself. As she does so* TONY *steps behind her and kisses her neck.*) You fool, don't do that. Anyone might see us.

TONY: I don't care.

PEARL: I do. Arthur's as jealous as cat's meat.

TONY: Arthur's playing the pianola.

PEARL: There's nothing wrong with my hair.

TONY: Of course there isn't. You're perfectly divine tonight. I don't know what there is about you.

PEARL: You're a foolish creature, Tony.

TONY: Let's go in the garden.

PEARL: No, they'll be wondering where we are.

TONY: Hang it all, it's not so extraordinary to take a stroll instead of dancing.

PEARL: I don't want to take a stroll.

TONY: Pearl.

PEARL: Yes?

(*She looks at him. For a moment they stare at one another in silence. A hot flame of passion leaps up suddenly between them, and envelops them, so that they forget everything but that they are man and woman. The air seems all at once heavy to breathe.* PEARL, *like a bird in a net, struggles to escape; their voices sink, and unconsciously they speak in whispers.*)

PEARL: Don't be a fool, Tony.

TONY (*hoarsely*): Let's go down to the tea-house.

PEARL: No, I won't.

TONY: We shall be quite safe there.

PEARL: I daren't. It's too risky.

TONY: Oh, damn the risk!

PEARL (*agitated*): I can't!

TONY: I'll go down there and wait.

PEARL (*breathlessly*): But—if they wonder where I am.

TONY: They'll think you've gone up to your room.

PEARL: I won't come, Tony.

TONY: I'll wait for you.

(*As he goes out, ARTHUR FENWICK comes in. PEARL gives a slight start, but quickly recovers herself.*)

FENWICK: Look here, I'm not going on pounding away at that wretched pianola unless you come and dance, Pearl.

PEARL (*exhausted*): I'm tired, I don't want to dance any more.

FENWICK: Poor child, you look quite pale.

PEARL: Do I? I thought I'd put plenty of rouge on. Am I looking revolting?

FENWICK: You always look adorable. You're wonderful. I can't think what you see in an old fellow like me.

PEARL: You're the youngest man I've ever known.

FENWICK: How well you know the thing to say to please me!

(*He is just going to take her in his arms, but instinctively she draws back.*)

PEARL: Let's play poker now, shall we?

FENWICK: Not if you're tired, darling.

PEARL: I'm never too tired for that.

FENWICK: You don't know how I adore you. It's a privilege to be allowed to love you.

PEARL (*sure of herself again*): Oh, what nonsense! You'll make me vain if you say things like that.

FENWICK: You do love me a little, don't you? I want your love so badly.

PEARL: Why, I dote on you, you silly old thing.

(*She takes his face in her hands and kisses him, avoids his arms that seek to encircle her, and goes towards the door.*)

FENWICK: Where are you going?

PEARL: I'm just going to my room to arrange my face.

FENWICK: My God, how I love you, girlie! There's nothing in the world I wouldn't do for you.

PEARL: Really?

FENWICK: Nothing.

PEARL: Then ring for Pole and tell him to set out the card-table and bring the counters.

FENWICK: And I was prepared to give you a sable coat or a diamond tiara.

PEARL: I much prefer chinchilla and emeralds.

FENWICK (*taking her hand*): Must you really go and arrange your face?

PEARL: Really!

FENWICK: Be quick then. I can hardly bear you out of my sight.

(*He kisses her hand.*)

PEARL (*looking at him tenderly*): Dear Arthur.

(*She goes out. FENWICK rings the bell. Then he goes on the terrace and calls out.*)

FENWICK: Thornton, we're going to play poker. Get them to come along, will you?

CLAY (*outside*): Right-ho!

(*POLE comes in.*)

FENWICK: Oh, Pole, get the card-table ready.

POLE: Very good, sir.

FENWICK: And we shall want the counters. Let's have those mother-o'-pearl ones that I brought down last time I was here.

POLE: Very good, sir.

(*The* PRINCESS *comes in.* POLE *proceeds to bring a card-table into the centre of the room and unfolds it. He gets a box of counters out of a drawer, and puts them on the table.*)

FENWICK: Pearl has just gone to her room. She'll be here in one minute.

PRINCESS (*looking at the preparations*): This looks like more dissipation.

FENWICK: We were going to have a little game of poker. I don't think we ought to play very long. Pearl is looking terribly tired.

PRINCESS: I don't wonder. She's so energetic.

FENWICK: She does too much. Just now when I came in she was quite white. I'm really very uneasy about her. You see, she never spares herself.

PRINCESS: Fortunately she's extremely strong.

FENWICK: She has a constitution of iron. She's a very wonderful woman. It's very seldom you meet a woman like Pearl. She's got a remarkable brain. I've frequently discussed business with her, and I've been amazed at her clear grasp of complicated matters. I owe a great deal to her. And she's good, Princess, she's good. She's got a heart of gold.

PRINCESS: I'm sure she has.

FENWICK: She'll always do a good turn to anybody. She's the most generous, the most open-handed woman I've ever met.

(*The* DUCHESSE *comes in as he says these words.*)

Duchesse: Who is this?

Fenwick: We were talking of our hostess.

Duchesse: I see.

(*She has her bag in her hand; when the others are not looking she hides it behind a sofa.*)

Fenwick: I have no hesitation in saying that Pearl is the most remarkable woman in England. Why, she's got half the Cabinet in her pocket. She's very powerful.

Duchesse: I have often thought that if she'd lived in the reign of Charles II she would have been a duchess in her own right.

Fenwick (*innocently*): Maybe. She would adorn any sphere. She's got everything—tact, brains, energy, beauty.

Duchesse: Virtue.

Fenwick: If I were the British people, I'd make her Prime Minister.

Princess (*smiling*): You're an excellent friend, Mr. Fenwick.

Fenwick: Of course, you've heard of her hostel for young women alone in London?

Duchesse (*sweetly*): Yes, there was a great deal about it in the papers, wasn't there?

Fenwick: That's a thing I've always admired in Pearl. She has a thoroughly modern understanding of the value of advertisement.

Duchesse: Yes, she has, hasn't she?

Fenwick: Well, believe me, she conceived the idea of that hostel, built it, endowed it, organized it, all on her own. It cost twenty thousand pounds.

Duchesse: But surely, Mr. Fenwick, you paid the twenty thousand pounds. Pearl hasn't got sums like that to throw away on charity.

Fenwick: I gave the money, but the money isn't the important thing. The idea, the organization, the success, are all due to Pearl.

DUCHESSE: It has certainly been one of the best adver-
tised of recent philanthropic schemes.

(THORNTON CLAY, BESSIE, BLEANE *and* FLEMING *come
in.*)

CLAY: We're all dying to play poker.
FENWICK: The table is ready.
BESSIE: Where is Pearl?
FENWICK: She's gone to her room. She'll be back in a
minute.

(*They gather round the table and sit down.*)

BESSIE: You're going to play, Princess?
PRINCESS: Oh, I don't think so, I'll look on. I'm going to
bed in a minute.
BESSIE: Oh, you must play.

(*The* PRINCESS *smiles, shrugs her shoulders and ap-
proaches the table.*)

FENWICK: Leave a place for Pearl.
DUCHESSE: You must leave one for Tony, too.
CLAY: What's he doing?
DUCHESSE: He'll be here presently.
FENWICK: Shall I give out the counters? What would
you like to play for?
PRINCESS: Don't let it be too high.
DUCHESSE: How tiresome of you, Flora! I think I'm in
luck tonight.
FENWICK: We don't want to ruin anyone. Shilling
antes. Will that suit you?
PRINCESS: Very well.
FENWICK (*to* CLAY): The whites are a shilling, Thorn-
ton, reds two, and blues five bob. Mr. Harvey, you might
count some out, will you?
FLEMING: Sure.

(*The three of them start counting out the counters.*)

DUCHESSE: Oh, how stupid of me, I haven't got my bag.

FENWICK: Never mind, we'll trust you.

DUCHESSE: Oh, I'd rather pay at once. It saves so much bother. Besides, I hate not having my bag.

PRINCESS: One always wants to powder one's nose if one hasn't got it.

DUCHESSE: Bessie dear, I left it in Pearl's new tea-house. Do run and fetch it for me.

BESSIE: Certainly.

BLEANE: No, I'll go.

BESSIE: You don't know the way. I can go through the bushes. It's only twenty yards. You stop and count out the counters.

(*She goes out.*)

FENWICK: There's five pounds here. Will you take them, Princess?

PRINCESS: Thank you. Here's my money.

DUCHESSE: I'll give you my fiver as soon as Bessie brings my bag.

CLAY: How on earth came you to leave it in the tea-house?

DUCHESSE: I'm so careless. I'm always leaving my bag about.

FLEMING: Here's another five pounds.

PRINCESS: What beautiful counters they are!

FENWICK: I'm glad you like them. I gave them to Pearl. They've got her initials on them.

CLAY: Let's have a hand before Pearl comes. Lowest deals.

(*They all cut.*)

FLEMING: Table stakes, I suppose?

FENWICK: Oh yes, it makes it a much better game.

CLAY: Your deal, Fenwick.

FENWICK: Ante up, Princess.

PRINCESS: I beg your pardon.

(*She pushes forward a counter.* FENWICK *deals. The others take up their cards.*)

FENWICK: Two shillings to come in.

FLEMING: I'm coming in.

BLEANE: I always come in.

FENWICK: I oughtn't to, but I shall all the same. Are you going to make good your ante, Princess?

PRINCESS: I may just as well, mayn't I?

FENWICK: That's how I've made a fortune. By throwing good money after bad. Would you like a card?

PRINCESS: I'll have three.

(FENWICK *gives them to her.*)

CLAY: The Princess has got a pair of deuces.

FLEMING: I'll have one.

(FENWICK *gives it to him.*)

BLEANE: One never gets that straight, Harvey. I'll take five.

FENWICK: That's what I call a real sport.

CLAY: Nonsense. It just means he can't play.

BLEANE: It would be rather a sell for you if I got a flush.

CLAY: It would, but you haven't.

(FENWICK *has given him cards and* BLEANE *looks at them.*)

BLEANE: You're quite right. I haven't.

(*He flings them down. Through the next speeches the business with the cards follows the dialogue.*)

FENWICK: Don't you want any cards, Duchesse?

DUCHESSE: No, I'm out of it.

CLAY: I'll have three. I thought you were in luck.

DUCHESSE: Wait a minute. You'll be surprised.

FENWICK: Dealer takes two.

CLAY: Who bets?

PRINCESS: I'm out of it.

CLAY: I said it was a pair of deuces.

FLEMING: I'll bet five shillings.

CLAY: I'll take it and raise five shillings.

FENWICK: I suppose I must risk my money. What have I got to put down? Ten shillings?

FLEMING: There's five shillings, and I'll raise you five shillings more.

CLAY: No, I've had enough.

FENWICK: I'll take you and raise you again.

FLEMING: Very well. And once more.

FENWICK: I'll see you.

(BESSIE *comes in. The* DUCHESSE *has been watching for her.* BESSIE *is excessively disturbed.*)

DUCHESSE: Ah, there's Bessie.

FENWICK (*to* FLEMING): What have you got?

DUCHESSE: Did you find my bag?

BESSIE (*with a gasp*): No, it wasn't there.

DUCHESSE: Oh, but I remember distinctly leaving it there. I'll go and look for it myself. Mr. Fenwick, will you come with me?

BESSIE: No, don't—you can't go into the tea-house.

PRINCESS (*surprised*): Bessie, is anything the matter?

BESSIE (*in a strained voice*): The door of the tea-house is locked.

DUCHESSE: Oh, it can't be. I saw Pearl and Tony go in there just now.

(BESSIE *suddenly hides her face and bursts into a flood of tears.*)

PRINCESS (*starting to her feet*): Minnie, you devil! What have you been doing?

DUCHESSE: Don't ask what I've been doing.

FENWICK: You must be mistaken. Pearl went up to her room.

DUCHESSE: Go and look for her. . . .

(FENWICK *is about to start from his chair. The* PRINCESS *puts her hand on his shoulders.*)

PRINCESS: Where are you going?

DUCHESSE: I saw her.

(*For a moment there is a pause.*)

CLAY (*in an embarrassed way*): Well, we'd better go on with our game, hadn't we?

(*The* PRINCESS *and* BLEANE *are bending over* BESSIE, *trying to get her to control herself.*)

FLEMING: That was your money, Mr. Fenwick.

FENWICK (*staring in front of him, with a red face and bloodshot eyes, under his breath*): The slut. The slut.

(*The* DUCHESSE *takes her bag from behind the cushion, gets out the stick for her lips, and her mirror, and begins to paint them.*)

CLAY: You'd better deal, Fleming. The Princess won't play, I expect.

DUCHESSE: Deal me cards. I want to play.

CLAY: Bleane, come on. We'd better go on with our game. Take Bessie's chips.

(BLEANE *comes forward.* FLEMING *deals the cards. A stormy silence hangs over the party, broken only by the short speeches referring to the game; they play trying to relieve the tension. They are all anxiously awaiting* PEARL, *afraid she will come, knowing she must, and dreading the moment; they are nervous and constrained.*)

CLAY: Your ante, Bleane.

(BLEANE *puts forward a counter. The cards are dealt
in silence.*)

CLAY: I'm coming in.

(FENWICK *looks at his cards, puts forward a couple
of counters, but does not speak.* FLEMING *puts
forward counters.*)

FLEMING: D'you want a card?
BLEANE: Three, please.
CLAY: Two.
FENWICK (*with an effort over himself*): I'll have three.

(FLEMING *deals them as they ask. Just as he has
given* FENWICK *his,* PEARL *comes in, followed by*
TONY. TONY *is smoking a cigarette.*)

PEARL: Oh, have you started already?
FENWICK (*violently*): Where have you been?
PEARL: I? My head was aching a little and I went for a
turn in the garden. I found Tony composing a sonnet to
the moon.
FENWICK: You said you were going to your room.
PEARL: What are you talking about?

(*She looks round, sees the* DUCHESSE's *look of angry
triumph, and gives a slight start.*)

DUCHESSE: Once too often, my dear, once too often.

(PEARL *takes no notice. She sees* BESSIE. BESSIE *has
been staring at her with miserable eyes, and now
she hides her face.* PEARL *realizes that everything is
discovered. She turns coolly to* TONY.)

PEARL: You damned fool, I told you it was too risky.

# ACT THREE

⚬•⚬•⚬•⚬•⚬•⚬•⚬•⚬•⚬•⚬•⚬•⚬•⚬•⚬•⚬•⚬•⚬•⚬•⚬•⚬•⚬•⚬•⚬•⚬•⚬•⚬•⚬•⚬•⚬

SCENE: *The same as in the last act, the morning-room at Kenton.*

*It is next day, Sunday, about three in the afternoon, and the sun is shining brightly.*

*The* PRINCESS, THORNTON CLAY *and* FLEMING *are sitting down.* FLEMING *lights another cigarette.*

PRINCESS: Is it good for you to smoke so many cigarettes?

FLEMING: I shouldn't think so.

CLAY: He must do something.

PRINCESS: Perhaps you can get up a game of tennis later on.

FLEMING: It's very hot for tennis.

CLAY: Besides, who will play?

PRINCESS: You two could have a single.

CLAY: If we only had the Sunday papers it would be something.

PRINCESS: You can hardly expect them in a place like this. I don't suppose there are many trains on Sunday.

CLAY: I wonder if dinner is going to be as cheerful as luncheon was.

FLEMING: Did Pearl send any explanation for not appearing at luncheon?

PRINCESS: I haven't an idea.

161

CLAY: I asked the butler where she was. He said she was lunching in bed. I wish I'd thought of that.

PRINCESS: I'm afraid we were rather silent.

CLAY: Silent! I shall never forget that luncheon. Minnie subdued—and silent. Tony sulky—and silent. Bessie frightened—and silent. Bleane embarrassed—and silent. Fenwick furious—and silent. I tried to be pleasant and chatty. It was like engaging the pyramids in small-talk. Both of you behaved very badly. You might have given me a little encouragement.

FLEMING: I was afraid of saying the wrong thing. The Duchesse and Bessie looked as if they'd burst into tears on the smallest provocation.

PRINCESS: I was thinking of Pearl. What a humiliation! What a horrible humiliation!

FLEMING: What d'you think she'll do now?

CLAY: That's what I'm asking myself. I have an idea that she won't appear again till we're all gone.

PRINCESS: I hope she won't. She's always so sure of herself, I couldn't bear to see her pale and mortified.

CLAY: She's got plenty of courage.

PRINCESS: I know. She may force herself to face us. It would be a dreadful ordeal for all of us.

FLEMING: D'you think she's feeling it very much?

PRINCESS: She wouldn't be human if she weren't. I don't suppose she slept any better last night than the rest of us. Poor thing, she must be a wreck.

FLEMING: It was a terrible scene.

PRINCESS: I shall never forget it. The things that Minnie said. I couldn't have believed such language could issue from a woman's throat. Oh, it was horrible.

CLAY: It was startling. I've never seen a woman so beside herself. And there was no stopping her.

FLEMING: And with Bessie there.

PRINCESS: She was crying so much, I doubt if she heard.

CLAY: I was thankful when Minnie had the hysterics and we were able to fuss over her and dab her face and slap her hands. It was a very welcome diversion.

FLEMING: Does she have attacks like that often?

CLAY: I know she did when the young man before Tony married an heiress. I think she has one whenever there's a crisis in the affairs of her heart.

FLEMING: For goodness' sake, Thornton, don't talk about it as if it were a joke.

CLAY (*surprised*): What's the matter, Fleming?

FLEMING: I think it's abominable to treat the whole thing so flippantly.

CLAY: Why, I was very sympathetic. I wasn't flippant. Who got the sal volatile? I got the sal volatile.

FLEMING (*with a shrug of the shoulders*): I daresay my nerves are a bit on edge. You see, before, I only thought things were rather queer. It's come as, well, as a shock to discover exactly what the relations are between all these people. And what I can't very easily get over is to realize that I'm the only member of the party who doesn't take it as a matter of course.

CLAY: We shall never make a man of the world of you, Fleming.

FLEMING: I'm afraid that didn't sound very polite, Princess. I beg your pardon.

PRINCESS: I should have few friends if I demanded the standard that you do. I've learned not to judge my neighbours.

FLEMING: Is it necessary to condone their vices?

PRINCESS: You don't understand. It's not entirely their fault. It's the life they lead. They've got too much money and too few responsibilities. English women in our station have duties that are part of their birthright, but we, strangers in a strange land, have nothing to do but enjoy ourselves.

FLEMING: Well, I thank God Bleane is a decent man, and he'll take Bessie out of all this.

(*The* DUCHESSE *comes in. Unlike the* PRINCESS, *who is in a summer frock, suitable for the country, the* DUCHESSE *wears a town dress and a hat.*)

PRINCESS: You've been changing your frock, Minnie.

DUCHESSE: Yes. I'm leaving this house in half an hour. I'd have gone this morning, if I'd been able to get away. I always thought it a detestable hole, but now that I've discovered there are only two trains on Sunday, one at nine, and the other at half-past four, I have no words to express my opinion of it.

CLAY: Yet you have an extensive vocabulary, Minnie.

DUCHESSE: I've been just as much a prisoner as if I'd been shut up with lock and key. I've been forced to eat that woman's food. I thought every mouthful would choke me.

PRINCESS: Do keep calm, Minnie. You know how bad it is for you to upset yourself.

DUCHESSE: As soon as I found there wasn't a train I sent over to the garage and said I wanted to be taken to London at once. Would you believe it, I couldn't get a car.

CLAY: Why not?

DUCHESSE: One of the cars went up to town early this morning, and the other is being overhauled. There's nothing but a luggage cart. I couldn't go to London in a luggage cart. As it is I shall have to go to the station in it. I shall look ridiculous.

CLAY: Have you ordered it?

DUCHESSE: Yes. It's to be round at the door in a few minutes.

CLAY: What on earth can Pearl have sent the car up to London for?

DUCHESSE: To show her spite.

PRINCESS: That's not like her.

DUCHESSE: My dear, she's been my greatest friend for fifteen years. I know her through and through, and I tell you that she hasn't got a single redeeming quality. And why does she want to have the car overhauled today? When you're giving a party the least you can do is to see that your cars are in running order.

PRINCESS: Oh, well, that was an accident. You can't blame her for that.

DUCHESSE: I only have one thing to be thankful for, and that is that she has had the decency to keep to her room. I will be just. It shows at least that she has some sense of shame.

CLAY: You know, Minnie, Pearl has a good heart. She didn't mean to cause you pain.

DUCHESSE: Are you trying to excuse her, Thornton?

CLAY: No, I think her conduct is inexcusable.

DUCHESSE: So do I. I mean to have nothing more to do with her. It's a judgment on me. I disliked her the first time I saw her. One should always trust one's first impressions. Now my eyes are opened. I will never speak to her again. I will cut her dead. I hope you'll tell her that, Thornton.

CLAY: If that's a commission you're giving me, it's not a very pleasant one.

PRINCESS: Will you let me have a word or two with Minnie?

CLAY: Why, of course. Come along, Fleming.

(CLAY *and* FLEMING HARVEY *go into the garden.*)

DUCHESSE: My dear, if you're going to ask me to turn the other cheek, don't. Because I'm not going to. I'm going to do all I can to revenge myself on that woman. I'm going to expose her. I'm going to tell everyone how she's treated me. When I was her guest.

PRINCESS: You must take care what you say for your own sake, Minnie.

DUCHESSE: I know quite enough about her to make her position in London impossible. I'm going to ruin her.

PRINCESS: What about Tony?

DUCHESSE: Oh, I've finished with him. Ah! I'm not the kind of woman to stand that sort of treatment. I hope he'll end in the gutter.

PRINCESS: Don't you care for him any more?

DUCHESSE: My dear, if he was starving, and went down on his bended knees to me for a piece of bread, I wouldn't give it to him. He revolts me.

PRINCESS: Well, I'm very glad. It distressed me to see you on those terms with a boy like that. You're well rid of him.

DUCHESSE: My dear, you needn't tell me that. He's a thorough wrong 'un, and that's all there is about it. He hasn't even had the decency to try and excuse himself. He hasn't even made an attempt to see me.

PRINCESS (*gives her a quick look*): After all, he never really cared for you. Anyone could see that.

DUCHESSE (*her voice breaking*): Oh, don't say that, Flora. I couldn't bear it. He loved me. Until that woman came between us I know he loved me. He couldn't help loving me. I did everything in the world for him. (*She bursts into tears.*)

PRINCESS: Minnie. My dear, don't give way. You know what a worthless creature he is. Haven't you any self-respect?

DUCHESSE: He's the only man I've ever loved. I could hardly bear him out of my sight. What shall I do without him?

PRINCESS: Take care, here he is.

(TONY *comes in. He is startled at seeing the* DUCH-ESSE. *She turns away and hurriedly dries her tears.*)

TONY: Oh, I beg your pardon. I didn't know anyone was here. I was looking for some cigarettes.

(*He stands there awkwardly, not knowing whether to go or stay. The* PRINCESS *looks at him reflectively. There is a moment's silence. Then she shrugs her shoulders and goes out. He looks at the* DUCHESSE *who stands with her back to him. He hesitates a moment, then, almost on the tips of his toes, walks over to the cigarettes, fills his case, takes another look at the* DUCHESSE, *and is in the act of tip-toeing out of the room when she stops him with her question.*)

DUCHESSE: Where are you going?

TONY: Nowhere in particular.

DUCHESSE: Then you'd better stay here.

TONY: I thought you wished to be alone.

DUCHESSE: Is that why you've kept away from me all day?

(*He sinks sulkily into an armchair. The* DUCHESSE *finally turns round and faces him.*)

DUCHESSE: Haven't you got anything to say for yourself at all?

TONY: What's the good of talking?

DUCHESSE: You might at least say you're sorry for the pain you've caused me. If you'd had any affection for me you wouldn't have done all you could to avoid me.

TONY: I knew you'd only make a scene.

DUCHESSE: Good heavens, you surely don't expect me not to make a scene.

TONY: The whole thing's very unfortunate.

DUCHESSE: Ha! Unfortunate. You break my heart and then you say it's unfortunate.

TONY: I didn't mean that. I meant it was unfortunate that you caught us out.

DUCHESSE: Oh, hold your stupid tongue. Every word you say is more unfortunate than the last.

TONY: It's because I knew you'd take offence at everything I said that I thought the best thing I could do was to keep out of the way.

DUCHESSE: You're heartless, heartless. If you'd had any decent feeling you couldn't have eaten the lunch you did. But you munched away, munched, munched, munched, till I could have killed you.

TONY: Well, I was hungry.

DUCHESSE: You oughtn't to have been hungry.

TONY: What are you going to do about it?

DUCHESSE: About your appetite? Pray to God your next mouthful chokes you.

TONY: No, about the other.

DUCHESSE: I'm going to leave this house this afternoon.

TONY: D'you want me to come, too?

DUCHESSE: What d'you suppose it matters to me whether you go or stay?

TONY: If you go I shall have to go, too.

DUCHESSE: You ought to start soon then. It's four miles to the station. I shall be obliged if you will not get in the same carriage as me.

TONY: I'm not going to walk. They can run me down in a car.

DUCHESSE: There's nothing but a luggage cart, and I'm going in that.

TONY: Isn't there room for me?

DUCHESSE: No.

TONY: When d'you want me to move out of my flat?

DUCHESSE: What has that got to do with me?

TONY: You know very well that I can't pay the rent.

DUCHESSE: That's your look-out.

TONY: I shall go to the colonies.

DUCHESSE: That's the very best thing you can do. I hope you'll have to break stones, and dig, and paint—with lead paint. I hope you're miserable.

TONY: Oh, well, it'll have its compensations.

DUCHESSE: Such as?

TONY: I shall be my own master. I was about fed up with this, I can tell you.

DUCHESSE: Yes, you can say that now.

TONY: D'you think it was all jam, never being able to call my soul my own? I was sick to death of it.

DUCHESSE: You cad!

TONY: Well, you may just as well know the truth.

DUCHESSE: D'you mean to say you never cared for me? Not even at the beginning?

(*He shrugs his shoulders, but does not answer. She speaks the next phrases in little gasps gradually weakening as her emotion overcomes her. He stands before her in sulky silence.*)

DUCHESSE: Tony, I've done everything in the world for you. I've been like a mother to you. How *can* you be so ungrateful. You haven't got any heart. If you had you'd have asked me to forgive you. You'd have made some attempt to . . . Don't you *want* me to forgive you?

TONY: What d'you mean by that?

DUCHESSE: If you'd only asked me, if you'd only shown you were sorry, I'd have been angry with you, I wouldn't have spoken to you for a week, but I'd have forgiven you —I'd have forgiven you, Tony. But you never gave me a chance. It's cruel of you, cruel!

TONY: Well, anyhow, it's too late now.

DUCHESSE: Do you want it to be too late?

TONY: It's no good grousing about the past. The thing's over now.

DUCHESSE: Aren't you sorry?

TONY: I don't know. I suppose I am in a way. I don't want to make you unhappy.

DUCHESSE: If you wanted to be unfaithful to me, why didn't you prevent me from finding out? You didn't even trouble to take a little precaution.

TONY: I was a damned fool, I know that.

DUCHESSE: Are you in love with that woman?

TONY: No.

DUCHESSE: Then why did you? Oh, Tony, how could you?

TONY: If one felt about things at night as one does next morning, life would be a dashed sight easier.

DUCHESSE: If I said to you, Let's let bygones be bygones and start afresh, what would you say, Tony?

(*She looks away. He rests his eyes on her reflectively.*)

TONY: We've made a break now. We'd better leave it at that. I shall go out to the colonies.

DUCHESSE: Tony, you don't mean that seriously. You could never stand it. You know, you're not strong. You'll only die.

TONY: Oh, well, one can only die once.

Duchesse: I'm sorry for all I said just now, Tony. I didn't mean it.

Tony: It doesn't matter.

Duchesse: I can't live without you, Tony.

Tony: I've made up my mind. It's no good talking.

Duchesse: I'm sorry I was horrid to you, Tony. I'll never be again. Won't you forget it? Oh, Tony, won't you forgive me? I'll do anything in the world for you if only you won't leave me.

Tony: It's a rotten position I'm in. I must think of the future.

Duchesse: Oh, but Tony, I'll make it all right for you.

Tony: It's very kind of you, but it's not good enough. Let's part good friends, Minnie. If I've got to walk to the station, it's about time I was starting. (*He holds out his hand to her.*)

Duchesse: D'you mean to say it's good-bye? Good-bye for ever? Oh, how can you be so cruel!

Tony: When one's made up one's mind to do a thing, it's best to do it at once.

Duchesse: Oh, I can't bear it. I can't bear it. (*She begins to cry.*) Oh, what a fool I was! I ought to have pretended not to see anything. I wish I'd never known. Then you wouldn't have thought of leaving me.

Tony: Come, my dear, pull yourself together. You'll get over it.

Duchesse (*desperately*): Tony, if you want to marry me—I'm willing to marry you.

(*A pause.*)

Tony: I should be just as dependent on you. D'you think it would be jolly for me having to come to you for every five pounds I wanted?

Duchesse: I'll settle something on you so that you'll be independent. A thousand a year. Will that do?

Tony: You are a good sort, Minnie. (*He goes over and sits down beside her.*)

Duchesse: You will be kind to me, won't you?

TONY: Rather! And look here, you needn't give me
that two-seater. I shall be able to drive the Rolls-Royce.

DUCHESSE: You didn't want to go to the colonies, did
you?

TONY: Not much.

DUCHESSE: Oh, Tony, I do love you so.

TONY: That's right.

DUCHESSE: We won't stay another minute in this
house. Ring the bell, will you? You'll come with me in
the luggage cart?

TONY (*touching the bell*): I much prefer that to walking.

DUCHESSE: It's monstrous that there shouldn't be a
motor to take luggage to the station. It's a most uncomfortable house to stay in.

TONY: Oh, beastly. D'you know that I didn't have a
bathroom attached to my bedroom?

(POLE *comes in.*)

DUCHESSE: Is the luggage cart ready, Pole?

POLE: I'll enquire, your grace.

DUCHESSE: My maid is to follow in the morning with
the luggage. Mr. Paxton will come with me. (*to* TONY)
What about your things?

TONY: Oh, they'll be all right. I brought my man with
me.

POLE: Her ladyship is just coming downstairs, your
grace.

DUCHESSE: Oh, is she? Thank you, that'll do, Pole.

POLE: Very good, your grace.

(*He goes out. As soon as he closes the door behind
him the* DUCHESSE *springs to her feet.*)

DUCHESSE: I won't see her. Tony, see if Thornton is on
the terrace.

TONY: All right. (*He goes to the French window.*) Yes.
I'll call him, shall I? Clay, come here a minute, will you?

(*He goes out.* THORNTON CLAY *comes in, followed immediately by the* PRINCESS *and* FLEMING.)

DUCHESSE: Thornton, I'm told Pearl is coming downstairs.

CLAY: At last.

DUCHESSE: I won't see her. Nothing will induce me to see her.

PRINCESS: My dear, what is to be done? We can't make her remain upstairs in her own house.

DUCHESSE: No, but Thornton can speak to her. She's evidently ashamed of herself. I only ask one thing, that she should keep out of the way till I'm gone.

CLAY: I'll do my best.

DUCHESSE: I'm going to walk up and down till the luggage cart is ready. I haven't taken my exercise today.

(*She goes out.*)

CLAY: If Pearl is in a temper that's not a very pleasant message to give her.

PRINCESS: You won't find her in a temper. If she's dreadfully upset, tell her what Minnie says gently.

FLEMING: Here is Bessie. (*She comes in.*) It appears that Pearl is just coming downstairs.

BESSIE: Is she?

PRINCESS: Have you seen her this morning, Bessie?

BESSIE: No. She sent her maid to ask me to go to her, but I had a headache and couldn't.

(*They look at her curiously. She is inclined to be abrupt and silent. It may be imagined that she has made up her mind to some course, but what that is the others cannot tell.* FLEMING *goes over and sits beside her.*)

FLEMING: I'm thinking of going back to America next Saturday, Bessie.

BESSIE: Dear Fleming, I shall be sorry to lose you.

FLEMING: I expect you'll be too busy to think about me. You'll have to see all kinds of people, and then there's your trousseau to get.

BESSIE: I wish you could come over to Paris with me, Princess, and help me with it.

PRINCESS: I? (*She gets an inkling of what* BESSIE *means.*) Of course, if I could be of any help to you, dear child. . . .

(*She takes* BESSIE'S *hand and gives her a fond smile.* BESSIE *turns away to hide a tear that for a moment obscures her eyes.*)

Perhaps it's a very good idea. We must talk about it.

(PEARL *comes in. She is perfectly cool and collected. Radiant in a wonderful, audacious gown; she is looking her best and knows it. There is nothing in her manner to indicate the smallest recollection of the episode that took place on the preceding evening.*)

PEARL (*brightly*): Good-morning.

CLAY: Good-afternoon.

PEARL: I knew everyone would abuse me for coming down so late. It was such a lovely day I thought it was a pity to get up.

CLAY: Don't be paradoxical, Pearl, it's too hot.

PEARL: The sun streamed into my room, and I said, It's a sin not to get up on a morning like this. And the more I said I ought to get up, the more delightful I found it to lie in bed. How is your head, Bessie?

BESSIE: Oh, it's better, thank you.

PEARL: I was sorry to hear you weren't feeling up to the mark.

BESSIE: I didn't sleep very well.

PEARL: What have you done with your young man?

BESSIE: Harry? He's writing letters.

PEARL: Spreading the glad tidings, I suppose. You ought to write to his mother, Bessie. It would be a graceful attention. A charming, frank little letter, the sort of thing one would expect an *ingénue* to write. Straight from the heart.

CLAY: I'm sure you'd love to write it yourself, Pearl.

PEARL: And we must think about sending an announcement to the Morning Post.

FLEMING: You think of everything, Pearl.

PEARL: I take my duties as Bessie's chaperon very seriously. I've already got a brilliant idea for the gown I'm going to wear at the wedding.

FLEMING: Gee!

PEARL: My dear Fleming, don't say Gee, it's so American. Say By Jove.

FLEMING: I couldn't without laughing.

PEARL: Laffing. Why can't you say laughing?

FLEMING: I don't want to.

PEARL: How obstinate you are. Of course, now that Bessie is going to marry an Englishman she'll have to take lessons. I know an excellent woman. She's taught all the American peeresses.

FLEMING: You surprise me.

PEARL: She's got a wonderful method. She makes you read aloud. And she has long lists of words that you have to repeat twenty times a day—half instead of haf, and barth instead of bath, and carnt instead of can't.

FLEMING: By Jove instead of Gee?

PEARL: Peeresses don't say By Jove, Fleming. She teaches them to say Good heavens instead of Mercy.

FLEMING: Does she make money by it?

PEARL: Pots. She's a lovely woman. Eleo Dorset had an accent that you could cut with a knife when she first came over, and in three months she hadn't got any more than I have.

BESSIE (*getting up. To* FLEMING): D'you think it's too hot for a turn in the garden?

FLEMING: Why, no.

BESSIE: Shall we go then?

(*They go out together.*)

PEARL: What's the matter with Bessie? She must have swallowed a poker last night. No wonder she couldn't sleep. It's enough to give anyone indigestion.

CLAY: You know that Minnie is going this afternoon, Pearl?

PEARL: Yes, so I heard. It's such a bore there are no cars to take her to the station. She'll have to go in the luggage cart.

CLAY: She doesn't wish to see you.

PEARL: Oh, but I wish to see her.

CLAY: I daresay.

PEARL: I must see her.

CLAY: She asked me to tell you that she only wished you to do one thing, and that is to keep out of the way till she's gone.

PEARL: Then you can go and tell her that unless she sees me she shan't have the luggage cart.

CLAY: Pearl!

PEARL: That's my ultimatum.

CLAY: Can you see me taking a message like that to the Duchesse?

PEARL: It's four miles to the station, and there's not a scrap of shade all the way.

CLAY: After all, it's not a very unreasonable request she's making.

PEARL: If she wants the luggage cart she must come and say good-bye to me like a lady.

CLAY (*to the* PRINCESS): What am I to do? We used up all the sal volatile last night.

PRINCESS: I'll tell her if you like. D'you really insist on seeing her, Pearl?

PEARL: Yes, it's very important. (*The* PRINCESS *goes out.* PEARL *watches her go with a smile.*) I'm afraid Flora is shocked. She shouldn't know such people.

CLAY: Really, Pearl, your behaviour is monstrous.

Pearl: Never mind about my behaviour. Tell me how luncheon went off.

Clay: My dear, it was like a gathering of relations who hate one another, after the funeral of a rich aunt who's left all her money to charity.

Pearl: It must have been priceless. I'd have given anything to be there.

Clay: Why weren't you?

Pearl: Oh, I knew there'd be scenes, and I'm never at my best in a scene before luncheon. One of the things I've learnt from the war is that a general should choose his own time for a battle.

Clay: Minnie moved heaven and earth to get away this morning.

Pearl: I knew she couldn't. I knew none of them could go till the afternoon.

Clay: The train service is atrocious.

Pearl: George says that is one of the advantages of the place. It keeps it rural. There's one at nine and another at half-past four. I knew that not even the most violent disturbances would get people up at eight who never by any chance have breakfast till ten. As soon as I awoke I took the necessary steps.

Clay (interrupting): You slept?

Pearl: Oh, yes, I slept beautifully. There's nothing like a little excitement to give me a good night.

Clay: Well, you certainly had some excitement. I've rarely witnessed such a terrific scene.

Pearl: I sent out to the garage and gave instructions that the old Rolls-Royce was to be taken down at once and the other was to go to London.

Clay: What for?

Pearl: Never mind. You'll know presently. Then I did a little telephoning.

Clay: Why were you so anxious to prevent anybody from leaving the house?

Pearl: I couldn't have persuaded myself that my party was a success if half my guests had left me on Sunday morning. I thought they might change their minds by the afternoon.

CLAY: If that's your only reason, I don't think it's a very good one.

PEARL: It isn't. I will be frank with you, Thornton. I can imagine that a very amusing story might be made out of this episode. I never mind scandal, but I don't expose myself to ridicule if I can help it.

CLAY: My dear Pearl, surely you can trust the discretion of your guests. Who do you think will give it away?

PEARL: You.

CLAY: I? My dear Pearl, I give you my word of honour...

PEARL (calmly): My dear Thornton, I don't care twopence about your word of honour. You're a professional entertainer, and you'll sacrifice everything to a good story. Why, don't you remember that killing story about your father's death? You dined out a whole season on it.

CLAY: Well, it was a perfectly killing story. No one would have enjoyed it more than my poor old father.

PEARL: I'm not going to risk anything, Thornton. I think it's much better there should be no story to tell.

CLAY: No one can move the clock backwards, Pearl. I couldn't help thinking at luncheon that there were the elements of a very good story indeed.

PEARL: And you'll tell it, Thornton. Then I shall say: My dear, does it sound probable? They all stayed quite happily till Monday morning; Sturrey and the Arlingtons dined on the Sunday night, and we had a very merry evening. Besides, I was lunching with Minnie only two days afterwards. And I shall say: Poor Thornton, he *is* such a liar, isn't he?

CLAY: I confess that if you are reconciled with Minnie it will take a great deal of the point away from my story. What about Arthur Fenwick?

PEARL: He's a sensualist, and the sensual are always sentimental.

CLAY: He scared me dreadfully at luncheon. He was eating a dressed crab, and his face grew every minute more purple. I was expecting him to have an apoplectic fit.

PEARL: It's not an unpleasant death, you know, Thornton, to have a stroke while you're eating your favourite dish.

CLAY: You know, there are no excuses for you, Pearl.

PEARL: Human nature excuses so much, Thornton.

CLAY: You really might lave left Tony alone. This habit you have of snitching has got you into trouble before.

PEARL: People are so selfish. It just happens that I find no man so desirable as one that a friend of mine is in love with. I make allowances for the idiosyncrasies of my friends. Why shouldn't they make allowances for mine?

(*The* DUCHESSE *comes in, erect and haughty, with the air of Boadicea facing the Roman legions.* PEARL *turns to her with an ingratiating smile.*)

PEARL: Ah, Minnie.

DUCHESSE: I'm told the only way I can leave this house is by submitting to the odious necessity of seeing you.

PEARL: I wish you wouldn't go, Minnie. Lord Sturrey is coming over to dinner tonight, and so are the Arlingtons. I always take a lot of trouble to get the right people together, and I hate it when anybody fails me at the last minute.

DUCHESSE: D'you think anything would have induced me to stay so long if there'd been any possibility of getting away?

PEARL: It wouldn't have been nice to go without saying good-bye to me.

DUCHESSE: Don't talk nonsense, Pearl.

PEARL: D'you know that you behaved very badly last night, and I ought to be extremely angry with you?

DUCHESSE: I? Thornton, the woman's as mad as a hatter.

PEARL: You really oughtn't to have made a scene before Harry Bleane. And, you know, to tell Arthur wasn't playing the game. If you wanted to tell anyone, why didn't you tell George?

DUCHESSE: In the first place, he wasn't here. He never is.

PEARL: I know. He says that now society has taken to coming down to the country for week-ends he prefers London.

DUCHESSE: I'll never forgive you. Never. Never. Never. You'd got Arthur Fenwick. Why weren't you satisfied with him? If you wanted to have an affair with anyone, why didn't you take Thornton? He's almost the only one of your friends with whom you haven't. The omission is becoming almost marked.

PEARL: Thornton never makes love to me except when other people are looking. He can be very passionate in the front seat of my box at the opera.

CLAY: This conversation is growing excessively personal. I'll leave you.

(*He goes out.*)

PEARL: I'm sorry I had to insist on your seeing me, but I had something quite important to say to you.

DUCHESSE: Before you go any further, Pearl, I wish to tell you that I'm going to marry Tony.

PEARL (*aghast*): Minnie! Oh, my dear, you're not doing it to spite me? You know, honestly, he doesn't interest me in the slightest. Oh, Minnie, do think carefully.

DUCHESSE: It's the only way I can keep him.

PEARL: D'you think you'll be happy?

DUCHESSE: What should you care if I'm happy?

PEARL: Of course I care. D'you think it's wise? You're giving yourself into his hands. Oh, my dear, how can you risk it?

DUCHESSE: He said he was going out to the colonies. I love him. . . . I believe you're really distressed. How strange you are, Pearl! Perhaps it's the best thing for me. He may settle down. I was very lonely sometimes, you know. Sometimes, when I had the blues, I almost wished I'd never left home.

PEARL: And I've been moving heaven and earth to get him a job. I've been on the telephone this morning to all the Cabinet Ministers I know, and at last I've done it. That's what I wanted to tell you. I thought you'd be so pleased. I suppose now he won't want it.

DUCHESSE: Oh, I'm sure he will. He's very proud, you know. That's one of the things I liked in him. He had to be dependent on me, and that's partly why he always wanted to marry me.

PEARL: Of course, you'll keep your title.

DUCHESSE: Oh, yes, I shall do that.

PEARL (going towards her as if to kiss her): Well, darling, you have my very, very best wishes.

DUCHESSE (drawing back): I'm not going to forgive you, Pearl.

PEARL: But you've forgiven Tony.

DUCHESSE: I don't blame him. He was led away.

PEARL: Come, Minnie, don't be spiteful. You might let bygones by bygones.

DUCHESSE: Nothing will induce me to stay in this house another night.

PEARL: It's a very slow train, and you'll have to go without your tea.

DUCHESSE: I don't care.

PEARL: You won't arrive in London till half-past eight, and you'll have to dine in a restaurant.

DUCHESSE: I don't care.

PEARL: You'll be grubby and hot. Tony will be hungry and out of temper. And you'll look your age.

DUCHESSE: You promised me the luggage cart.

PEARL (with a sigh): You shall have it; but you'll have to sit on the floor, because it hasn't got any seats.

DUCHESSE: Pearl, it's not going to break down on the way to the station?

PEARL: Oh, no. How can you suspect me of playing a trick like that on you? . . . (with a tinge of regret) It never occurred to me.

(THORNTON CLAY *comes in.*)

CLAY: Pearl, I thought you'd like to know that Fenwick is coming to say good-bye to you.

DUCHESSE: I'll go and tell Tony about the job you've got him. By the way, what is it?

PEARL: Oh, it's something in the Education Office.

DUCHESSE: How very nice. What do they do there?

PEARL: Nothing. But it'll keep him busy from ten to four.

(*The* DUCHESSE *goes out.*)

PEARL: She's going to marry him.

CLAY: I know.

PEARL: I'm a wonderful matchmaker. First Bessie and Harry Bleane, and now Minnie and Tony Paxton. I shall have to find someone for you, Thornton.

CLAY: How on earth did you manage to appease her?

PEARL: I reasoned with her. After all, she should be glad the boy has sown his wild oats before he marries. And besides, if he were her husband, of course she wouldn't expect fidelity from him; it seems unnatural to expect it when he isn't.

CLAY: But she's going all the same.

PEARL: I've got a quarter of an hour yet. Give me your handkerchief, will you?

CLAY (*handing it to her*): You're not going to burst into tears?

PEARL (*She rubs her cheeks violently.*): I thought I ought to look a little wan and pale when Arthur comes in.

CLAY: You'll never love me, Pearl. You tell me all your secrets.

PEARL: Shall I tell you what to do about it? Take the advice I give to Americans who come over to London and want to see the Tower: say you've been, and don't go.

CLAY: D'you think you can bring Arthur round?

PEARL: I'm sure I could if he loved me.

CLAY: My dear, he dotes on you.

PEARL: Don't be a fool, Thornton. He loves his love for me. That's quite a different thing. I've only got one chance. He sees himself as the man of iron. I'm going to play the dear little thing racket.

CLAY: You're a most unscrupulous woman, Pearl.

PEARL: Not more than most. Please go. I think he ought to find me alone.

(CLAY *goes out.* PEARL *seats herself in a pensive attitude and looks down at the carpet; in her hand she holds dejectedly an open volume of poetry. Presently* ARTHUR FENWICK *comes in. She pretends not to see him. He is the strong man, battered but not beaten, struggling with the emotion which he tries to master.*)

FENWICK: Pearl!

PEARL (*with a jump*): Oh, how you startled me. I didn't hear you come in.

FENWICK: I daresay you're surprised to see me. I thought it was necessary that we should have a short conversation before I left this house.

PEARL (*looking away*): I'm glad to see you once more.

FENWICK: You understand that everything is over between us.

PEARL: If you've made up your mind, there's nothing for me to say. I know that nothing can move you when you've once done that.

FENWICK (*drawing himself up a little*): No. That has always been part of my power.

PEARL: I wouldn't have you otherwise.

FENWICK: I don't want to part from you in anger, Pearl. Last night I could have thrashed you within an inch of your life.

PEARL: Why didn't you? D'you think I'd have minded that from the man I loved?

FENWICK: You know I could never hit a woman.

PEARL: I thought of you all through the long hours of the night, Arthur.

FENWICK: I never slept a wink.

PEARL: One would never think it. You must be made of iron.

FENWICK: I think I am sometimes.

PEARL: Am I very pale?

FENWICK: A little.

PEARL: I feel a perfect wreck.

FENWICK: You must go and lie down. It's no good making yourself ill.

PEARL: Oh, don't bother about me, Arthur.

FENWICK: I've bothered about you so long. It's difficult for me to get out of the habit all at once.

PEARL: Every word you say stabs me to the heart.

FENWICK: I'll get done quickly with what I had to tell you and then go. It's merely this. Of course, I shall continue the allowance I've always made you.

PEARL: Oh, I couldn't take it. I couldn't take it.

FENWICK: You must be reasonable, Pearl. This is a matter of business.

PEARL: It's a question I refuse to discuss. Nothing would have induced me to accept your help if I hadn't loved you. Now that there can be nothing more between us—no, no, the thought outrages me.

FENWICK: I was afraid that you'd take up that attitude. Remember that you've only got eight thousand a year of your own. You can't live on that.

PEARL: I can starve.

FENWICK: I must insist, Pearl, for my own sake. You've adopted a style of living which you would never have done if you hadn't had me at the back of you. I'm morally responsible, and I must meet my obligations.

PEARL: We can only be friends in future, Arthur.

FENWICK: I haven't often asked you to do anything for me, Pearl.

PEARL: I shall return your presents. Let me give you my pearl necklace at once.

FENWICK: Girlie, you wouldn't do that.

PEARL (*pretending to try and take the necklace off*): I can't undo the clasp. Please help me.

(*She goes up to him and turns her back so that he may get at it.*)

FENWICK: I won't. I won't.

PEARL: I'll tear it off my neck.

FENWICK: Pearl, you break my heart. Do you care for me so little that you can't bear to wear the trifling presents I gave you?

PEARL: If you talk to me like that I shall cry. Don't you see that I'm trying to keep my self-control?

FENWICK: This is dreadful. This is even more painful than I anticipated.

PEARL: You see, strength is easy to you. I'm weak. That's why I put myself in your hands. I felt your power instinctively.

FENWICK: I know, I know, and it was because I felt you needed me that I loved you. I wanted to shelter you from the storms and buffets of the world.

PEARL: Why didn't you save me from myself, Arthur?

FENWICK: When I look at your poor, pale little face I wonder what you'll do without me, girlie.

PEARL (*her voice breaking*): It'll be very hard. I've grown so used to depending on you. Whenever anything has gone wrong, I've come to you and you've put it right. I was beginning to think there was nothing you couldn't do.

FENWICK: I've always welcomed obstacles. I like something to surmount. It excites me.

PEARL: You seemed to take all my strength from me. I felt strangely weak beside you.

FENWICK: It wasn't necessary that we should both be strong. I loved you because you were weak. I liked you to come to me in all your troubles. It made me feel so good to be able to put everything right for you.

PEARL: You've always been able to do the impossible.

FENWICK (*impressively*): I have never found anything impossible.

PEARL (*deeply moved*): Except to forgive.

FENWICK: Ah, I see you know me. I never forget. I never forgive.

PEARL: I suppose that's why people feel there's something strangely Napoleonic about you.

FENWICK: Maybe. And yet—though you're only a woman, you've broken me, Pearl, you've broken me.

PEARL: Oh no, don't say that. I couldn't bear that. I want you to go on being strong and ruthless.

FENWICK: Something has gone out of my life for ever. I almost think you've broken my heart. I was so proud of you. I took so much pleasure in your success. Why, whenever I saw your name in the society columns of the papers it used to give me a thrill of satisfaction. What's going to become of you now, girlie? What's going to become of you now?

PEARL: I don't know; I don't care.

FENWICK: This fellow, does he care for you? Will he make you happy?

PEARL: Tony? He's going to marry the Duchesse. (FENWICK *represses a start.*) I shall never see him again.

FENWICK: Then if I leave you, you'll have nobody but your husband.

PEARL: Nobody.

FENWICK: You'll be terribly lonely, girlie.

PEARL: You will think of me sometimes, Arthur, won't you?

FENWICK: I shall never forget you, girlie. I shall never forget how you used to leave your fine house in Mayfair and come and lunch with me down town.

PEARL: You used to give me such delicious things to eat.

FENWICK: It was a treat to see you in your beautiful clothes sharing a steak with me and a bottle of beer. I can order a steak, Pearl, can't I?

PEARL: And d'you remember those delicious little onions that we used to have? (*She seems to taste them.*) M

... M ... M ... It makes my mouth water to think of them.

FENWICK: There are few women who enjoy food as much as you do, Pearl.

PEARL: D'you know, next time you dined with me, I'd made up my mind to give you an entirely English dinner. Scotch broth, herrings, mixed grill, saddle of lamb, and then enormous marrow bones.

(FENWICK *can hardly bear the thought, his face grows red, his eyes bulge, and he gasps.*)

FENWICK: Oh, girlie! (*with utter abandonment*) Let's have that dinner. (*He seizes her in his arms and kisses her.*) I can't leave you. You need me too much.

PEARL: Arthur, Arthur, can you forgive me?

FENWICK: To err is human, to forgive divine.

PEARL: Oh, how like you that is!

FENWICK: If you must deceive me, don't let me ever find out. I love you too much.

PEARL: I won't, Arthur, I promise you I won't.

FENWICK: Come and sit on the sofa and let me look at you. I seem to see you for the first time.

PEARL: You know, you wouldn't have liked the walk to the station. It's four miles in the sun. You're a vain old thing, and your boots are always a little too small for you.

(BESSIE *comes in. She stops as she sees* PEARL *and* FENWICK *sitting hand in hand.*)

PEARL: Are you going out, Bessie?

BESSIE: As soon as Harry has finished his letters, we're going for a walk.

PEARL (*to* FENWICK): You mustn't squeeze my hand in Bessie's presence, Arthur.

FENWICK: You're a very lucky girl, Bessie, to have a sister like Pearl. She's the most wonderful woman in the world.

PEARL: You're talking nonsense, Arthur. Go and put some flannels on. It makes me quite hot to look at you in that suit. We'll try and get up a little tennis after tea.

FENWICK: Now, you mustn't tire yourself, Pearl. Remember those white cheeks of yours.

PEARL (with a charming look at him): Oh, I shall soon get my colour back now.

(She gives him her hand to kiss and he goes out. PEARL takes a little mirror out of her bag and looks at herself reflectively.)

PEARL: Men are very trivial, foolish creatures. They have kind hearts. But their heads. Oh dear, oh dear, it's lamentable. And they're so vain, poor dears, they're so vain.

BESSIE: Pearl, tomorrow, when we go back to London, I'm going away.

PEARL: Are you? Where?

BESSIE: The Princess is going to take me over to Paris for a few days.

PEARL: Oh, is that all? Don't stay away too long. You ought to be in London just at present.

BESSIE: On my return I'm proposing to stay with the Princess.

PEARL (coldly): Nonsense.

BESSIE: I wasn't asking your permission, Pearl. I was telling you my plans.

PEARL (looks at her for a moment reflectively): Are you going to make me a scene, too? I've already gone through two this afternoon. I'm rather tired of them.

BESSIE: Please don't be alarmed. I've got nothing more to say.

(She makes as though to leave the room.)

PEARL: Don't be a little fool, Bessie. You've been staying with me all the season. I can't allow you to leave my house and go and live with Flora. We don't want to go out of our way to make people gossip.

BESSIE: Please don't argue with me, Pearl. It's not my business to reproach you for anything you do. But it isn't my business, either, to stand by and watch.

PEARL: You're no longer a child, Bessie.

BESSIE: I've been blind and foolish. Because I was happy and having a good time, I never stopped to ask for explanations of this, that and the other. I never thought.... The life was so gay and brilliant—it never struck me that underneath it all—Oh, Pearl, don't make me say what I have in my heart, but let me go quietly.

PEARL: Bessie, dear, you must be reasonable. Think what people would say if you suddenly left my house. They'd ask all sort of questions, and heaven knows what explanations they'd invent. People aren't charitable, you know. I don't want to be hard on you, but I can't afford to let you do a thing like that.

BESSIE: Now that I know what I do, I should never respect myself again if I stayed.

PEARL: I don't know how you can be so unkind.

BESSIE: I don't want to be that, Pearl. But it's stronger than I am. I must go.

PEARL (*with emotion*): I'm so fond of you, Bessie. You don't know how much I want you with me. After all, I've seen so little of you these last few years. It's been such a comfort to me to have you. You were so pretty and young and sweet, it was like a ray of April sunshine in the house.

BESSIE: I'm afraid you think women are as trivial, foolish creatures as men, Pearl.

(PEARL *looks up and sees that* BESSIE *is not in the least taken in by the pathetic attitude.*)

PEARL (*icily*): Take care you don't go too far, Bessie.

BESSIE: There's no need for us to quarrel. I've made up my mind, and there's the end of it.

PEARL: Flora's a fool. I shall tell her that I won't have

her take you away from me. You'll stay with me until you're married.

BESSIE: D'you want me to tell you that I can hardly bear to speak to you? You fill me with shame and disgust. I want never to see you again.

PEARL: Really, you drive me beyond endurance. I think I must be the most patient woman in the world to put up with all I've had to put up with today. After all, what have I done? I was a little silly and incautious. By the fuss you all make one would think no one had ever been incautious and silly before. Besides, it hasn't got anything to do with you. Why don't you mind your own business?

BESSIE (*bitterly*): You talk as though your relations with Arthur Fenwick were perfectly natural.

PEARL: Good heavens, you're not going to pretend you didn't know about Arthur. After all, I'm no worse than anybody else. Why, one of the reasons we Americans like London is that we can live our own lives and people accept things philosophically. Eleo Gloster, Sadie Twickenham, Maimie Hartlepool—you don't imagine they're faithful to their husbands? They didn't marry them for that.

BESSIE: Oh, Pearl, how can you? How can you? Haven't you any sense of decency at all? When I came in just now and saw you sitting on the sofa with that gross, vulgar, sensual old man—oh! (*She makes a gesture of disgust.*) You can't love him. I could have understood if ... but—oh, it's so disgraceful, it's so hideous. What can you see in him? He's nothing but rich.... (*She pauses, and her face changes as a thought comes to her, and coming, horrifies her.*) It's not because he's rich? Pearl! Oh!

PEARL: Really, Bessie, you're very silly, and I'm tired of talking to you.

BESSIE: Pearl, it's not that? Answer me. Answer me.

PEARL (*roughly*): Mind your own business.

BESSIE: He was right, then, last night, when he called you that. He was so right that you didn't even notice it.

A few hours later you're sitting hand in hand with him.
A slut. That's what he called you. A slut. A slut.

PEARL: How dare you! Hold your tongue. How dare
you!

BESSIE: A kept woman. That's what you are.

PEARL (*recovering herself*): I'm a fool to lose my
temper with you.

BESSIE: Why should you? I'm saying nothing but the
truth.

PEARL: You're a silly little person, Bessie. If Arthur
helps me a little, that's his affair, and mine. He's got
more money than he knows what to do with, and it
amuses him to see me spend it. I could have twenty
thousand a year from him if I chose.

BESSIE: Haven't you got money of your own?

PEARL: You know exactly what I've got. Eight thousand a year. D'you think I could have got the position I
have on that? You're not under the impression all the
world comes to my house because of my charm, are you?
I'm not. You don't think the English want us here? You
don't think they like us marrying their men? Good heavens, when you've known England as long as I have
you'll realize that in their hearts they still look upon us as
savages and Red Indians. We have to force ourselves
upon them. They come to me because I amuse them.
Very early in my career I discovered that the English can
never resist getting something for nothing. If a dancer is
the rage, they'll see her at my house. If a fiddler is in
vogue, they'll hear him at my concert. I give them balls.
I give them dinners. I've made myself the fashion, I've
got power, I've got influence. But everything I've got—
my success, my reputation, my notoriety—I've bought it,
bought it, bought it.

BESSIE: How humiliating!

PEARL: And, finally, I've bought you a husband.

BESSIE: That's not true. He loves me.

PEARL: D'you think he'd have loved you if I hadn't
shown you to him in these surroundings, if I hadn't
dazzled him by the brilliant people among whom he

found you? You don't know what love is made of. D'you think it's nothing that he should hear a Prime Minister pay you compliments? Of course I bought him.

BESSIE (*aghast*): It's horrible.

PEARL: You know the truth now. It'll be very useful to you in your married life. Run away and take your little walk with Harry Bleane. I'm going to arrange my face.

(*She goes out.* BESSIE *is left ashamed and stunned.* BLEANE *comes in.*)

BLEANE: I'm afraid I've kept you waiting. I'm so sorry.

BESSIE (*dully*): It doesn't matter at all.

BLEANE: Where shall we go? You know the way about these parts, and I don't.

BESSIE: Harry, I want you to release me. I can't marry you.

BLEANE (*aghast*): Why?

BESSIE: I want to go back to America. I'm frightened.

BLEANE: Of me?

BESSIE: Oh no, I know that you're a dear, good creature; I'm frightened of what I may become.

BLEANE: But I love you, Bessie.

BESSIE: Then that's all the more reason for me to go. I must tell you frankly. I'm not in love with you, I only like you. I would never have dreamt of marrying you, if you hadn't been who you are. I wanted to have a title. That's why Pearl married her husband, and that's why the Duchesse married. Let me go, Harry.

BLEANE: I knew you didn't love me, but I thought you might come to in time. I thought if I tried I could make you love me.

BESSIE: You didn't know that I was nothing but a self-seeking, heartless snob.

BLEANE: I don't care what you say of yourself, I know that you can be nothing but what is true and charming.

BESSIE: After what you've seen last night? After what you know of this house? Aren't you disgusted with all of us?

Bleane: You can't think I could class you with the Duchesse and ... (*He stops.*)

Bessie: Pearl at my age was no different from what I am. It's the life.

Bleane: But perhaps you won't want to lead it. The set you've been living in here isn't the only set in England. It makes a stir because it's in the public eye. Its doings are announced in the papers. But it isn't a very good set, and there are plenty of people who don't very much admire it.

Bessie: You must let me try and say what I have in my heart. And be patient with me. You think I can make myself at home in your life. I've had a hint of it now and then. I've seen a glimpse of it through Pearl's laughter and the Duchesse's sneers. It's a life of dignity, of responsibilities, and of public duty.

Bleane (*with a rueful smile*): You make it very strenuous.

Bessie: It comes naturally to the English girls of your class. They've known it all their lives, and they've been brought up to lead it. But we haven't. To us it's just tedious, and its dignity is irksome. We're bored, and we fall back on the only thing that offers, pleasure. You've spoken to me about your house. It means everything to you because it's associated with your childhood and all your people before you. It could only mean something to me if I loved you. And I don't.

Bleane: You've made me so wretched. I don't know what to say to you.

Bessie: If I make you wretched now, it's so that we may both be saved a great deal of unhappiness later on. I'm glad I don't care for you, for it would make it so much harder for me to go. And I've got to go. I can't marry you. I want to go home. If I marry ever I want to marry in my own country. That is my place.

Bleane: Don't you think you could wait a little before you decide finally?

Bessie: Don't put difficulties in my way. Don't you see that we're not strong enough for the life over here? It goes to our head; we lose our bearings; we put away our own code, and we can't adopt the code of the country we come to. We drift. There's nothing for us to do but amuse ourselves, and we fall to pieces. But in America we're safe. And perhaps America wants us. When we come over here we're like soldiers deserting our country in time of war. Oh, I'm homesick for America. I didn't know how much it meant to me till now. Let me go back, Harry.

BLEANE: If you don't want to marry me, of course, I'm not going to try and make you.

BESSIE: Don't be angry, and be my friend always.

BLEANE: Always.

BESSIE: After all, three months ago you didn't know me. In three months more you will have forgotten me. Then marry some English girl, who can live your life and share your thoughts. And be happy.

(PEARL *comes in. She has rouged her cheeks, and she has once more the healthy colour which is usual with her. She is evidently jubilant.*)

PEARL: The car has just come back from London. (*She goes to the French window and calls.*) Minnie!

BESSIE: I shall tell Pearl tomorrow.

BLEANE: I won't post my letters then. I'll go and get them out of the box.

BESSIE: Forgive me.

(*He goes out. The* DUCHESSE *and* CLAY *appear at the window.*)

DUCHESSE: Did you call me?

PEARL: The car has just come back from London, so it can take you to the station.

DUCHESSE: That's a mercy. I didn't at all like the idea of going to the station in the luggage cart. Where is Flora? I must say good-bye to her.

Pearl: Oh, there's plenty of time now. The car will run you down in ten minutes.

(Tony *comes in, then the* Princess *and* Fleming.)

Duchesse: Tony, the car has returned, and is going to take us to the station.

Tony: Thank God for that! I should have looked a perfect fool in that luggage cart.

Clay: But what on earth did you send the car to London for, anyway?

Pearl: In one minute you'll see.

(Arthur Fenwick *comes in. He has changed into flannels.*)

Fenwick: Who is that gentleman that's just arrived, Pearl?

Pearl: The man of mystery.

(*The* Butler *comes in, followed by* Ernest, *and after announcing him goes out.*)

Pole: Mr. Ernest.
Duchesse: Ernest!
Clay: Ernest?

(*He is a little dark man, with large eyes, and long hair neatly plastered down. He is dressed like a tailor's dummy, in black coat, white gloves, silk hat, patent leather boots. He is a dancing master, and overwhelmingly gentlemanly. He speaks in mincing tones.*)

Ernest: Dear Lady Grayston.
Pearl (*shaking hands with him*): I'm so glad you were able to come. (*to the others*) You were talking about Ernest last night, and I thought we would have nothing to do this evening and he would cheer and comfort us. I

sent the car up to London with orders to bring him back dead or alive.

ERNEST: My dear Lady Grayston, I'm sure I'll get into no end of trouble. I had all sorts of calls to pay this afternoon, and I was dining out, and I'd promised to go to a little hop that the dear Duchess of Gloster was giving. But I felt I couldn't refuse *you*. You've always been such a good friend to me, dear Lady Grayston. You must excuse me coming in my town clothes, but your chauffeur said there wasn't a moment to lose, so I came just as I am.

PEARL: But you look a perfect picture.

ERNEST: Oh, don't say that, dear Lady Grayston; I know this isn't the sort of thing one ought to wear in the country.

PEARL: You remember the Duchesse de Surennes?

ERNEST: Oh, of course I remember the Duchesse.

DUCHESSE: Dear Ernest!

ERNEST: Dear Duchesse!

DUCHESSE: I thought I was never going to see you again, Ernest.

ERNEST: Oh, don't say that, it sounds too sad.

PEARL: It's such a pity you must go, Minnie. Ernest could have shown you all sorts of new steps.

ERNEST: Oh, dear Duchesse, you're not going the very moment I come down? That is unkind of you.

DUCHESSE (*with an effort*): I must go. I must go.

ERNEST: Have you been practicing that little step I showed you the other day? My dear friend, the Marchioness of Twickenham—not the *old* one, you know, the *new* one—is beginning to do it so well.

DUCHESSE (*struggling with herself*): Have we time, Pearl? I should like Ernest to dance just one two-step with me.

PEARL: Of course there's time. Thornton, set the gramophone.

(THORNTON CLAY *at once starts it, and the notes of the two-step tinkle out.*)

DUCHESSE: You don't mind, Ernest, do you?
ERNEST: I love dancing with you, Duchesse.

(*They take up their positions.*)

DUCHESSE: Just one moment. It always makes me so nervous to dance with you, Ernest.
ERNEST: Oh, now, don't be silly, dear Duchesse.

(*They begin to dance.*)

ERNEST: Now hold your shoulders like a lady. Arch your back, my dear, arch your back. Don't look like a sack of potatoes. If you put your foot there, I shall kick it.
DUCHESSE: Oh, Ernest, don't be cross with me.
ERNEST: I shall be cross with you, Duchesse. You don't pay any attention to what I say. You must give your mind to it.
some vim into it. That's what I always say about these modern dances: you want two things, vim and nous.
DUCHESSE (*plaintively*): Ernest!
ERNEST: Now don't cry. I'm saying all this for your good, you know. What's wrong with you is that you've got no passion.
DUCHESSE: Oh, Ernest, how can you say such a thing. I've always looked upon myself as a very passionate woman.
ERNEST: I don't know anything about that, dear Duchesse, but you don't get it into your dancing. That's what I said the other day to the dear Marchioness of Twickenham—not the *new* one, you know, the *old* one— You must put passion into it, I said. That's what these modern dances want—passion, passion.
DUCHESSE: I do! I do!
ERNEST: And don't dance like an old fish-wife. Put
DUCHESSE: I see exactly what you mean, Ernest.
ERNEST: And you must dance with your eyes as well,

you know. You must look as if you had a knife in your garter, and as if you'd kill me if I looked at another woman. Don't you see how I'm looking, I'm looking as though I meant, Curse her! how I love her. There!

(*The music stops and they separate.*)

DUCHESSE: I have improved, Ernest, haven't I?
ERNEST: Yes, you've improved, dear Duchesse, but you want more practice.
PEARL: Minnie, why on earth don't you stay, and Ernest will give you a real lesson this evening.
ERNEST: That's what you want, Duchesse.

(*The* DUCHESSE *wrestles with her soul.*)

DUCHESSE: Tony, d'you think we can stop?
TONY: I didn't want to go away. It's rotten going up to town this evening. What on earth are we going to do with ourselves when we get there?
DUCHESSE: Very well, Pearl, if it'll please you, we'll stop.
PEARL: That is nice of you, Minnie.
DUCHESSE: You're very naughty sometimes, Pearl, but you have a good heart, and I can't help being fond of you.
PEARL (*with outstretched arms*): Minnie!
DUCHESSE: Pearl!

(*They clasp one another and affectionately embrace.*)

ERNEST: What an exquisite spectacle—two ladies of title kissing one another.
BESSIE (*to* FLEMING): They're not worth making a fuss about. I'm sailing for America next Saturday!

# THE
# CONSTANT
# WIFE

# CHARACTERS

CONSTANCE

JOHN MIDDLETON, F.R.C.S.

BERNARD KERSAL

MRS. CULVER

MARIE-LOUISE

MARTHA

BARBARA

MORTIMER DURHAM

BENTLEY

---

*The action of the play takes place in John's house
in Harley Street.*

# ACT ONE

SCENE: CONSTANCE'S *drawing-room. It is a room furnished with singularly good taste.* CONSTANCE *has a gift for decoration and has made this room of hers both beautiful and comfortable.*

*It is afternoon.*

MRS. CULVER *is seated alone. She is an elderly lady with a pleasant face and she is dressed in walking costume. The door is opened and* BENTLEY *the butler introduces* MARTHA CULVER. *This is her daughter and a fine young woman.*

BENTLEY: Miss Culver. (*He goes out.*)

MARTHA (*with astonishment*): Mother.

MRS. CULVER (*very calmly*): Yes, darling.

MARTHA: You're the last person I expected to find here. You never told me you were coming to see Constance.

MRS. CULVER (*good-humouredly*): I didn't intend to till I saw in your beady eye that *you* meant to. I thought I'd just as soon be here first.

MARTHA: Bentley says she's out.

MRS. CULVER: Yes. . . . Are you going to wait?

MARTHA: Certainly.

Mrs. Culver: Then I will, too.

Martha: That'll be very nice.

Mrs. Culver: Your words are cordial, but your tone is slightly frigid, my dear.

Martha: I don't know what you mean by that, mother.

Mrs. Culver: My dear, we've known one another a great many years, haven't we? More than we always find it convenient to mention.

Martha: Not at all. I'm thirty-two. I'm not in the least ashamed of my age. Constance is thirty-six.

Mrs. Culver: And yet we still think it worth while to be a trifle disingenuous with one another. Our sex takes a natural pleasure in dissimulation.

Martha: I don't think anyone can accuse me of not being frank.

Mrs. Culver: Frankness of course is the pose of the moment. It is often a very effective screen for one's thoughts.

Martha: I think you're being faintly disagreeable to me, mother.

Mrs. Culver: I, on the other hand, think you're inclined to be decidedly foolish.

Martha: Because I want to tell Constance something she ought to know?

Mrs. Culver: Ah, I *was* right then. And it's to tell her that you've broken an engagement, and left three wretched people to play cut-throat.

Martha: It is.

Mrs. Culver: And may I ask why you think Constance ought to know?

Martha: Why? Why? Why? That's one of those questions that really don't need answering.

Mrs. Culver: I've always noticed that the questions that really don't need answering are the most difficult to answer.

Martha: It isn't at all difficult to answer. She ought to know the truth because it's the truth.

Mrs. Culver: Of course truth is an excellent thing, but before one tells it one should be quite sure that one does so for the advantage of the person who hears it rather than for one's own self-satisfaction.

MARTHA: Mother, Constance is a very unhappy person.

MRS. CULVER: Nonsense. She eats well, sleeps well, dresses well, and she's losing weight. No woman can be unhappy in those circumstances.

MARTHA: Of course if you won't understand it's no use my trying to make you. You're a darling, but you're the most unnatural mother. Your attitude simply amazes me.

(*The door opens and* BENTLEY *ushers in* MRS. FAW-CETT. MRS. FAWCETT *is a trim, business-like woman of forty.*)

BENTLEY: Mrs. Fawcett.

MRS. CULVER: Oh, Barbara, how very nice to see you.

BARBARA (*going up to her and kissing her*): Bentley told me you were here and Constance was out. What are you doing?

MRS. CULVER: Bickering.

BARBARA: What about?

MRS. CULVER: Constance.

MARTHA: I'm glad you've come, Barbara. . . . Did you know that John was having an affair with Marie-Louise?

BARBARA: I hate giving a straight answer to a straight question.

MARTHA: I suppose everyone knows but us. How long have you known? They say it's been going on for months. I can't think how it is we've only just heard it.

MRS. CULVER (*ironically*): It speaks very well for human nature that with the masses of dear friends we have it's only today that one of them broke the news to us.

BARBARA: Perhaps the dear friend only heard it this morning.

MARTHA: At first I refused to believe it.

MRS. CULVER: Only quite, quite at first, darling. You surrendered to the evidence with an outraged alacrity that took my breath away.

MARTHA: Of course I put two and two together. After

the first shock I understood everything. I'm only astonished that it never occurred to me before.

BARBARA: Are you very much upset, Mrs. Culver?

MRS. CULVER: Not a bit. I was brought up by a very
strict mother to believe that men were naturally wicked.
I am seldom surprised at what they do and never upset.

MARTHA: Mother has been simply maddening. She
treats it as though it didn't matter a row of pins.

MRS. CULVER: Constance and John have been married
for fifteen years. John is a very agreeable man. I've
sometimes wondered whether he was any more faithful
to his wife than most husbands, but as it was really no
concern of mine I didn't let my mind dwell on it.

MARTHA: Is Constance your daughter or is she not your
daughter?

MRS. CULVER: You certainly have a passion for straight
questions, my dear. The answer is yes.

MARTHA: And are you prepared to sit there quietly and
let her husband grossly deceive her with her most intimate friend?

MRS. CULVER: So long as she doesn't know I can't see
that she's any the worse. Marie-Louise is a nice little
thing, silly of course, but that's what men like, and if
John is going to deceive Constance it's much better that
it should be with someone we all know.

MARTHA (*to* BARBARA): Did you ever hear a respectable woman—and mother is respectable. . . .

MRS. CULVER (*interrupting*): Oh, quite.

MARTHA: Talk like that?

BARBARA: You think that something ought to be done
about it?

MARTHA: I am determined that something shall be
done about it.

MRS. CULVER: Well, my dear, I'm determined that
there's at least one thing you shan't do and that is to tell
Constance.

BARBARA (*a trifle startled*): Is that what you want to
do?

MARTHA: Somebody ought to tell her. If mother won't I must.

BARBARA: I'm extremely fond of Constance. Of course I've known what was going on for a long time and I've been dreadfully worried.

MARTHA: John has put her into an odious position. No man has the right to humiliate his wife as he has humiliated Constance. He's made her perfectly ridiculous.

MRS. CULVER: If women were ridiculous because their husbands are unfaithful to them, there would surely be a great deal more merriment in the world than there is.

BARBARA (*delighted to have a good gossip*): You know they were lunching together today?

MARTHA: We hadn't heard that. But they were dining together the night before last.

MRS. CULVER (*brightly*): We know what they had to eat for dinner. Do you know what they had to eat for luncheon?

MARTHA: Mother.

MRS. CULVER: Well, I thought she seemed rather uppish about the lunch.

MARTHA: You have no sense of decency, mother.

MRS. CULVER: Oh, my dear, don't talk to me about decency. Decency died with dear Queen Victoria.

BARBARA (*to* MRS. CULVER): But you can't approve of John having an open and flagrant intrigue with Constance's greatest friend.

MRS. CULVER: It may be that with advancing years my arteries have hardened. I am unable to attach any great importance to the philanderings of men. I think it's their nature. John is a very hard-working surgeon. If he likes to lunch and dine with a pretty woman now and then I don't think he's much to blame. It must be very tiresome to have three meals a day with the same woman for seven days a week. I'm a little bored myself at seeing Martha opposite me at the dinner-table. And men can't stand boredom as well as women.

MARTHA: I'm sure I'm very much obliged to you, mother.

BARBARA (*significantly*): But they're not only lunching and dining together.

MRS. CULVER: You fear the worst, my dear?

BARBARA (*with solemnity*): I know the worst.

MRS. CULVER: I always think that's such a comfort. With closed doors and no one listening to us, so long as a man is kind and civil to his wife do you blame him very much if he strays occasionally from the narrow path of virtue?

MARTHA: Do you mean to say that you attach no importance to husbands and wives keeping their marriage vows?

MRS. CULVER: I think wives should.

BARBARA: But that's grossly unfair. Why should *they* any more than men?

MRS. CULVER: Because on the whole they like it. We ascribe a great deal of merit to ourselves because we're faithful to our husbands. I don't believe we deserve it for a minute. We're naturally faithful creatures and we're faithful because we have no particular inclination to be anything else.

BARBARA: I wonder.

MRS. CULVER: My dear, you are a widow and perfectly free. Have you really had any great desire to do anything that the world might say you shouldn't?

BARBARA: I have my business. When you work hard eight hours a day you don't much want to be bothered with love. In the evening the tired business woman wants to go to a musical comedy or play cards. She doesn't want to be worried with adoring males.

MARTHA: By the way, how is your business?

BARBARA: Growing by leaps and bounds. As a matter of fact I came here today to ask Constance if she would like to come in with me.

MRS. CULVER: Why should she? John earns plenty of money.

BARBARA: Well, I thought if things came to a crisis she might like to know that her independence was assured.

MRS. CULVER: Oh, you want them to come to a crisis, too?

BARBARA: No, of course I don't. But, you know, they can't go on like this. It's a miracle that Constance hasn't heard yet. She's bound to find out soon.

MRS. CULVER: I suppose it's inevitable.

MARTHA: I hope she'll find out as quickly as possible. I still think it's mother's duty to tell her.

MRS. CULVER: Which I have no intention of doing.

MARTHA: And if mother won't I think I ought.

MRS. CULVER: Which I have no intention of permitting.

MARTHA: He's humiliated her beyond endurance. Her position is intolerable. I have no words to express my opinion of Marie-Louise, and the first time I see her I shall tell her exactly what I think of her. She's a horrid, ungrateful, mean and contemptible little cat.

BARBARA: Anyhow, I think it would be a comfort to Constance to know that if anything happened she has me to turn to.

MRS. CULVER: But John would make her a handsome allowance. He's a very generous man.

MARTHA (*indignantly*): Do you think Constance would accept it?

BARBARA: Martha's quite right, Mrs. Culver. No woman in those circumstances would take a penny of his money.

MRS. CULVER: That's what she'd say. But she'd take care that her lawyer made the best arrangement he could. Few men know with what ingenuity we women can combine the disinterested gesture with a practical eye for the main chance.

BARBARA: Aren't you rather cynical, Mrs. Culver?

MRS. CULVER: I hope not. But when women are alone together I don't see why they shouldn't tell the truth now and then. It's a rest from the weary round of pretending to be something that we quite well know we're not.

MARTHA (*stiffly*): I'm not aware that I've ever pretended to be anything I wasn't.

MRS. CULVER: I dare say not, my dear. But I've always thought you were a little stupid. You take after your poor father. Constance and I have the brains of the family.

(CONSTANCE *comes into the room. She is a handsome woman of six and thirty. She has been out and wears a hat.*)

BARBARA (*eagerly*): Constance.

CONSTANCE: I'm so sorry I wasn't in. How nice of you all to wait. How are you, mother darling?

(*She kisses them one after another.*)

MARTHA: What have you been doing all day, Constance?

CONSTANCE: Oh, I've been shopping with Marie-Louise. She's just coming up.

BARBARA (*with dismay*): Is she here?

CONSTANCE: Yes. She's telephoning.

MARTHA (*ironically*): You and Marie-Louise are quite inseparable.

CONSTANCE: I like her. She amuses me.

MARTHA: Were you lunching together?

CONSTANCE: No, she was lunching with a beau.

MARTHA: (*with a glance at* MRS. CULVER): Oh, really. (*breezily*) John always comes home to luncheon, doesn't he?

CONSTANCE (*with great frankness*): When he doesn't have to be at the hospital too early.

MARTHA: Was he lunching with you today?

CONSTANCE: No. He was engaged.

MARTHA: Where?

CONSTANCE: Good heavens, I don't know. When you've been married as long as I have you never ask your husband where he's going.

MARTHA: I don't know why not.

CONSTANCE (*smiling*): Because he might take it into his head to ask *you*.

MRS. CULVER: And also because if you're a wise woman you have confidence in your husband.

CONSTANCE: John has never given me a moment's uneasiness yet.

MARTHA: You're lucky.

CONSTANCE (*with her tongue in her cheek*): Or wise.

(MARIE-LOUISE *appears. She is a very pretty little thing, beautifully dressed, of the clinging, large-eyed type.*)

MARIE-LOUISE: Oh, I didn't know there was a party.

MRS. CULVER: Martha and I are just going.

CONSTANCE: You know my mother, Marie-Louise.

MARIE-LOUISE: Of course I do.

CONSTANCE: She's a very nice mother.

MRS. CULVER: With her head screwed on the right way and very active for her years.

(MARIE-LOUISE *kisses* BARBARA *and* MARTHA.)

MARIE-LOUISE: How do you do.

MARTHA (*looking at her dress*): That's new, isn't it, Marie-Louise?

MARIE-LOUISE: Yes, I've never had it on before.

MARTHA: Oh, did you put it on because you were lunching with a beau?

MARIE-LOUISE: What makes you think I was lunching with a beau?

MARTHA: Constance told me so.

CONSTANCE: It was only a guess on my part. (*to* MARIE-LOUISE) When we met I noticed that your eyes were shining and you had that pleased, young look a woman always gets when some one has been telling her she's the most adorable thing in the world.

MARTHA: Tell us who it was, Marie-Louise.

CONSTANCE: Do nothing of the kind, Marie-Louise. Keep it a secret and give us something to gossip about.

BARBARA: How is your husband, dear?

MARIE-LOUISE: Oh, he's very well. I've just been telephoning to him.

BARBARA: I never saw anyone adore his wife so obviously as he adores you.

MARIE-LOUISE: Yes, he's sweet, isn't he?

BARBARA: But doesn't it make you a little nervous sometimes? It must be nerve-racking to be obliged to live up to such profound devotion. It would be a dreadful shock if he ever found out that you were not everything he thought you.

CONSTANCE (*charmingly*): But Marie-Louise is everything he thinks her.

MARIE-LOUISE: And even if I weren't I think it would require more than the evidence of his eyes to persuade him.

CONSTANCE: Listen. There's John. (*She goes to the door and calls.*) John! John!

JOHN (*downstairs*): Hulloa.

CONSTANCE: Are you coming up? Marie-Louise is here.

JOHN: Yes, I'm just coming.

CONSTANCE: He's been operating all the afternoon. I expect he's tired out.

MARTHA (*with a look at* MARIE-LOUISE): I dare say he only had a sandwich for luncheon.

(JOHN *comes in. He is a tall, spare man of about forty.*)

JOHN: Good Lord, I never saw such a lot of people. How is my mother-in-law?

MRS. CULVER: Mother-in-lawish.

JOHN (*kissing her—to* BARBARA): You know, I only married Constance because her mother wouldn't have me.

MRS. CULVER: I was too young at the time to marry a boy twenty years younger than myself.

CONSTANCE: It hasn't prevented you from flirting outrageously with the creature ever since. It's lucky I'm not a jealous woman.

JOHN: What have you been doing all day, darling?

CONSTANCE: I've been shopping with Marie-Louise.

JOHN (*shaking hands with* MARIE-LOUISE): Oh, how do you do? Did you lunch together?

MARTHA: No, she lunched with a beau.

JOHN: I wish it had been me. (*to* MARIE-LOUISE) What have you been doing with yourself lately? We haven't seen you for ages.

MARIE-LOUISE: You're never about. Constance and I almost live in one another's pockets.

JOHN: How's that rich husband of yours?

MARIE-LOUISE: I've just been speaking to him. Isn't it a bore, he's got to go down to Birmingham for the night.

CONSTANCE: You'd better come and dine with us.

MARIE-LOUISE: Oh, it's awfully nice of you. But I'm tired out. I shall just go to bed and have an egg.

JOHN: I was just going to tell you, Constance. I shan't be in this evening. I've got an acute appendix to do.

CONSTANCE: Oh, what a nuisance.

MARTHA: You've got a wonderful profession, John. If you ever want to do anything or go anywhere you've only got to say you've got an operation and no one can prove it's a lie.

CONSTANCE: Oh, my dear, you mustn't put suspicions into my innocent head. It would never occur to John to be so deceitful. (*to* JOHN) Would it?

JOHN: I think I'd have to go an awful long way before I managed to deceive you, darling.

CONSTANCE (*with a little smile*): Sometimes I think you're right.

MARIE-LOUISE: I do like to see a husband and wife so devoted to one another as you and John. You've been married fifteen years, haven't you?

JOHN: Yes. And it doesn't seem a day too much.

MARIE-LOUISE: Well, I must be running along. I'm late already. Good-bye, darling. Good-bye, Mrs. Culver.

CONSTANCE: Good-bye, darling. We've had such a nice afternoon.

MARIE-LOUISE (*giving her hand to* JOHN): Good-bye.

JOHN: Oh, I'll come downstairs with you.

MARTHA: I was just going, Marie-Louise. I'll come with you.

MARIE-LOUISE (*with presence of mind*): John, I wonder if you'd mind looking at my knee for a minute. It's been rather painful for the last day or two.

JOHN: Of course not. Come into my consulting-room. These knee-caps are troublesome things when you once get them out of order.

MARTHA (*firmly*): I'll wait for you. You won't be long, will you? We might share a taxi.

MARIE-LOUISE: I've got my car.

MARTHA: Oh, how nice! You can give me a lift then.

MARIE-LOUISE: Of course. I shall be delighted.

(JOHN *opens the door for* MARIE-LOUISE. *She goes out and he follows her.* CONSTANCE *has watched this little scene coolly, but with an alert mind.*)

MARTHA: What is the matter with her knee?

CONSTANCE: It slips.

MARTHA: What happens then?

CONSTANCE: She slips too.

MARTHA: Are you never jealous of these women who come and see John in his consulting-room?

CONSTANCE: He always has a nurse within call in case they should attempt to take liberties with him.

MARTHA (*amiably*): Is the nurse there now?

CONSTANCE: And anyway I can't help thinking that the sort of woman who wants to be made love to in a consulting-room with a lively odour of antiseptics is the sort of woman who wears horrid undies. I could never bring myself to be jealous of her.

MARTHA: Marie-Louise gave me two of her chemises to copy only the other day.

CONSTANCE: Oh, did she give you the cerise one with

the Irish lace insertions? I thought that sweet. I've copied that.

BARBARA: It's true that Marie-Louise is very pretty.

CONSTANCE: Marie-Louise is a darling. But she and John have known each other far too long. John likes her of course, but he says she has no brain.

MARTHA: Men don't always say what they think.

CONSTANCE: Fortunately, or we shouldn't always know what they feel.

MARTHA: Don't you think John has any secrets from you?

CONSTANCE: I'm sure of it. But of course a good wife always pretends not to know the little things her husband wishes to keep hidden from her. That is an elementary rule in matrimonial etiquette.

MARTHA: Don't forget that men were deceivers ever.

CONSTANCE: My dear, you talk like a confirmed spinster. What woman was ever deceived that didn't want to be? Do you really think that men are mysterious? They're children. Why, my dear, John at forty isn't nearly so grown up as Helen at fourteen.

BARBARA: How is your girl, Constance?

CONSTANCE: Oh, she's very well. She loves boarding-school, you know. They're like little boys, men. Sometimes of course they're rather naughty and you have to pretend to be angry with them. They attach so much importance to such entirely unimportant things that it's really touching. And they're so helpless. Have you never nursed a man when he's ill? It wrings your heart. It's just like a dog or a horse. They haven't got the sense to come in out of the rain, poor darlings. They have all the charming qualities that accompany general incompetence. They're sweet and good and silly and tiresome and selfish. You can't help liking them, they're so ingenuous and so simple. They have no complexity or finesse. I think they're sweet, but it's absurd to take them seriously. You're a wise woman, mother. What do you think?

MRS. CULVER: I think you're not in love with your husband.

Constance: What nonsense.

(John *comes in.*)

John: Marie-Louise is waiting for you, Martha. I've just put a little bandage round her knee.

Constance: I hope you weren't rough.

Martha (*to* Constance): Good-bye, dear. Are you coming, mother?

Mrs. Culver: Not just yet.

Martha: Good-bye, Barbara.

(Martha *and* John *go out.*)

Barbara: Constance, I've got a suggestion to make to you. You know that my business has been growing by leaps and bounds and I simply cannot get along alone any more. I was wondering if you'd like to come in with me.

Constance: Oh, my dear, I'm not a business woman.

Barbara: You've got marvellous taste and you have ideas. You could do all the decorating and I'd confine myself to buying and selling furniture.

Constance: But I've got no capital.

Barbara: I've got all the capital I want. I must have help and I know no one more suitable than you. We'd go fifty-fifty and I think I can promise that you'd make a thousand to fifteen hundred a year.

Constance: I've been an idle woman so long. I think I'd find it dreadfully hard to work eight hours a day.

Barbara: Won't you think it over? It's very interesting, you know. You're naturally energetic. Don't you get bored with doing nothing all the time?

Constance: I don't think John would like it. After all, it would look as though he couldn't afford to support me.

Barbara: Oh, not nowadays, surely. There's no reason why a woman shouldn't have a career just as much as a man.

Constance: I think my career is looking after John—

running a house for him, entertaining his friends and making him happy and comfortable.

BARBARA: Don't you think it rather a mistake to put all your eggs in one basket? Supposing that career failed you?

CONSTANCE: Why should it?

BARBARA: Of course I hope it won't. But men, you know, are fluctuating and various. Independence is a very good thing, and a woman who stands on her own feet financially can look upon the future with a good deal of confidence.

CONSTANCE: It's sweet of you, but so long as John and I are happy together I think I should be a fool to do anything that would vex him.

BARBARA: Of course I'm in no immediate hurry. One never knows what the future will bring forth. I want you to know that if you change your mind the job is open to you. I don't think I shall ever find any one so competent as you. You have only to say the word.

CONSTANCE: Oh, Barbara, you are kind to me. It's a splendid offer and I'm ever so grateful to you. Don't think me horrid if I say I hope I shall never need to accept it.

BARBARA: Of course not. Good-bye, darling.

CONSTANCE: Good-bye, dear.

(*They kiss, and* BARBARA *goes out.* CONSTANCE *rings the bell.*)

MRS. CULVER: Are you quite happy, dear?

CONSTANCE: Oh, quite. Don't I look it?

MRS. CULVER: I'm bound to say you do. So far as I can judge by the look of you I should say you haven't a trouble in the world.

CONSTANCE: You'd be wrong. My cook has given notice and she makes the best meringues I've ever eaten.

MRS. CULVER: I like John.

CONSTANCE: So do I. He has all the solid qualities that make a man a good husband, an agreeable temper, a sense of humour and an entire indifference to petty extravagance.

MRS. CULVER: How right you are, darling, to realize that those are the solid qualities.

CONSTANCE: It's not the seven deadly virtues that make a man a good husband, but the three hundred pleasing amiabilities.

MRS. CULVER: Of course one has to compromise in life. One has to make the best of things. One mustn't expect too much from people. If one wants to be happy in one's own way one must let others be happy in theirs. If one can't get this, that and the other the wise thing is to make up one's mind to do without it. The great thing is not to let vanity warp one's reasonable point of view.

CONSTANCE: Mother, Mother, pull yourself together.

MRS. CULVER: Everybody's so clever nowadays. They see everything but the obvious. I've discovered that I only have to say it quite simply in order to be thought a most original and amusing old lady.

CONSTANCE: Spare me, darling.

MRS. CULVER (*affectionately*): If at any time anything went wrong with you, you would tell your mother, wouldn't you?

CONSTANCE: Of course.

MRS. CULVER: I hate the thought that you might be unhappy and let a foolish pride prevent you from letting me console and advise you.

CONSTANCE (*with feeling*): It wouldn't, Mother dear.

MRS. CULVER: I had rather an odd experience the other day. A little friend of mine came to see me and told me that her husband was neglecting her. I asked her why she told me and not her own mother. She said that her mother had never wanted her to marry and it would mortify her now to have to say that she had made a mistake.

CONSTANCE: Oh, well, John never neglects me, mother.

MRS. CULVER: Of course I gave her a good talking to. She didn't get much sympathy from me.

CONSTANCE (*with a smile*): That was very unkind, wasn't it?

MRS. CULVER: I have my own ideas about marriage. If a man neglects his wife it's her own fault, and if he's systematically unfaithful to her in nine cases out of ten she only has herself to blame.

CONSTANCE (*ringing the bell*): Systematically is a grim word.

MRS. CULVER: No sensible woman attaches importance to an occasional slip. Time and chance are responsible for that.

CONSTANCE: And shall we say, masculine vanity?

MRS. CULVER: I told my little friend that if her husband was unfaithful to her it was because he found other women more attractive. Why should she be angry with him for that? Her business was to be more attractive than they.

CONSTANCE: You are not what they call a feminist, mother, are you?

MRS. CULVER: After all, what is fidelity?

CONSTANCE: Mother, do you mind if I open the window?

MRS. CULVER: It is open.

CONSTANCE: In that case do you mind if I shut it? I feel that when a woman of your age asks such a question I should make some sort of symbolic gesture.

MRS. CULVER: Don't be ridiculous. Of course I believe in fidelity for women. I suppose no one has ever questioned the desirability of that. But men are different. Women should remember that they have their homes and their name and position and their family, and they should learn to close their eyes when it's possible they may see something they are not meant to.

(*The* BUTLER *comes in.*)

BENTLEY: Did you ring, madam?

CONSTANCE: Yes. I am expecting Mr. Bernard Kersal. I'm not at home to anybody else.

BENTLEY: Very good, madam.

CONSTANCE: Is Mr. Middleton in?

BENTLEY: Yes, madam. He's in the consulting-room.

CONSTANCE: Very well.

(*The* BUTLER *goes out.*)

MRS. CULVER: Is that a polite way of telling me that I had better take myself off?

CONSTANCE: Of course not. On the contrary I particularly want you to stay.

MRS. CULVER: Who is this mysterious gentleman?

CONSTANCE: Mother. Bernard.

MRS. CULVER: That says nothing to me at all. Not Saint Bernard, darling?

CONSTANCE: Pull yourself together, my pet. You must remember Bernard Kersal. He proposed to me.

MRS. CULVER: Oh, my dear, you cannot expect me to remember the names of all the young men who proposed to you.

CONSTANCE: Yes, but he proposed more than any of the others.

MRS. CULVER: Why?

CONSTANCE: I suppose because I refused him. I can't think of any other reason.

MRS. CULVER: He made no impression on me.

CONSTANCE: I don't suppose he tried to.

MRS. CULVER: What did he look like?

CONSTANCE: He was tall.

MRS. CULVER: They were all tall.

CONSTANCE: He had brown hair and brown eyes.

MRS. CULVER: They all had brown hair and brown eyes.

CONSTANCE: He danced divinely.

MRS. CULVER: They all danced divinely.

CONSTANCE: I very nearly married him, you know.

MRS. CULVER: Why didn't you?

CONSTANCE: I think he was a trifle too much inclined to lie down on the floor and let me walk over him.

MRS. CULVER: In short he had no sense of humour.

CONSTANCE: I was quite certain that he loved me, and I was never absolutely sure that John did.

MRS. CULVER: Well, you're sure now, dear, aren't you?

CONSTANCE: Oh, yes. John adores me.

MRS. CULVER: And what's this young man coming for today?

CONSTANCE: He's not such a very young man any more. He was twenty-nine then and so he must be nearly forty-five now.

MRS. CULVER: He isn't still in love with you?

CONSTANCE: I shouldn't think so. Do you think it possible after fifteen years? It's surely very unlikely. Don't look at me like that, mother. I don't like it.

MRS. CULVER: Don't talk stuff and nonsense to me, child. Of course you know if he's in love with you or not.

CONSTANCE: But I haven't seen him since I married John. You see he lives in Japan. He's a merchant or something in Kobe. He was here during the war on leave. But that was when I was so dreadfully ill and I didn't see him.

MRS. CULVER: Oh! Why's he here now then? Have you been corresponding with him?

CONSTANCE: No. One can't write letters to any one one never sees for fifteen years. He always sends me flowers on my birthday.

MRS. CULVER: That's rather sweet of him.

CONSTANCE: And the other day I had a letter from him saying he was in England and would like to see me. So I asked him to come today.

MRS. CULVER: I wondered why you were so smart.

CONSTANCE: Of course he may be terribly changed. Men go off so dreadfully, don't they? He may be bald and fat now.

MRS. CULVER: He may be married.

CONSTANCE: Oh, if he were I don't think he'd want to come and see me, would he?

MRS. CULVER: I see you're under the impression that he's still in love with you.

CONSTANCE: Oh, I'm not.

MRS. CULVER: Then why are you so nervous?

CONSTANCE: It's only natural that I shouldn't want him to think me old and haggard. He adored me, mother. I suppose he still thinks of me as I was then. It wouldn't be very nice if his face fell about a yard and a half when he came into the room.

MRS. CULVER: I think I'd much better leave you to face the ordeal alone.

CONSTANCE: Oh, no, mother, you must stay. I particularly want you. You see, he may be awful and I may wish I'd never seen him again. It'll be so much easier if you're here. I may not want to be alone with him at all.

MRS. CULVER: Oh.

CONSTANCE (*with a twinkle in her eye*): On the other hand I may.

MRS. CULVER: It seems to me you're putting me in a slightly embarrassing situation.

CONSTANCE: Now listen. If I think he's awful we'll just talk about the weather and the crops for a few minutes and then we'll have an ominous pause and stare at him. That always makes a man feel a perfect fool and the moment a man feels a fool he gets up and goes.

MRS. CULVER: Sometimes they don't know how to, poor dears, and the earth will never open and swallow them up.

CONSTANCE: On the other hand if I think he looks rather nice I shall just take out my handkerchief and carelessly place it on the piano.

MRS. CULVER: Why?

CONSTANCE: Darling, in order that you may rise to your aged feet and say, well, you really must be running along.

MRS. CULVER: Yes, I know that, but why should you carelessly place your handkerchief on the piano?

CONSTANCE: Because I am a creature of impulse. I shall have an impulse to place my handkerchief on the piano.

MRS. CULVER: Oh, very well. But I always mistrust impulses.

(BENTLEY *enters and announces* BERNARD KERSAL. *He is a tall good-looking man, sunburned and of healthy appearance. He is evidently very fit and he carries his forty-five years well.*)

BENTLEY: Mr. Kersal.

CONSTANCE: How do you do? Do you remember my mother?

BERNARD (*shaking hands with her*): I'm sure she doesn't remember me.

(CONSTANCE *takes a small handkerchief out of her bag.*)

MRS. CULVER: That is the soft answer that turneth away wrath.

CONSTANCE: It's rather late for tea, isn't it? Would you like a drink?

(*As she says this she goes toward the bell and places her handkerchief on the piano.*)

BERNARD: No, thanks. I've just this moment had one.

CONSTANCE: To brace you for seeing me?

BERNARD: I was nervous.

CONSTANCE: Have I changed as much as you expected?

BERNARD: Oh, that's not what I was nervous about.

MRS. CULVER: Is it really fifteen years since you saw Constance?

BERNARD: Yes. I didn't see her when I was last in England. When I got demobbed I had to go out to Japan again and get my business together. I haven't had a chance to come home before.

(CONSTANCE *has been giving her mother significant looks, but her mother does not notice them.* CONSTANCE *takes a second handkerchief out of her bag and when the opportunity arises places it neatly on the piano beside the first one.)*

Mrs. Culver: And are you home for long?

Bernard: A year.

Mrs. Culver: Have you brought your wife with you?

Bernard: I'm not married.

Mrs. Culver: Oh, Constance said you were married to a Japanese lady.

Constance: Nonsense, Mother. I never said anything of the sort.

Mrs. Culver: Oh, perhaps I was thinking of Julia Linton. She married an Egyptian pasha. I believe she's very happy. At all events he hasn't killed her yet.

Bernard: How is your husband?

Constance: He's very well. I dare say he'll be in presently.

Bernard: Haven't you got a little sister? I suppose she's out now?

Mrs. Culver: He means Martha. She's come out and gone in again.

Constance: She was not so very much younger than me, you know. She's thirty-two now.

*(Mrs. Culver has taken no notice of the handkerchiefs and in desperation Constance takes a third from her bag and places it beside the other two.)*

Mrs. Culver: Do you like the East, Mr. Kersal?

Bernard: One has a pretty good time there, you know.

*(Now Mrs. Culver catches sight of the three handkerchiefs and starts.)*

Mrs. Culver: I wonder what the time is.

Constance: It's late, Mother. Are you dining out tonight? I suppose you want to have a lie-down before you dress for dinner.

MRS. CULVER: I hope I shall see you again, Mr. Kersal.
BERNARD: Thank you very much.

(CONSTANCE *accompanies her to the door.*)

MRS. CULVER: Good-bye, darling. (*in a whisper*) I couldn't remember if the handkerchiefs meant go or stay.
CONSTANCE: You had only to use your eyes. You can see at a glance that he is the kind of man one would naturally want to have a heart-to-heart talk with after fifteen years.
MRS. CULVER: You only confused me by putting more and more handkerchiefs on the piano.
CONSTANCE: For goodness' sake go, Mother. (*aloud*) Good-bye, my sweet. I'm sorry you've got to run away so soon.
MRS. CULVER: Good-bye.

(*She goes out and* CONSTANCE *comes back into the room.*)

CONSTANCE: Did you think it very rude of us to whisper? Mother has a passion for secrets.
BERNARD: Of course not.
CONSTANCE: Now let's sit down and make ourselves comfortable. Let me look at you. You haven't changed much. You're a little thinner and perhaps a little more lined. Men are so lucky, if they have any character they grow better-looking as they grow older. Do you know I'm thirty-six now?
BERNARD: What does that matter?
CONSTANCE: Shall I tell you something? When you wrote and suggested coming here I was delighted at the thought of seeing you again and wrote at once making a date. And then I was panic-stricken. I would have given almost anything not to have sent that letter. And all today I've had such a horrible feeling at the pit of my stomach. Didn't you see my knees wobble when you came into the room?

BERNARD: In God's name, why?

CONSTANCE: Oh, my dear, I think you must be a little stupid. I should be a perfect fool if I didn't know that when I was a girl I was very pretty. It's rather a pang when you are forced to the conclusion that you're not quite so pretty as you were. People don't tell one. One tries to hide it from oneself. Anyhow I thought I'd rather know the worst. That's one of the reasons I asked you to come.

BERNARD: Whatever I thought you can hardly imagine that I should be deliberately rude.

CONSTANCE: Of course not. But I watched your face. I was afraid I'd see there: By God, how she's gone off.

BERNARD: And did you?

CONSTANCE: You were rather shy when you came in. You weren't thinking of me.

BERNARD: It's quite true, fifteen years ago you were a pretty girl. Now you're lovely. You're ten times more beautiful than you were then.

CONSTANCE: It's nice of you to say so.

BERNARD: Don't you believe it?

CONSTANCE: I think you do. And I confess that's sufficiently gratifying. Now tell me, why aren't you married? It's time you did, you know, or it'll be too late. You'll have a very lonely old age if you don't.

BERNARD: I never wanted to marry anyone but you.

CONSTANCE: Oh, come, you're not going to tell me that you've never been in love since you were in love with me?

BERNARD: No, I've been in love half a dozen times, but when it came to the point I found I still loved you best.

CONSTANCE: I like you for saying that. I shouldn't have believed it if you'd said you'd never loved anybody else and I should have been vexed with you for thinking me such a fool as to believe it.

BERNARD: You see, it was you I loved in the others. One because she had hair like yours and another because her smile reminded me of your smile.

CONSTANCE: I hate to think that I've made you unhappy.

BERNARD: But you haven't. I've had a very good time; I've enjoyed my work; I've made a bit of money and I've had a lot of fun. I don't blame you for having married John instead of me.

CONSTANCE: Do you remember John?

BERNARD: Of course I do. He was a very nice fellow. I dare say he's made you a better husband than I should have. I've had my ups and downs. I'm very irritable sometimes. John's been able to give you everything you wanted. You were much safer with him. By the way, I suppose I can still call you Constance?

CONSTANCE: Of course. Why not? Do you know, I think you have a very nice nature, Bernard.

BERNARD: Are you happy with John?

CONSTANCE: Oh, very. I don't say that he has never given me a moment's uneasiness. He did once, but I took hold of myself and saw that I mustn't be silly. I'm very glad I did. I think I can quite honestly say that ours has been a very happy and successful marriage.

BERNARD: I'm awfully glad to hear that. Do you think it's cheek to ask if John loves you?

CONSTANCE: I'm sure he loves me.

BERNARD: And do you love him?

CONSTANCE: Very much.

BERNARD: May I make you a short speech?

CONSTANCE: If I may interrupt at suitable moments.

BERNARD: I hope you're going to let me see a great deal of you during this year I've got at home.

CONSTANCE: I want to see a great deal of you.

BERNARD: There's just one thing I want to get off my chest and then I needn't refer to it again. I am just as madly in love with you as I was when I asked you to marry me fifteen years ago. I think I shall remain in love with you all my life. I'm too old a dog to learn new tricks. But I want you to know that you needn't have the smallest fear that I shall make a nuisance of myself. I should think it an awfully caddish thing to try to come between you and John. I suppose we all want to be happy, but I don't believe the best way of being that is to try to upset other people's happiness.

Constance: That's not such a very long speech after all. At a public dinner they would hardly even call it a few remarks.

Bernard: All I ask for is your friendship and if in return I care to give you my love I don't see that it's any one's business but my own.

Constance: I don't think it is. I think I can be a very good friend, Bernard.

(*The door opens and* John *comes in.*)

John: Oh, I'm sorry. I didn't know you were engaged.

Constance: I'm not. Come in. This is Bernard Kersal.

John: How do you do?

Bernard: I'm afraid you don't remember me.

John: If you ask me point-blank I think it's safer to confess I don't.

Constance: Don't be so silly, John. He used to come to mother's.

John: Before we were married, d'you mean?

Constance: Yes. You spent several week-ends with us together.

John: My dear, that was fifteen years ago. I'm awfully sorry not to remember you, but I'm delighted to see you now.

Constance: He's just come back from Japan.

John: Oh, well, I hope we shall see you again. I'm just going along to the club to have a rubber before dinner, darling. (*to* Bernard) Why don't you dine here with Constance? I've got an acute appendix and she'll be all alone, poor darling.

Bernard: Oh, that's awfully kind of you.

Constance: It would be a friendly act. Are you free?

Bernard: Always to do a friendly act.

Constance: Very well. I shall expect you at eight-fifteen.

# ACT TWO

SCENE: *The same.*

*A fortnight has passed.*

MARTHA *in walking costume and a hat is looking at an illustrated paper.*

BENTLEY *comes in.*

BENTLEY: Mr. Kersal is here, Miss.

MARTHA: Oh! Ask him if he won't come up.

BENTLEY: Very good, Miss. (*He goes out and in a moment comes in again to announce* BERNARD, *and then goes.*) Mr. Kersal.

MARTHA: Constance is dressing. She won't be very long.

BERNARD: Oh, I see. Well, there's no violent hurry.

MARTHA: You're taking her to Ranelagh, aren't you?

BERNARD: That was the idea. I know some of the fellows who are playing today.

MARTHA: Are you having a good time in London?

BERNARD: Marvellous. When a man's lived in the East as long as I have, he's apt to feel rather out of it when he comes home. But Constance and John have been ripping to me.

MARTHA: Do you like John?

BERNARD: Yes. He's been awfully kind.

MARTHA: Do you know, I remember you quite well.

229

BERNARD: Oh, you can't. You were a kid when I used to come down and stay with your mother.

MARTHA: I was sixteen. Do you imagine I wasn't thrilled to the marrow by Constance's young men?

BERNARD: There were a good many of them. I should have thought your marrow got callous.

MARTHA: But you were one of the serious ones. I always thought you terribly romantic.

BERNARD: I was terribly romantic. I think it's becoming in the young.

MARTHA: I don't think it's unbecoming in the not quite as young.

BERNARD: Don't think I'm romantic now. I make a considerable income and I'm putting on weight. The price of silk has ousted love's young dream in my manly bosom.

MARTHA: You're an unconscionable liar.

BERNARD: To which I can only retort that you're excessively rude.

MARTHA: You were madly in love with Constance in those days, weren't you?

BERNARD: You know, it's so long ago I forget.

MARTHA: I advised her to marry you rather than John.

BERNARD: Why?

MARTHA: Well, for one thing you lived in Japan. I would have married any one who would take me there.

BERNARD: I live there still.

MARTHA: Oh, I don't want to marry you.

BERNARD: I couldn't help suspecting that.

MARTHA: I could never really quite understand what she saw in John.

BERNARD: I suppose she loved him.

MARTHA: I wonder if she ever regrets that she married John rather than you.

BERNARD: Well, don't. She's perfectly satisfied with John and wouldn't change him for anything in the world.

MARTHA: It's exasperating, isn't it?

BERNARD: I don't think so. It must make it much more

comfortable for a husband and wife to be content with one another.

MARTHA: You're in love with her still, aren't you?

BERNARD: Not a bit.

MARTHA: Upon my soul, you've got a nerve. Why, you donkey, you're giving it away all the time. Do you know what you look like when she's in the room? Have you any idea how your eyes change when they rest on her? When you speak her name it sounds as though you were kissing it.

BERNARD: I thought you were an odious child when you were sixteen, Martha, and now that you're thirty-two I think you're a horrible woman.

MARTHA: I'm not really. But I'm very fond of Constance and I'm inclined to be rather fond of you.

BERNARD: Don't you think you could show your attachment by minding your own business?

MARTHA: Why does it make you angry because I've told you that no one can see you with Constance for five minutes without knowing that you adore her?

BERNARD: My dear, I'm here for one year. I want to be happy. I don't want to give trouble or cause trouble. I value my friendship with Constance and I hate the idea that anything should interfere with it.

MARTHA: Hasn't it occurred to you that she may want more than your friendship?

BERNARD: No, it has not.

MARTHA: You need not jump down my throat.

BERNARD: Constance is perfectly happy with her husband. You must think me a damned swine if you think I'm going to butt in and try to smash up a perfectly wonderful union.

MARTHA: But, you poor fool, don't you know that John has been notoriously unfaithful to Constance for ages?

BERNARD: I don't believe it.

MARTHA: Ask any one you like. Mother knows it. Barbara Fawcett knows it. Every one knows it but Constance.

BERNARD: That certainly isn't true. Mrs. Durham told

me when I met her at dinner two or three days ago that John and Constance were the most devoted couple she'd ever known.

MARTHA: Did Marie-Louise tell you that?

BERNARD: She did.

(MARTHA *begins to laugh. She can hardly restrain herself.*)

MARTHA: The nerve. Marie-Louise. Oh, my poor Bernard. Marie-Louise is John's mistress.

BERNARD: Marie-Louise is Constance's greatest friend.

MARTHA: Yes.

BERNARD: If this is a pack of lies I swear I'll damned well wring your neck.

MARTHA: All right.

BERNARD: That was a silly thing to say. I'm sorry.

MARTHA: Oh, I don't mind. I like a man to be violent. I think you're just the sort of man Constance needs.

BERNARD: What the devil do you mean by that?

MARTHA: It can't go on. Constance is being made perfectly ridiculous. Her position is monstrous. I thought she ought to be told and as every one else seemed to shirk the job I was prepared to do it myself. My mother was so disagreeable about it, I've had to promise not to say a word.

BERNARD: You're not under the delusion that I'm going to tell her?

MARTHA: No, I don't really think it would come very well from you. But things can't go on. She's bound to find out. All I want you to do is to . . . well, stand by.

BERNARD: But Marie-Louise has got a husband. What about him?

MARTHA: His only ambition in life is to make a million. He's the sort of fool who thinks a woman loves him just because he loves her. Marie-Louise can turn him round her little finger.

BERNARD: Has Constance never suspected?

MARTHA: Never. You've only got to look at her. Really, her self-confidence sometimes is positively maddening.

BERNARD: I wonder if it wouldn't be better that she never did find out. She's so happy. She's entirely care-free. You've only got to look at that open brow and those frank, trustful eyes.

MARTHA: I thought you loved her.

BERNARD: Enough to want her happiness above all things.

MARTHA: You *are* forty-five, aren't you? I forgot that for a moment.

BERNARD: Dear Martha. You have such an attractive way of putting things.

(CONSTANCE's *voice on the stairs is heard calling*: "Bentley, Bentley.")

MARTHA: Oh, there's Constance. I can't imagine where mother is. I think I'll go into the brown room and write a letter.

(BERNARD *takes no notice of what she says nor does he make any movement when she goes out. A moment later* CONSTANCE *comes in.*)

CONSTANCE: Have I kept you waiting?

BERNARD: It doesn't matter.

CONSTANCE: Hulloa! What's up?

BERNARD: With me? Nothing. Why?

CONSTANCE: You look all funny. Why are your eyes suddenly opaque?

BERNARD: I didn't know they were.

CONSTANCE: Are you trying to hide something from me?

BERNARD: Of course not.

CONSTANCE: Have you had bad news from Japan?

BERNARD: No. Far from it. Silk is booming.

CONSTANCE: Then you're going to tell me that you've just got engaged to a village maiden.

BERNARD: No, I'm not.

CONSTANCE: I hate people who keep secrets from me.

BERNARD: I have no secrets from you.

CONSTANCE: Do you think I don't know your face by now?

BERNARD: You'll make me vain. I would never have ventured to think that you took the trouble to look twice at my ugly face.

CONSTANCE (*with sudden suspicion*): Wasn't Martha here when you came? She hasn't gone, has she?

BERNARD: She's waiting for her mother. She's gone into another room to write letters.

CONSTANCE: Did you see her?

BERNARD (*trying to be very casual*): Yes. We had a little chat about the weather.

CONSTANCE (*immediately grasping what has happened*): Oh——Don't you think we ought to be starting?

BERNARD: There's plenty of time. It's no good getting there too early.

CONSTANCE: Then I'll take off my hat.

BERNARD: And it's jolly here, isn't it? I love your room.

CONSTANCE: Do you think it's a success? I did it myself. Barbara Fawcett wants me to go into the decorating business. She's in it, you know, and she's making quite a lot of money.

BERNARD (*smiling to hide his anxiety in asking the question*): Aren't you happy at home?

CONSTANCE (*breezily*): I don't think it necessarily means one's unhappy at home because one wants an occupation. One may very easily grow tired of going to parties all the time. But as a matter of fact I refused Barbara's offer.

BERNARD (*insisting*): You are happy, aren't you?

CONSTANCE: Very.

BERNARD: You've made *me* very happy during this last fortnight. I feel as though I'd never been away. You've been awfully kind to me.

CONSTANCE: I'm very glad you think so. I don't know that I've done anything very much for you.

BERNARD: Yes, you have. You've let me see you.

CONSTANCE: I let the policeman at the corner do that, you know.

BERNARD: You mustn't think that because I take care only to talk to you of quite casual things I don't still love you with all my heart.

CONSTANCE (*quite coolly*): We agreed when first you came back that your feelings were entirely your business.

BERNARD: Do you mind my loving you?

CONSTANCE: Oughtn't we all to love one another?

BERNARD: Don't tease me.

CONSTANCE: My dear, I can't help being pleased and flattered and rather touched. It is rather wonderful that any one should care for me. . . .

BERNARD (*interrupting*): So much?

CONSTANCE: After so many years.

BERNARD: If any one had asked me fifteen years ago if I could love you more than I loved you then I should have said it was impossible. I love you ten times more than I ever loved you before.

CONSTANCE (*going on with her own speech*): But I don't in the least want you to make love to me now.

BERNARD: I know. I'm not going to. I know you far too well.

CONSTANCE (*amused and a trifle taken aback*): I don't quite know what you've been doing for the last five minutes.

BERNARD: I was merely stating a few plain facts.

CONSTANCE: Oh, I beg your pardon. I thought it was something quite different. I'm afraid you might mistake my meaning if I said I'm quite curious to see how you *do* make love.

BERNARD (*good-humouredly*): I have a notion that you're laughing at me.

CONSTANCE: In the hope of teaching you to laugh at yourself.

BERNARD: I've been very good during the last fortnight, haven't I?

CONSTANCE: Yes, I kept on saying to myself: I wonder if a pat of butter really would melt in his mouth.

BERNARD: Well, for just a minute I'm going to let myself go.

CONSTANCE: I wouldn't if I were you.

BERNARD: Yes, but you're not. I want to tell you just once that I worship the ground you tread on. There's never been any one in the world for me but you.

CONSTANCE: Oh, nonsense. There have been half a dozen. We are seven.

BERNARD: They were all you. I love you with all my heart. I admire you more than any woman I've ever met. I respect you. I'm an awful fool when it comes to the point. I don't know how to say all I've got in my heart without feeling like a perfect ass. I love you. I want you to know that if ever you're in trouble I should look upon it as the greatest possible happiness to be allowed to help you.

CONSTANCE: That's very kind of you. I don't see why I should be in any trouble.

BERNARD: Always and in all circumstances you can count on me absolutely. I will do anything in the world for you. If ever you want me you have only to give me a sign. I should be proud and happy to give my life for you.

CONSTANCE: It's sweet of you to say so.

BERNARD: Don't you believe it?

CONSTANCE (*with a charming smile*): Yes.

BERNARD: I should like to think that it meant—oh, not very much, but just a little to you.

CONSTANCE (*almost shaken*): It means a great deal. I thank you.

BERNARD: Now we won't say anything more about it.

CONSTANCE (*recovering her accustomed coolness*): But why did you think it necessary to say all this just now?

BERNARD: I wanted to get it off my chest.

CONSTANCE: Oh, really.

BERNARD: You're not angry with me?

CONSTANCE: Oh, Bernard, I'm not that kind of a fool at all. . . . It's a pity that Martha doesn't marry.

BERNARD: Don't think that I'm going to marry her.

CONSTANCE: I don't. I merely thought that a husband would be a pleasant and useful occupation for her. She's quite a nice girl, you know. A liar, of course, but otherwise all right.

BERNARD: Oh?

CONSTANCE: Yes, a terrible liar, even for a woman. . . . Shall we start now? It's no good getting there when the polo is over.

BERNARD: All right. Let's start.

CONSTANCE: I'll put my hat on again. By the way, you haven't had a taxi waiting all this time, have you?

BERNARD: No, I've got a car. I thought I'd like to drive you down myself.

CONSTANCE: Open or shut?

BERNARD: Open.

CONSTANCE: Oh, my dear, then I must get another hat. A broad brim like this is such a bore in an open car.

BERNARD: Oh, I am sorry.

CONSTANCE: It doesn't matter a bit. I shall only be a minute. And why on earth shouldn't one be comfortable if one can?

(*She goes out. In a moment* BENTLEY *shows in* MARIE-LOUISE.)

MARIE-LOUISE: Oh, how do you do. (*to* BENTLEY) Will you tell Mr. Middleton at once?

BENTLEY: Yes, madam.

(*Exit* BENTLEY.)

MARIE-LOUISE (*rather flustered*): I particularly wanted to see John for a minute and there are patients waiting to see him, so I asked Bentley if he couldn't come here.

BERNARD: I'll take myself off.

Marie-Louise: I'm awfully sorry, but it's rather urgent. John hates to be disturbed like this.

Bernard: I'll go into the next room.

Marie-Louise: Are you waiting for Constance?

Bernard: Yes, I'm taking her to Ranelagh. She's changing her hat.

Marie-Louise: I see. Bentley told me she was upstairs. Good-bye. I shall only be a minute. (Bernard *goes into the adjoining room just as* John *comes in.*) Oh, John, I'm sorry to drag you away from your patients.

John: There's nothing urgent. They can wait for a few minutes. (Bernard *has closed the door behind him, and* John's *tone changes. They speak now in a low voice and quickly.*) Is anything the matter?

Marie-Louise: Mortimer.

John: What about Mortimer?

Marie-Louise: I'm convinced he suspects.

John: Why?

Marie-Louise: He was so funny last night. He came into my room to say good-night to me. He sat on my bed. He was chatting nicely and he was asking what I'd been doing with myself all the evening. . . .

John: Presumably you didn't tell him.

Marie-Louise: No, I said I'd been dining here. And suddenly he got up and just said good-night and went out. His voice was so strange that I couldn't help looking at him. He was as red as a turkey cock.

John: Is that all?

Marie-Louise: He never came in to say good-morning to me before he went to the City.

John: He may have been in a hurry.

Marie-Louise: He's never in too much of a hurry for that.

John: I think you're making a mountain of a mole heap.

Marie-Louise: Don't be stupid, John. Can't you see I'm as nervous as a cat?

John: I can. But I'm trying to persuade you there's nothing to be nervous about.

MARIE-LOUISE: What fools men are. They never will see that it's the small things that matter. I tell you I'm frightened out of my wits.

JOHN: You know there's a devil of a distance between suspicion and proof.

MARIE-LOUISE: Oh, I don't think he could prove anything. But he can make himself awfully unpleasant. Supposing he put ideas in Constance's head?

JOHN: She'd never believe him.

MARIE-LOUISE: If the worst came to worst I could manage Mortimer. He's awfully in love with me. That always gives one such an advantage over a man.

JOHN: Of course you can twist Mortimer round your little finger.

MARIE-LOUISE: I should die of shame if Constance knew. After all, she's my greatest friend and I'm absolutely devoted to her.

JOHN: Constance is a peach. Of course I don't believe there's anything in this at all, but if there were, I'd be in favour of making a clean breast of it to Constance.

MARIE-LOUISE: Never!

JOHN: I expect she'd kick up a row. Any woman would. But she'd do anything in the world to help us out.

MARIE-LOUISE: A lot you know about women. She'd help you out, I dare say. But she'd stamp on me with both feet. That's only human nature.

JOHN: Not Constance's.

MARIE-LOUISE: Upon my word, it's lucky I'm fairly sure of you, John, or the way you talk of Constance would really make me jealous.

JOHN: Thank God you can smile. You're getting your nerve back.

MARIE-LOUISE: It's been a comfort to talk it over. It doesn't seem so bad now.

JOHN: I'm sure you've got nothing to be frightened about.

MARIE-LOUISE: I dare say it was only my fancy. It was a stupid risk to take all the same.

John: Perhaps. Why did you look so devilish pretty?

Marie-Louise: Oughtn't you to be getting back to your wretched patients?

John: I suppose so. Will you stop and see Constance?

Marie-Louise: I may as well. It would look rather odd if I went away without saying how d'you do to her.

John (going): I'll leave you then. And don't worry.

Marie-Louise: I won't. I dare say it was only a guilty conscience. I'll go and have my hair washed.

(As John is about to go, Martha comes in followed by Bernard.)

Martha (with an almost exaggerated cordiality): I had no idea you were here, Marie-Louise.

Marie-Louise: It's not very important.

Martha: I was just writing letters, waiting for mother, and Bernard's only just told me.

Marie-Louise: I wanted to see John about something.

Martha: I hope you haven't got anything the matter with you, darling.

Marie-Louise: No. Mortimer's been looking rather run-down lately and I want John to persuade him to take a holiday.

Martha: Oh, I should have thought he'd be more likely to take a physician's advice than a surgeon's in a thing like that.

Marie-Louise: He's got a tremendous belief in John, you know.

Martha: In which I'm sure he's justified. John is so very reliable.

John: What can I do for you, Martha? If you'd like me to cut out an appendix or a few tonsils I shall be happy to oblige you.

Martha: My dear John, you've only left me the barest necessities of existence as it is. I don't think I could manage with anything less than I have.

John: My dear, as long as a woman has a leg to stand

on she need not despair of exciting her surgeon's sympathy and interest.

(CONSTANCE *comes in with* MRS. CULVER.)

MARIE-LOUISE (*kissing her*): Darling.

CONSTANCE: How is your knee, still slipping?

MARIE-LOUISE: It always gives me more or less trouble, you know.

CONSTANCE: Yes, of course. I think you're very patient. In your place I should be furious with John. Of course I would never dream of consulting him if I had anything the matter with me.

MRS. CULVER: I'm sorry I've been so long, Martha. Have you been very impatient?

MARTHA: No, I've been passing the time very pleasantly.

MRS. CULVER: For others, darling, or only for yourself?

CONSTANCE: I met mother on the stairs and she came up with me while I changed my hat. Bernard is taking me down to Ranelagh.

JOHN: Oh, that'll be jolly.

BERNARD: We shall be dreadfully late.

CONSTANCE: Does it matter?

BERNARD: No.

(BENTLEY *comes in with a card on a small salver and takes it to* CONSTANCE. *She looks at the card and hesitates.*)

CONSTANCE: How very odd.

JOHN: What's the matter, Constance?

CONSTANCE: Nothing. (*For an instant she reflects.*) Is he downstairs?

BENTLEY: Yes, madam.

CONSTANCE: I don't know why he should send up a card. Show him up.

BENTLEY: Very good, madam.

(*Exit* Bentley.)

John: Who is it, Constance?

Constance: Come and sit down, Marie-Louise.

Marie-Louise: I must go and so must you.

Constance: There's plenty of time. Do you like this hat?

Marie-Louise: Yes. I think it's sweet.

Constance: What are *you* doing here, John? Haven't you got any patients today?

John: Yes, there are two or three waiting. I'm just going down. As a matter of fact I thought I deserved a cigarette. (*He puts his hand to his hip pocket.*) Hang, I've mislaid my cigarette-case. You haven't seen it about, Constance?

Constance: No, I haven't.

John: I looked for it everywhere this morning. I can't think where I left it. I must ring up the nursing-home and ask if I left it there.

Constance: I hope you haven't lost it.

John: Oh, no. I'm sure I haven't. I've just put it somewhere.

(*The door opens and* Bentley *announces the visitor.*)

Bentley: Mr. Mortimer Durham.

Marie-Louise: (*startled out of her wits*): Oh!

Constance (*quickly, seizing her wrist*): Sit still, you fool.

(Mortimer Durham *comes in. He is a stoutish biggish man of about forty, with a red face and an irascible manner. At the moment he is a prey to violent emotion.* Bentley *goes out.*)

Hulloa, Mortimer. What are you doing in these parts at this hour? Why on earth did you send up a card?

(*He stops and looks around.*)

MARIE-LOUISE: What is the matter, Mortimer?

MORTIMER (*to* CONSTANCE, *with difficulty restraining his fury*): I thought you might like to know that your husband is my wife's lover.

MARIE-LOUISE: Morty!

CONSTANCE: (*keeping a firm hand on* MARIE-LOUISE *and very coolly to* MORTIMER): Oh? What makes you think that?

MORTIMER (*taking a gold cigarette-case out of his pocket*): Do you recognize this? I found it under my wife's pillow last night.

CONSTANCE: Oh, I am relieved. I couldn't make out where I'd left it. (*taking it from him*) Thank you so much.

MORTIMER (*angrily*): It's not yours.

CONSTANCE: Indeed it is. I was sitting on Marie-Louise's bed and I must have slipped it under the pillow without thinking.

MORTIMER: It has John's initials on it.

CONSTANCE: I know. It was presented to him by a grateful patient and I thought it much too nice for him, so I just took it.

MORTIMER: What sort of fool do you take me for, Constance?

CONSTANCE: My dear Morty, why should I say it was my cigarette-case if it wasn't?

MORTIMER: They had dinner together.

CONSTANCE: My poor Morty, I know that. You were going to a City banquet or something, and Marie-Louise rang up and asked if she might come and take pot-luck with us.

MORTIMER: Do you mean to say she dined here?

CONSTANCE: Isn't that what she told you?

MORTIMER: Yes.

CONSTANCE: It's quite easy to prove. If you won't take my word for it we can ring for the butler, and you can ask him yourself. . . . Ring the bell, John, will you?

Mortimer (*uneasily*): No, don't do that. If you give me your word, of course I must take it.

Constance: That's very kind of you. I'm grateful to you for not exposing me to the humiliation of making my butler corroborate my statement.

Mortimer: If Marie-Louise was dining here why were you sitting on her bed?

Constance: John had to go out and do an operation, and Marie-Louise wanted to show me the things she'd got from Paris, so I walked round to your house. It was a lovely night. You remember that, don't you?

Mortimer: Damn it, I've got more important things to do than look at the night.

Constance: We tried them all on and then we were rather tired, so Marie-Louise got into bed and I sat down and we talked.

Mortimer: If you were tired why didn't you go home and go to bed?

Constance: John had promised to come round and fetch me.

Mortimer: And did he? At what time did he come?

John: I couldn't manage it. The operation took much longer than I expected. It was one of those cases where when you once start cutting you really don't know where to stop. You know the sort of thing, don't you, Mortimer?

Mortimer: No, I don't. How the devil should I?

Constance: All that is neither here nor there. This is a terrible accusation you've made against John and Marie-Louise and I'm very much upset. But I will remain perfectly calm till I've heard everything. Now let me have your proofs.

Mortimer: My proofs? What d'you mean? The cigarette-case. When I found the cigarette-case I naturally put two and two together.

Constance (*with her eyes flashing*): I quite understand, but why did you make them five?

Mortimer (*emphatically, in order not to show that he is wavering*): It isn't possible that I should have made a mistake.

CONSTANCE: Even the richest of us may err. I remember when Mr. Pierpont Morgan died, he was found to own seven million dollars worth of worthless securities.

MORTIMER (*uneasily*): You don't know what a shock it was, Constance. I had the most implicit confidence in Marie-Louise. I was knocked endways. I've been brooding over it ever since till I was afraid I should go mad.

CONSTANCE: And do you mean to say that you've come here and made a fearful scene just because you found my cigarette-case in Marie-Louise's room? I can't believe it. You're a man of the world and a business man. You're extremely intelligent. Surely you have something to go upon. You must be holding something back. Don't be afraid of hurting my feelings. You've said so much now that I must insist on your saying everything. I want the truth and the whole truth.

(*There is a pause.* MORTIMER *looks from* MARIE-LOUISE, *who is quietly weeping, to* CONSTANCE, *with the utmost bewilderment.*)

MORTIMER: I'm afraid I've made a damned fool of myself.

CONSTANCE: I'm afraid you have.

MORTIMER: I'm awfully sorry, Constance. I beg your pardon.

CONSTANCE: Oh, don't bother about me. You've exposed me to the most bitter humiliation. You've sown seeds of distrust between me and John which can never be . . .

(*She looks for a word.*)

MRS. CULVER (*supplying it*): Fertilized.

CONSTANCE (*ignoring it*): Uprooted. But I don't matter. It's Marie-Louise's pardon you must beg.

MORTIMER (*humbly*): Marie-Louise.

MARIE-LOUISE: Don't touch me. Don't come near me.

MORTIMER (*to* CONSTANCE, *miserably*): You know what jealousy is.

CONSTANCE: Certainly not. I think it's a most ugly and despicable vice.

MORTIMER (*to* MARIE-LOUISE): Marie-Louise, I'm sorry. Won't you forgive me?

MARIE-LOUISE: You've insulted me before all my friends. You know how devotedly I love Constance. You might have accused me of having an affair with anyone else—but not John.

CONSTANCE: Not her greatest friend's husband. The milkman or the dustman if you like, but not her greatest friend's husband.

MORTIMER: I've been a perfect swine. I don't know what came over me. I really wasn't responsible for my actions.

MARIE-LOUISE: I've loved you all these years. No one has ever loved you as I've loved you. Oh, it's cruel, cruel.

MORTIMER: Come away, darling. I can't say here what I want to say.

MARIE-LOUISE: No, no, no.

CONSTANCE (*putting her hand on his arm, gently*): I think you'd better leave her here for a little while, Morty. I'll talk to her when you've gone. She's naturally upset. A sensitive little thing like that.

MORTIMER: We're dining with the Vancouvers at 8:15.

CONSTANCE: For eight-thirty. I promise I'll send her home in good time to dress.

MORTIMER: She'll give me another chance?

CONSTANCE: Yes, yes.

MORTIMER: I'd do anything in the world for her. (CONSTANCE *puts her fingers to her lips and then points significantly to the pearl chain she is wearing. For a second* MORTIMER *does not understand, but as soon as her notion dawns on him he gives a pleased nod.*) You're the cleverest woman in the world. (*As he goes out he stops and holds out his hand to* JOHN.) Will you shake hands with me, old man? I made a mistake and I'm man enough to acknowledge it.

JOHN (*very cordially*): Not at all, old boy. I quite agree that it did look fishy, the cigarette-case. If I'd dreamt that Constance was going to leave an expensive thing like that lying about all over the place, I'm hanged if I'd have let her pinch it.

MORTIMER: You don't know what a weight it is off my mind. I felt a hundred when I came here, and now I feel like a two-year-old.

(*He goes out. The moment the door is closed behind him there is a general change in every attitude. The tension disappears and there is a feeling of relief.*)

JOHN: Constance, you're a brick. I shall never forget this. Never, so long as I live. And by George, what presence of mind you showed. I went hot and cold all over, and you never batted an eye-lash.

CONSTANCE: By the way, here is your cigarette-case. You'd better have a ring made and hang it on your key-chain.

JOHN: No, no. Keep it. I'm too old to take these risks.

CONSTANCE: By the way, did anyone see you go into Morty's house last night?

JOHN: No, we let ourselves in with Marie-Louise's latch key.

CONSTANCE: That's all right then. If Mortimer asks the servants they can tell him nothing. I had to take that chance.

MARIE-LOUISE (*with a little gesture of ashamed dismay*): Oh, Constance, what must you think of me?

CONSTANCE: I? Exactly the same as I thought before. I think you're sweet, Marie-Louise.

MARIE-LOUISE: You have every right to be angry with me.

CONSTANCE: Perhaps, but not the inclination.

MARIE-LOUISE: Oh, it's not true. I've treated you shamefully. You've made me feel such a pig. And you had your chance to get back on me and you didn't take it. I'm so ashamed.

CONSTANCE (*amused*): Because you've been having an affair with John, or because you've been found out?

MARIE-LOUISE: Oh, Constance, don't be heartless. Say anything you like, curse me, stamp on me, but don't smile at me. I'm in a terrible position.

CONSTANCE: And you want me to make a scene. I know and I sympathize. (*very calmly*) But the fact is that Mortimer told me nothing I didn't know before.

MARIE-LOUISE (*aghast*): Do you mean to say that you've known all along?

CONSTANCE: All along, darling. I've been spending the last six months in a desperate effort to prevent my friends and relations from telling me your ghastly secret. It's been very difficult sometimes. Often mother's profound understanding of life, Martha's passion for truth at any price, and Barbara's silent sympathy, have almost worn me down. But until today the t's were not definitely crossed nor the i's distinctly dotted, and I was able to ignore the facts that were staring me—rather rudely, I must say—in the face.

MARIE-LOUISE: But why, why? It's not human. Why didn't you do anything?

CONSTANCE: That, darling, is my affair.

MARIE-LOUISE (*thinking she understands*): Oh, I see.

CONSTANCE (*rather tartly*): No, you don't. I have always been absolutely faithful to John. I have not winked at your intrigue in order to cover my own.

MARIE-LOUISE (*beginning to be a little put out*): I almost think you've been laughing at me up your sleeve all the time.

CONSTANCE (*good-humouredly*): Oh, my dear, you mustn't be offended just because I've taken away from you the satisfaction of thinking that you have been deceiving me all these months. I should hate you to think me capable of an intentional meanness.

MARIE-LOUISE: My head's going round and round.

CONSTANCE: Such a pretty head, too. Why don't you go and lie down? You want to look your best if you're dining with the Vancouvers.

MARIE-LOUISE: I wonder where Mortimer is?

CONSTANCE: You know that pearl necklace you showed me the other day and you said that Mortimer thought it cost a lot of money—well, he's gone to Cartier's to buy it for you.

MARIE-LOUISE (*excitedly*): Oh, Constance, do you think he has?

CONSTANCE: I think all men are born with the knowledge that when they have wounded a woman's soul—and our souls are easily wounded—the only cure is a trifling, but expensive jewel.

MARIE-LOUISE: Do you think he'll have the sense to bring it home with him so that I can wear it tonight?

CONSTANCE: Oh, my dear, don't be such a fool as to accept it with alacrity. Remember that Mortimer has grievously insulted you, he's made the most shocking accusation that a man can make against his wife, he's trampled on your love and now he's destroyed your trust in him.

MARIE-LOUISE: Oh, how right you are, Constance.

CONSTANCE: Surely I need not tell you what to do. Refuse to speak to him, but never let him get a word of defence in edgeways. Cry enough to make him feel what a brute he is, but not enough to make your eyes swell. Say you'll leave him and run sobbing to the door, but take care to let him stop you before you open it. Repeat yourself. Say the same thing over and over again—it wears them down—and if he answers you take no notice, but just say it again. And at last when you've reduced him to desperation, when his head is aching as though it would split, when he's sweating at every pore, when he's harassed and miserable and haggard and broken—then consent as an unmerited favour, as a sign of your forgiving temper and the sweetness of your nature, to accept, no, don't consent, *deign* to accept the pearl necklace for which the wretch has just paid ten thousand pounds.

MARIE-LOUISE (*with peculiar satisfaction*): Twelve, darling.

Constance: And don't thank him. That wouldn't be
playing the game. Let him thank *you* for the favour you
do him in allowing him to make you a paltry gift. Have
you got your car here?

Marie-Louise: No, I was in such a state when I came
I took a taxi.

Constance: John, do take Marie-Louise down and put
her in a taxi.

John: All right.

Marie-Louise: No, not John. I couldn't. After all, I
have some delicacy.

Constance: Oh, have you? Well, let Bernard go.

Bernard: I shall be pleased.

Constance (*to* Bernard): But come back, won't you?

Bernard: Certainly.

Marie-Louise (*kissing* Constance): This has been a
lesson to me, darling. I'm not a fool, Constance. I can
learn.

Constance: At least prudence, I hope.

(Marie-Louise *goes out followed by* Bernard Kersal.)

John: How did you guess that Marie-Louise had said
she was dining here?

Constance: She's too crafty a woman to invent a new
lie when an old one will serve.

John: It would have been awkward if Mortimer had
insisted on asking Bentley if it was true.

Constance: I knew he wouldn't dare. It's only if a
man's a gentleman that he won't hesitate to do an un-
gentlemanly thing. Mortimer is on the boundary line and
it makes him careful.

Martha (*significantly*): Don't you imagine your patients are growing a trifle restless, John?

John: I like to keep them waiting. They grow more
and more nervous as the minutes pass and when I
recommend an operation that will cost them two hundred and fifty pounds they are too shaken to protest.

Martha (*pursing her lips*): I can't imagine you'll very

much like to hear what I'm determined to say to Constance.

JOHN: It's because I shrewdly suspect that you have some very unpleasant things to say about me that I am prepared reluctantly to neglect the call of duty and listen to you with my own ears.

CONSTANCE: She's been exercising miracles of restraint for the last three months, John. I think she has a right to let herself go now.

JOHN: If she's suffering from suppressed desires she's come to the wrong establishment. She ought to go to a psycho-analyst.

MARTHA: I've only got one thing to say, John, and I'm perfectly willing that you should hear it. (*to* CONSTANCE) I don't know what your reasons were for shielding that abominable woman. I can only suppose you wanted to avoid more scandal than was necessary. . . .

MRS. CULVER (*interrupting*): Before you go any further, my dear, you must let me put my word in. (*to* CONSTANCE) My dear child, I beg you not to decide anything in a hurry. We must all think things over. First of all you must listen to what John has to say for himself.

MARTHA: What can he have to say for himself?

CONSTANCE (*ironically*): What indeed?

JOHN: Not the right thing anyway. I've seen too much of married life. . . .

CONSTANCE (*interrupting, with a smile*): Let us be just. Other people's rather than your own.

JOHN (*going on*): To imagine that even the Archangel Gabriel could say the right thing.

CONSTANCE: I've no reason, however, to suppose that the Archangel Gabriel could ever find himself in such a predicament.

JOHN: I'm for it and I'm prepared to take what's coming to me.

CONSTANCE (*to the world in general*): No man could say handsomer than that.

JOHN: I'm expecting you to make a scene, Constance. It's your right and your privilege. I'm willing to bear it.

Give me hell. I deserve it. Drag me up and down the room by the hair of the head. Kick me in the face. Stamp on me. I'll grovel. I'll eat the dust. My name is mud. Mud.

CONSTANCE: My poor John, what is there to make a scene about?

JOHN: I know how badly I've treated you. I had a wife who was good, loving and faithful, devoted to my interests, a perfect mother and an excellent housekeeper. A woman ten times too good for me. If I'd had the smallest spark of decency I couldn't have treated you like this. I haven't a word to say for myself.

MARTHA (*interrupting him*): You've humiliated her to all her friends.

JOHN: I've behaved neither like a gentleman nor a sportsman.

MARTHA: Your conduct is inexcusable.

JOHN: I haven't a leg to stand on.

MARTHA: Even if you didn't love her, you might have treated her with respect.

JOHN: I've been as heartless as a crocodile and as unscrupulous as a typhoid bacillus.

CONSTANCE: Between you, of course, you're leaving me very little to say.

MARTHA: There *is* nothing to say. You're quite right. This is the sort of occasion when it's beneath a woman's dignity to make a scene. It just shows how little John knows women to think that you could demean yourself to vulgar abuse. (*to* JOHN) I suppose you'll have the decency to put no obstacle in the way of Constance's getting her freedom.

MRS. CULVER: Oh, Constance, you're not going to divorce him?

MARTHA: Mother, you're so weak. How can she go on living with a man for whom she has no respect? What would her life be with this creature whom she can only mistrust and despise? Besides, you have to think of their child. How can Constance allow her daughter to be contaminated by the society of a person of this character?

CONSTANCE: John has always been an excellent father. Let us give the devil his due.

MRS. CULVER: Don't be too hard, darling. I can understand that at the moment you feel bitter, but it would be very sad if you let your bitterness warp your judgment.

CONSTANCE: I don't feel in the least bitter. I wish I looked as sweet as I feel.

MRS. CULVER: You can't deceive a mother, my dear. I know the angry resentment that you feel. Under the unfortunate circumstances it's only too natural.

CONSTANCE: When I look into my heart I can't find a trace of resentment, except perhaps for John's being so stupid as to let himself be found out.

JOHN: Let me say this in justification for myself, Constance. I did my little best to prevent it. Angels could do no more.

CONSTANCE: And angels presumably have not the pernicious habit of smoking straight-cut cigarettes.

JOHN: When you once get the taste for them, you prefer them to gippies.

MRS. CULVER: Don't be cynical, darling. That is the worst way to ease an aching heart. Come to your mother's arms, my dear, and let us have a good cry together. And then you'll feel better.

CONSTANCE: It's sweet of you, mother, but honestly I couldn't squeeze a tear out of my eyes if my life depended on it.

MRS. CULVER: And don't be too hard. Of course John is to blame. I admit that. He's been very, very naughty. But men are weak and women are so unscrupulous. I'm sure he's sorry for all the pain he's caused you.

MARTHA: What puzzles me is that you didn't do something the moment you discovered that John was having an affair.

CONSTANCE: To tell you the truth, I thought it no business of mine.

MARTHA (*indignantly*): Aren't you his wife?

CONSTANCE: John and I are very lucky people. Our marriage has been ideal.

MARTHA: How can you say that?

CONSTANCE: For five years we adored each other. That's much longer than most people do. Our honeymoon lasted five years and then we had a most extraordinary stroke of luck: we ceased to be in love with one another simultaneously.

JOHN: I protest, Constance. I've never ceased to be absolutely devoted to you.

CONSTANCE: I never said you had, darling. I'm convinced of it. I've never ceased to be devoted to you. We've shared one another's interests, we've loved to be together, I've exulted in your success and you've trembled in my illness. We've laughed at the same jokes and sighed over the same worries. I don't know any couple that's been bound together by a more genuine affection. But honestly, for the last ten years have you been in love with me?

JOHN: You can't expect a man who's been married for fifteen years. . . .

CONSTANCE: My dear, I'm not asking for excuses. I'm only asking for a plain answer.

JOHN: In the long run I enjoy your society much more than anybody else's. There's no one I like so much as you. You're the prettiest woman I've ever known and I shall say the same when you're a hundred.

CONSTANCE: But does your heart leap into your mouth when you hear my footstep on the stairs, and when I come into the room, is your first impulse to catch me in your manly arms? I haven't noticed it.

JOHN: I don't want to make a fool of myself.

CONSTANCE: Then I think you've answered my question. You're no more in love with me than I am with you.

JOHN: You never said a word of this before.

CONSTANCE: I think most married couples tell one another far too much. There are some things that two people may know very well, but which it's much more tactful for them to pretend they don't.

JOHN: How did you find out?

CONSTANCE: I'll tell you. One night as we were dancing together, all at once I noticed that we weren't keeping such good step as we generally did. It was because my mind was wandering. I was thinking how it would suit me to do my hair like a woman who was dancing alongside of us. Then I looked at you and I saw you were thinking what pretty legs she'd got. I suddenly realized that you weren't in love with me any more and at the same moment I realized that it was a relief, because I wasn't in love with you.

JOHN: I must say it never occurred to me for a moment.

CONSTANCE: I know. A man thinks it quite natural that he should fall out of love with a woman, but it never strikes him for a moment that a woman can do anything so unnatural as to fall out of love with him. Don't be upset at that, darling, that is one of the charming limitations of your sex.

MARTHA: Do you mean mother and me to understand that since then John has been having one affair after another and you haven't turned a hair?

CONSTANCE: Since this is the first time he's been found out, let us give him the benefit of the doubt and hope that till now he has never strayed from the strict and narrow path. You're not angry with me, John?

JOHN: No, darling, not angry. But I *am* a little taken aback. I think you've been making rather a damned fool of me. It never struck me that your feelings for me had changed so much. You can't expect me to like it.

CONSTANCE: Oh, come now, you must be reasonable. You surely wouldn't wish me to have languished for all these years in a hopeless passion for you when you had nothing to give me in return but friendship and affection. Think what a bore it is to have someone in love with you whom you're not in love with.

JOHN: I can't conceive of your ever being a bore, Constance.

CONSTANCE (*kissing her hand to him*): Don't you realize that we must thank our lucky stars? We are the favoured of the gods. I shall never forget those five years of exquisite happiness you gave me when I loved you, and I shall never cease to be grateful to you, not because you loved me, but because you inspired me with love. Our love never degenerated into weariness. Because we ceased loving one another at the very same moment we never had to put up with quarrels and reproaches, recriminations and all the other paraphernalia of a passion that has ceased on one side and is still alive and eager on the other. Our love was like a cross-word puzzle in which we both hit upon the last word at the same moment. That is why our lives since have been so happy; that is why ours is a perfect marriage.

MARTHA: Do you mean to say that it meant nothing to you when you found out that John was carrying on with Marie-Louise?

CONSTANCE: Human nature is very imperfect. I'm afraid I must admit that at the first moment I was vexed. But only at the first moment. Then I reflected that it was most unreasonable to be angry with John for giving to another something that I had no use for. That would be too much like a dog in the manger. And then I was fond enough of John to be willing that he should be happy in his own way. And if he was going to indulge in an intrigue . . . isn't that the proper phrase, John?

JOHN: I have not yet made up my mind whether it really is an indulgence.

CONSTANCE: Then it was much better that the object of his affections should be so intimate a friend of mine that I could keep a maternal eye on him.

JOHN: Really, Constance.

CONSTANCE: Marie-Louise is very pretty so that my self-esteem was not offended, and so rich that it was certain John would have no reason to squander money on her to the inconvenience of myself. She's not clever enough to acquire any ascendancy over him, and so long as I kept his heart I was quite willing that she should have his senses. If you wanted to deceive me, John, I couldn't have chosen anyone with whom I would more willingly be deceived than Marie-Louise.

JOHN: I don't gather that you have been very grossly deceived, darling. You have such penetration that when you look at me I feel as though I were shivering without a stitch of clothing on.

MRS. CULVER: I don't approve of your attitude, Constance. In my day when a young wife discovered that her husband had been deceiving her, she burst into a flood of tears and went to stay with her mother for three weeks, not returning to her husband till he had been brought to a proper state of abjection and repentance.

MARTHA: Are we to understand, then, that you are not going to divorce John?

CONSTANCE: You know, I can never see why a woman should give up a comfortable home, a considerable part of her income and the advantage of having a man about to do all the tiresome and disagreeable things for her, because he has been unfaithful to her. She's merely cutting off her nose to spite her face.

MARTHA: I am at a loss for words. I cannot conceive how a woman of any spirit can sit down and allow her husband to make a perfect damned fool of her.

CONSTANCE: You've been very stupid, my poor John. In the ordinary affairs of life stupidity is much more tiresome than wickedness. You can mend the vicious, but what in Heaven's name are you to do with the foolish?

JOHN: I've been a fool, Constance. I know it, but I'm capable of learning by experience, so I can't be a damned fool.

CONSTANCE: You mean that in future you'll be more careful to cover your tracks?

MRS. CULVER: Oh, no, Constance, he means that this has been a lesson to him, and that in future you'll have no cause for complaint.

CONSTANCE: I've always been given to understand that men only abandon their vices when advancing years have made them a burden rather than a pleasure. John, I'm

happy to say, is still in the flower of his age. I suppose
you give yourself another fifteen years, John, don't you?

JOHN: Really, Constance, I don't know what you mean.
The things you say sometimes are positively embarrassing.

CONSTANCE: I think at all events we may take it that
Marie-Louise will have more than one successor.

JOHN: Constance, I give you my word of honour. . . .

CONSTANCE (*interrupting*): That is the only gift you
can make for which I can find no use. You see, so long as
I was able to pretend a blissful ignorance of your goings-
on we could all be perfectly happy. You were enjoying
yourself and I received a lot of sympathy as the outraged
wife. But now I do see that the position is very difficult.
You have put me in a position that is neither elegant nor
dignified.

JOHN: I'm awfully sorry, Constance.

MARTHA: You're going to leave him?

CONSTANCE: No, I'm not going to leave him. John, you
remember that Barbara offered to take me into her
business? I refused. Well, I've changed my mind and I'm
going to accept.

JOHN: But why? I don't see your point.

CONSTANCE: I'm not prepared any more to be entirely
dependent upon you, John.

JOHN: But, my dear, everything I earn is at your dispo-
sal. It's a pleasure for me to provide for your wants.
Heaven knows, they're not very great.

CONSTANCE: I know. Come, John, I've been very reasonable, haven't I? Don't try and thwart me when I want
to do something on which I've set my heart.

(*There is an instant's pause.*)

JOHN: I don't understand. But if you put it like that, I
haven't a word to say. Of course, you must do exactly as
you wish.

CONSTANCE: That's a dear. Now go back to your
patients or else I shall have to keep you as well as
myself.

JOHN: Will you give me a kiss?

CONSTANCE: Why not?

JOHN (*kissing her*): It's peace between us?

CONSTANCE: Peace and good-will. (JOHN *goes out*.) He is rather sweet, isn't he?

MRS. CULVER: What have you got on your mind, Constance?

CONSTANCE: I, mother? (*teasing her*) What do you suspect?

MRS. CULVER: I don't like the look of you.

CONSTANCE: I'm sorry for that. Most people find me far from plain.

MRS. CULVER: You've got some deviltry in mind, but for the life of me I can't guess it.

MARTHA: I can't see what you expect to get out of working with Barbara.

CONSTANCE: Between a thousand and fifteen hundred a year, I believe.

MARTHA: I wasn't thinking of the money, and you know it.

CONSTANCE: I'm tired of being the modern wife.

MARTHA: What do you mean by the modern wife?

CONSTANCE: A prostitute who doesn't deliver the goods.

MRS. CULVER: My dear, what would your father say if he heard you say such things?

CONSTANCE: Darling, need we conjecture the remarks of a gentleman who's been dead for five and twenty years? Had he any gift for repartee?

MRS. CULVER: None whatever. He was good, but he was stupid. That is why the gods loved him and he died young.

(BERNARD KERSAL *opens the door and looks in*.)

BERNARD: May I come in?

CONSTANCE: Oh, there you are. I wondered what had become of you.

BERNARD: When Marie-Louise saw my car at the door she asked me to drive her. I couldn't very well refuse.

CONSTANCE: So you took her home.

BERNARD: No, she said she was in such a state she must have her hair washed. I drove her to a place in Bond Street.

CONSTANCE: And what did she say to you?

BERNARD: She said, I don't know what you must think of me.

CONSTANCE: That is what most women say to a man when his opinion doesn't matter two straws to them. And what did you answer?

BERNARD: Well, I said, I prefer not to offer an opinion on a matter which is no business of mine.

CONSTANCE: Dear Bernard, one of the things I like most in you is that you always remain so perfectly in character. If the heavens fell you would still remain the perfect English gentleman.

BERNARD: I thought it the most tactful thing to say.

CONSTANCE: Well, mother, I won't detain you any longer. I know that you and Martha have a thousand things to do.

MRS. CULVER: I'm glad you reminded me. Come, Martha. Good-bye, darling. Good-bye, Mr. Kersal.

BERNARD: Good-bye.

CONSTANCE (to MARTHA): Good-bye, dear. Thank you for all your sympathy. You've been a great help in my hour of need.

MARTHA: I don't understand and it's no good saying I do.

CONSTANCE: Bless you. (MRS. CULVER and MARTHA go out. BERNARD closes the door after them.) Shall we be very late?

BERNARD: So late that it doesn't matter if we're a little later. I have something important to say to you.

CONSTANCE (teasing him a little): Important to me or important to you?

BERNARD: I can't tell you how distressed I was at that terrible scene.

CONSTANCE: Oh, didn't you think it had its lighter moments?

BERNARD: It's only this afternoon I learned the truth, and then I never imagined for a moment that you knew it, too. I can't tell you how brave I think it of you to have borne all this torture with a smiling face. If I admired you before, I admire you ten times more now.

CONSTANCE: You're very sweet, Bernard.

BERNARD: My heart bleeds when I think of what you've gone through.

CONSTANCE: It's not a very good plan to take other people's misfortunes too much to heart.

BERNARD: Hardly an hour ago I told you that if ever you wanted me I was only too anxious to do anything in the world for you. I little thought then that the time would come so soon. There's no reason now why I shouldn't tell you of the love that consumes me. Oh, Constance, come to me. You know that if things were as I thought they were between you and John nothing would have induced me to say a word. But now he has no longer any claims on you. He doesn't love you. Why should you go on wasting your life with a man who is capable of exposing you to all this humiliation? You know how long and tenderly I've loved you. You can trust yourself to me. I'll give my whole life to making you forget the anguish you've endured. Will you marry me, Constance?

CONSTANCE: My dear, John may have behaved very badly, but he's still my husband.

BERNARD: Only in name. You've done everything in your power to save a scandal and now if you ask him to let himself be divorced he's bound to consent.

CONSTANCE: Do you really think John has behaved so very badly to me?

BERNARD (astonished): You don't mean to say that you have any doubts in your mind about his relationship with Marie-Louise?

CONSTANCE: None.

BERNARD: Then what in God's name do you mean?

CONSTANCE: My dear Bernard, have you ever considered what marriage is among well-to-do people? In the working classes a woman cooks her husband's dinner, washes for him and darns his socks. She looks after the children and makes their clothes. She gives good value for the money she costs. But what is a wife in our class? Her house is managed by servants, nurses look after her children, if she has resigned herself to having any, and as soon as they are old enough she packs them off to school. Let us face it, she is no more than the mistress of a man of whose desire she has taken advantage to insist on a legal ceremony that will prevent him from discarding her when his desire has ceased.

BERNARD: She's also his companion and his helpmate.

CONSTANCE: My dear, any sensible man would sooner play bridge at his club than with his wife, and he'd always rather play golf with a man than with a woman. A paid secretary is a far better helpmate than a loving spouse. When all is said and done, the modern wife is nothing but a parasite.

BERNARD: I don't agree with you.

CONSTANCE: You see, my poor friend, you are in love and your judgment is confused.

BERNARD: I don't understand what you mean.

CONSTANCE: John gives me board and lodging, money for my clothes and amusements, a car to drive in and a certain position in the world. He's bound to do all that because fifteen years ago he was madly in love with me, and he undertook it; though, if you'd asked him, he would certainly have acknowledged that nothing is so fleeting as that particular form of madness called love. It was either very generous of him or very imprudent. Don't you think it would be rather shabby of me to take advantage now of his generosity or his want of foresight?

BERNARD: In what way?

CONSTANCE: He paid a very high price for something that he couldn't get cheaper. He no longer wants that. Why should I resent it? I know as well as anybody else that desire is fleeting. It comes and goes and no man can understand why. The only thing that's certain is that when it's gone it's gone forever. So long as John continues to provide for me what right have I to complain that he is unfaithful to me? He bought a toy, and if he no longer wants to play with it, why should he? He paid for it.

BERNARD: That might be all right if a man had only to think about himself. What about the woman?

CONSTANCE: I don't think you need waste too much sympathy on her. Like ninety-nine girls out of a hundred, when I married I looked upon it as the only easy, honourable and lucrative calling open to me. When the average woman who has been married for fifteen years discovers her husband's infidelity it is not her heart that is wounded but her vanity. If she had any sense, she would regard it merely as one of the necessary inconveniences of an otherwise pleasant profession.

BERNARD: Then the long and short of it is that you don't love me.

CONSTANCE: You think that my principles are all moonshine?

BERNARD: I don't think they would have much influence if you were as crazy about me as I am about you. Do you still love John?

CONSTANCE: I'm very fond of him, he makes me laugh, and we get on together like a house on fire, but I'm not in love with him.

BERNARD: And is that enough for you? Isn't the future sometimes a trifle desolate? Don't you want love?

(*A pause. She gives him a long reflective look.*)

CONSTANCE (*charmingly*): If I did I should come to you for it, Bernard.

BERNARD: Constance, what do you mean? Is it possible that you could ever care for me? Oh, my darling, I worship the ground you tread on.

(*He seizes her in his arms and kisses her passionately.*)

Constance (*releasing herself*): Oh, my dear, don't be so sudden. I should despise myself entirely if I were unfaithful to John so long as I am entirely dependent on him.

Bernard: But if you love me?

Constance: I never said I did. But even if I did, so long as John provides me with all the necessities of existence I wouldn't be unfaithful. It all comes down to the economic situation. He has bought my fidelity and I should be worse than a harlot if I took the price he paid and did not deliver the goods.

Bernard: Do you mean to say there's no hope for me at all?

Constance: The only hope before you at the moment is to start for Ranelagh before the game is over.

Bernard: Do you still want to go?

Constance: Yes.

Bernard: Very well. (*with a burst of passion*) I love you.

Constance: Then go down and start up the car, put a spot of oil in the radiator or something, and I'll join you in a minute. I want to telephone.

Bernard: Very well.

(*He goes out.* Constance *takes up the telephone.*)

Constance: Mayfair 2646 ... Barbara? It's Constance. That offer you made me a fortnight ago—is it still open? Well, I want to accept it. . . . No, no, nothing has happened. John is very well. He's always sweet, you know. It's only that I want to earn my own living. When can I start? The sooner the better.

# ACT THREE

•-•--•-•--•-•--•-•--•-•--•-•--•-•--•-•--•-•--•-•--•-•--•-•--•-•--•-•--•-•--•-•--•-•--•-•--•-•--•-•--•-•--•-•--•-•--•-•--•-•--•-•--•-•--•-•--•-•-

SCENE: *Still the same. A year has passed. It is afternoon.*
CONSTANCE *is seated at a desk writing letters. The*
BUTLER *shows in* BARBARA FAWCETT *and* MARTHA.

BENTLEY: Mrs. Fawcett and Miss Culver.

CONSTANCE: Oh! Sit down, I'm just finishing a note.

BARBARA: We met on the doorstep.

MARTHA: I thought I'd just look round and see if there was anything I could do to help you before you start.

CONSTANCE: That's very nice of you, Martha. I really don't think there is. I'm packed and ready, and for once I don't believe I've forgotten one of the things I shan't want.

BARBARA: I felt I must run in to say good-bye to you.

CONSTANCE: Now, my dear, you mustn't neglect your work the moment my back is turned.

BARBARA: Well, it's partly the work that's brought me. An order has just come in for a new house and they want an Italian room.

CONSTANCE: I don't like that look in your beady eye, Barbara.

BARBARA: Well, it struck me that as you're going to Italy you might go round the shops and buy any nice pieces that you can find.

265

CONSTANCE: Perish the thought. I've worked like a dog for a year and last night at six o'clock I downed tools. I stripped off my grimy overalls, wrung the sweat from my honest brow and scrubbed my horny hands. You said I could take six weeks' holiday.

BARBARA: I admit that you've thoroughly earned it.

CONSTANCE: When I closed the shop-door behind me, I ceased to be a British working-man and resumed the position of a perfect English lady.

MARTHA: I never saw you in such spirits.

CONSTANCE: Something accomplished, something done. But what I was coming to was this: for the next six weeks I refuse to give a moment's thought to bath-rooms or wallpapers, kitchen sinks, scullery floors, curtains, cushions and refrigerators.

BARBARA: I wasn't asking you to. I only wanted you to get some of that painted Italian furniture and a few mirrors.

CONSTANCE: No, I've worked hard and I've enjoyed my work, and now I'm going to enjoy a perfect holiday.

BARBARA: Oh, well, have it your own way.

MARTHA: Constance dear, I think there's something you ought to know.

CONSTANCE: I should have thought you had discovered by now that I generally know the things I ought to know.

MARTHA: You'll never guess whom I saw in Bond Street this morning.

CONSTANCE: Yes, I shall. Marie-Louise.

MARTHA: Oh!

CONSTANCE: I'm sorry to disappoint you, darling. She rang me up an hour ago.

MARTHA: But I thought she wasn't coming back for another month. She was going to stay away a year.

CONSTANCE: She arrived last night and I'm expecting her every minute.

MARTHA: Here?

CONSTANCE: Yes. She said she simply must run in and see me before I left.

MARTHA: I wonder what she wants.

CONSTANCE: Perhaps to pass the time of day. I think it's rather sweet of her, considering how busy she must be on getting back after so long.

BARBARA: She's been all over the place, hasn't she?

CONSTANCE: Yes, she's been in Malaya; Mortimer has interests there, you know, and in China, and now they've just come from India.

MARTHA: I often wondered if it was at your suggestion that they set off on that long tour immediately after that unfortunate scene.

CONSTANCE: Which, you must confess, no one enjoyed more than you, darling.

BARBARA: It was certainly the most sensible thing they could do.

MARTHA: Of course you know your own business best, darling, but don't you think it's a little unfortunate that you should be going away for six weeks just as she comes back?

CONSTANCE: We working-women have to take our holidays when we can.

BARBARA: Surely John has had his lesson. He's not going to make a fool of himself a second time.

MARTHA: Do you think he has really got over his infatuation, Constance?

CONSTANCE: I don't know at all. But here he is, you'd better ask him.

(*As she says these words,* JOHN *enters.*)

JOHN: Ask him what?

MARTHA (*not at all at a loss*): I was just wondering what you'd do with yourself during Constance's absence.

JOHN: I've got a lot of work, you know, and I shall go to the club a good deal.

MARTHA: It seems a pity that you weren't able to arrange things so that you and Constance should take your holidays together.

BARBARA: Don't blame me for that. I was quite willing to make my arrangements to suit Constance.

CONSTANCE: You see, I wanted to go to Italy and the only places John likes on the Continent are those in which it's only by an effort of the imagination that you can tell you're not in England.

MARTHA: What about Helen?

CONSTANCE: We've taken a house at Henley for August. John can play golf and go on the river, and I shall be able to come up to town every day to look after the business.

BARBARA: Well, dear, I'll leave you. I hope you'll have a wonderful holiday. You've deserved it. Do you know, I think I'm a very clever woman, John, to have persuaded Constance to work. She's been absolutely invaluable to me.

JOHN: I never liked the idea and I'm not going to say I did.

BARBARA: Haven't you forgiven me yet?

JOHN: She insisted on it and I had to make the best of a bad job.

BARBARA: Good-bye.

CONSTANCE (*kissing her*): Good-bye, dear. Take care of yourself.

MARTHA: I'll come with you, Barbara. Mother said she'd look in for a minute to say good-bye to you.

CONSTANCE: Oh, all right. Good-bye.

(*She kisses the two and accompanies them to the door. They go out.*)

JOHN: I say, Constance, I thought you had to go now because Barbara couldn't possibly get away.

CONSTANCE: Did I say that?

JOHN: Certainly.

CONSTANCE: Oh!

JOHN: If I'd dreamt that you could just as easily take your holiday when I take mine . . .

CONSTANCE (*interrupting*): Don't you think it's a mistake for husbands and wives to take their holidays together? The only reason one takes a holiday is for rest and change and recreation. Do you think a man really gets that when he goes away with his wife?

JOHN: It depends on the wife.

CONSTANCE: I know nothing more depressing than the sight of all those couples in a hotel dining-room, one little couple to one little table, sitting opposite to one another without a word to say.

JOHN: Oh, nonsense. You often see couples who are very jolly and cheerful.

CONSTANCE: Yes, I know, but look closely at the lady's wedding-ring and you'll see that it rests uneasily on the hand it adorns.

JOHN: We always get on like a house on fire and when I slipped a wedding-ring on your finger a bishop supervised the process. You're not going to tell me that I bore *you*.

CONSTANCE: On the contrary, you tickle me to death. It's that unhappy modesty of mine: I was afraid that you could have too much of my society. I thought it would refresh you if I left you to your own devices for a few weeks.

JOHN: If you go on pulling my leg so persistently I shall be permanently deformed.

CONSTANCE: Anyhow, it's too late now. My bags are packed, my farewells made, and nothing bores people so much as to see you tomorrow when they've made up their minds to get on without you for a month.

JOHN: H'm. Eyewash.... Look here, Constance, there's something I want to say to you.

CONSTANCE: Yes?

JOHN: Do you know that Marie-Louise has come back?

CONSTANCE: Yes. She said she'd try and look in to say how do you do before I started. It'll be nice to see her again after so long.

JOHN: I want you to do something for me, Constance.

CONSTANCE: What is it?

JOHN: Well, you've been a perfect brick to me, and hang it all, I can't take advantage of your good nature. I must do the square thing.

CONSTANCE: I'm afraid I don't quite understand.

JOHN: I haven't seen Marie-Louise since that day when Mortimer came here and made such a fool of himself. She's been away for nearly a year and taking all things into consideration I think it would be a mistake to resume the relations that we were on then.

CONSTANCE: What makes you think she wishes to?

JOHN: The fact that she rang you up the moment she arrived looks ominous to me.

CONSTANCE: Ominous? You know some women can't see a telephone without taking the receiver off and then, when the operator says, Number, please, they have to say something. I dare say ours was the first that occurred to Marie-Louise.

JOHN: It's no good blinking the fact that Marie-Louise was madly in love with me.

CONSTANCE: Well, we can neither of us blame her for that.

JOHN: I don't want to be unkind, but after all, circumstances have forced a break upon us and I think we had better look upon it as permanent.

CONSTANCE: Of course you must please yourself.

JOHN: I'm not thinking of myself, Constance. I'm thinking partly of course of Marie-Louise's good, but, I confess, chiefly of you. I could never look you in the face again if everything between Marie-Louise and me were not definitely finished.

CONSTANCE: I should hate you to lose so harmless and inexpensive a pleasure.

JOHN: Of course it'll be painful, but if one's made up one's mind to do a thing I think it's much better to do it quickly.

CONSTANCE: I think you're quite right. I'll tell you what I'll do, as soon as Marie-Louise comes I'll make an excuse and leave you alone with her.

JOHN: That wasn't exactly my idea.

CONSTANCE: Oh?

JOHN: It's the kind of thing that a woman can do so much better than a man. It struck me that it would come better from you than from me.

CONSTANCE: Oh, did it?

JOHN: It's a little awkward for me, but it would be quite easy for you to say—well, you know the sort of thing, that you have your self-respect to think of, and to cut a long story short, she must either give me up or you'll raise hell.

CONSTANCE: But you know what a soft heart I have. If she bursts into tears and says she can't live without you I shall feel so sorry for her that I shall say, Well, damn it all, keep him.

JOHN: You wouldn't do me a dirty trick like that, Constance.

CONSTANCE: You know that your happiness is my chief interest in life.

JOHN (*after a moment's hesitation*): Constance, I will be perfectly frank with you. I'm fed up with Marie-Louise.

CONSTANCE: Darling, why didn't you say that at once?

JOHN: Be a sport, Constance. You know that's not the kind of thing one can say to a woman.

CONSTANCE: I admit it's not the kind of thing she's apt to take very well.

JOHN: Women are funny. When they're tired of you they tell you so without a moment's hesitation and if you don't like it you can lump it. But if you're tired of them you're a brute and a beast and boiling oil's too good for you.

CONSTANCE: Very well, leave it to me. I'll do it.

JOHN: You're a perfect brick. But you'll let her down gently, won't you? I wouldn't hurt her feelings for the world. She's a nice little thing, Constance.

CONSTANCE: Sweet.

JOHN: And it's hard luck on her.

CONSTANCE: Rotten.

JOHN: Make her understand that I'm more sinned against than sinning. I don't want her to think too badly of me.

CONSTANCE: Of course not.

JOHN: But be quite sure it's definite.

CONSTANCE: Leave it to me.

JOHN: You're a ripper, Constance. By George, no man could want a better wife.

(*The* BUTLER *introduces* MARIE-LOUISE.)

BUTLER: Mrs. Durham.

(*The two women embrace warmly.*)

MARIE-LOUISE: Darling, how perfectly divine to see you again. It's too, too wonderful.

CONSTANCE: My dear, how well you're looking. Are those the new pearls?

MARIE-LOUISE: Aren't they sweet? But Mortimer bought me the most heavenly emeralds when we were in India. Oh, John, how are you?

JOHN: Oh, I'm all right, thanks.

MARIE-LOUISE: Aren't you a little fatter than when I saw you last?

JOHN: Certainly not.

MARIE-LOUISE: I've lost pounds. (*to* CONSTANCE) I'm so glad I caught you. I should have been so disappointed to miss you. (*to* JOHN) Where are you going?

JOHN: Nowhere. Constance is going alone.

MARIE-LOUISE: Is she? How perfectly divine. I suppose you can't get away. Are you making pots of money?

JOHN: I get along. Will you forgive me if I leave you? I've got to be off.

MARIE-LOUISE: Of course. You're always busy, aren't you?

JOHN: Good-bye.

MARIE-LOUISE: I hope we shall see something of you while Constance is away.

JOHN: Thank you very much.

MARIE-LOUISE: Mortimer's golf has improved. He'd love to play with you.

JOHN: Oh, yes, I should love it.

(*He goes out.*)

MARIE-LOUISE: I did so hope to find you alone. Constance, I've got heaps and heaps to tell you. Isn't it tactful of John to leave us? First of all I want to tell you how splendidly everything has turned out. You know you were quite right. I'm so glad I took your advice and made Mortimer take me away for a year.

CONSTANCE: Mortimer is no fool.

MARIE-LOUISE: Oh, no, for a man he's really quite clever. I gave him hell, you know, for ever having suspected me, and at last he was just eating out of my hand. But I could see he wasn't quite sure of me. You know what men are—when they once get an idea in their heads it's dreadfully difficult for them to get it out again. But the journey was an inspiration; I was absolutely angelic all the time, and he made a lot of money, so everything in the garden was rosy.

CONSTANCE: I'm very glad.

MARIE-LOUISE: I owe it all to you, Constance. I made Mortimer buy you a perfectly divine star sapphire in Ceylon. I told him he owed you some sort of reparation for the insult he'd put upon you. It cost a hundred and twenty pounds, darling, and we're taking it to Cartier's to have it set.

CONSTANCE: How thrilling.

MARIE-LOUISE: You mustn't think I'm ungrateful. Now listen, Constance, I want to tell you at once that you needn't distress yourself about me and John.

CONSTANCE: I never did.

MARIE-LOUISE: I know I behaved like a little beast, but I never thought you'd find out. If I had, well, you know me well enough to be positive that nothing would have induced me to have anything to do with him.

CONSTANCE: You're very kind.

MARIE-LOUISE: I want you to do something for me, Constance. Will you?

CONSTANCE: I'm always eager to oblige a friend.

MARIE-LOUISE: Well, you know what John is. Of course he's a dear and all that kind of thing, but the thing's over and it's best that he should realize it at once.

CONSTANCE: Over?

MARIE-LOUISE: Of course I know he's head over heels in love with me still. I saw that the moment I came into the room. One can't blame him for that, can one?

CONSTANCE: Men do find you fascinating.

MARIE-LOUISE: But one has to think of oneself sometimes in this world. He must see that it could never be the same after we discovered that you knew all about it.

CONSTANCE: I kept it from you as long as I could.

MARIE-LOUISE: One couldn't help feeling then that you were rather making fools of us. It seemed to take the romance away, if you see what I mean.

CONSTANCE: Dimly.

MARIE-LOUISE: You know, I wouldn't hurt John's feelings for the world, but it's no good beating about the bush and I'm quite determined to have the thing finished and done with before you go.

CONSTANCE: This is very sudden. I'm afraid it'll be an awful shock to John.

MARIE-LOUISE: I've quite made up my mind.

CONSTANCE: There isn't much time for a very long and moving scene, but I'll see if John is in still. Could you manage it in ten minutes?

MARIE-LOUISE: Oh, but *I* can't see him. I want you to tell him.

CONSTANCE: Me!

MARIE-LOUISE: You know him so well, you know just the sort of things to say to him. It's not very nice telling a man who adores you that you don't care for him in that way any more. It's so much easier for a third party.

CONSTANCE: Do you really think so?

MARIE-LOUISE: I'm positive of it. You see, you can say

that for your sake I've made up my mind that from now on we can be nothing but friends. You've been so wonderful to both of us, it would be dreadful if we didn't play the game now. Say that I shall always think of him tenderly and that he's the only man I've ever really loved, but that we must part.

CONSTANCE: But if he insists on seeing you?

MARIE-LOUISE: It's no good, Constance, I can't see him. I shall only cry and get my eyes all bunged up. You will do it for me, darling. Please.

CONSTANCE: I will.

MARIE-LOUISE: I got the most divine evening frock in pale green satin on my way through Paris, and it would look too sweet on you. Would you like me to give it to you? I've only worn it once.

CONSTANCE: Now tell me the real reason why you're so determined to get rid of John without a moment's delay.

(MARIE-LOUISE *looks at her and gives a little roguish smile.*)

MARIE-LOUISE: Swear you won't tell.

CONSTANCE: On my honour.

MARIE-LOUISE: Well, my dear, we met a perfectly divine young man in India. He was A.D.C. to one of the governors and he came home on the same boat with us. He simply adores me.

CONSTANCE: And of course you adore him.

MARIE-LOUISE: My dear, I'm absolutely mad about him. I don't know what's going to happen.

CONSTANCE: I think we can both give a pretty shrewd guess.

MARIE-LOUISE: It's simply awful to have a temperament like mine. Of course you can't understand, you're cold.

CONSTANCE (*very calmly*): You're an immoral little beast, Marie-Louise.

MARIE-LOUISE: Oh, I'm not. I have affairs—but I'm not promiscuous.

Constance: I should respect you more if you were an honest prostitute. She at least does what she does to earn her bread and butter. You take everything from your husband and give him nothing that he pays for. You are no better than a vulgar cheat.

Marie-Louise (*surprised and really hurt*): Constance, how can you say such things to me? I think it's terribly unkind of you. I thought you liked me.

Constance: I do. I think you a liar, a humbug and a parasite, but I like you.

Marie-Louise: You can't if you think such dreadful things about me.

Constance: I do. You're good-tempered and generous and sometimes amusing. I even have a certain affection for you.

Marie-Louise (*smiling*): I don't believe you mean a word you say. You know how devoted I am to you.

Constance: I take people as they are and I dare say that in another twenty years you'll be the pink of propriety.

Marie-Louise: Darling, I knew you didn't mean it, but you will have your little joke.

Constance: Now run along, darling, and I'll break the news to John.

Marie-Louise: Well, good-bye, and be gentle with him. There is no reason why we shouldn't spare him as much as possible. (*She turns to go and at the door—stops.*) Of course I've often wondered why with your looks you don't have more success than you do. I know now.

Constance: Tell me.

Marie-Louise: You see—you're a humourist and that always puts men off.

(*She goes out. In a moment the door is cautiously opened and* John *puts his head in.*)

John: Has she gone?
Constance: Come in. A fine night and all's well.

JOHN (*entering*): I heard the door bang. You broke it to her?

CONSTANCE: I broke it.

JOHN: Was she awfully upset?

CONSTANCE: Of course it was a shock, but she kept a stiff upper lip.

JOHN: Did she cry?

CONSTANCE: No. Not exactly. To tell you the truth I think she was stunned by the blow. But of course when she gets home and realizes the full extent of her loss, she'll cry like anything.

JOHN: I hate to see a woman cry.

CONSTANCE: It is painful, isn't it? But of course it's a relief to the nerves.

JOHN: I think you're rather cool about it, Constance. I am not feeling any too comfortable. I shouldn't like her to think I'd treated her badly.

CONSTANCE: I think she quite understands that you're doing it for my sake. She knows that you have still a very great regard for her.

JOHN: But you made it quite definite, didn't you?

CONSTANCE: Oh, quite.

JOHN: I'm really very much obliged to you, Constance.

CONSTANCE: Not at all.

JOHN: At all events I'm glad to think that you'll be able to set out on your holiday with a perfectly easy mind. By the way, do you want any money? I'll write you a cheque at once.

CONSTANCE: Oh, no, thank you. I've got plenty. I've earned fourteen hundred pounds during this year that I've been working.

JOHN: Have you, by Jove! That's a very considerable sum.

CONSTANCE: I'm taking two hundred of it for my holiday. I've spent two hundred on my clothes and on odds and ends and the remaining thousand I've paid into your account this morning for my board and lodging during the last twelve months.

JOHN: Nonsense, darling. I won't hear of such a thing. I don't want you to pay for your board and lodging.

CONSTANCE: I insist.

JOHN: Don't you love me any more?

CONSTANCE: What has that to do with it? Oh, you think a woman can only love a man if he keeps her. Isn't that rating your powers of fascination too modestly? What about your charm and good humour?

JOHN: Don't be absurd, Constance. I can perfectly well afford to support you in your proper station. To offer me a thousand pounds for your board and lodging is almost insulting.

CONSTANCE: Don't you think it's the kind of insult you could bring yourself to swallow? One can do a lot of amusing things with a thousand pounds.

JOHN: I wouldn't dream of taking it. I never liked the idea of your going into business. I thought you had quite enough to do looking after the house and so forth.

CONSTANCE: Have you been less comfortable since I began working?

JOHN: No, I can't say I have.

CONSTANCE: You can take my word for it, a lot of incompetent women talk a great deal of nonsense about housekeeping. If you know your job and have good servants it can be done in ten minutes a day.

JOHN: Anyhow, you wanted to work and I yielded. I thought in point of fact it would be a very pleasant occupation for you, but heaven knows I wasn't expecting to profit financially by it.

CONSTANCE: No, I'm sure you weren't.

JOHN: Constance, I could never help thinking that your determination had something to do with Marie-Louise.

(*There is a moment's pause and when* CONSTANCE *speaks it is not without seriousness.*)

CONSTANCE: Haven't you wondered why I never reproached you for your affair with Marie-Louise?

JOHN: Yes. I could only ascribe it to your unfathomable goodness.

CONSTANCE: You were wrong. I felt I hadn't the right to reproach you.

JOHN: What do you mean, Constance? You had every right. We behaved like a couple of swine. I may be a dirty dog, but, thank God, I know I'm a dirty dog.

CONSTANCE: You no longer desired me. How could I blame you for that? But if you didn't desire me, what use was I to you? You've seen how small a share I take in providing you with the comfort of a well-ordered home.

JOHN: You were the mother of my child.

CONSTANCE: Let us not exaggerate the importance of that, John. I performed a natural and healthy function of my sex. And all the tiresome part of looking after the child when she was born I placed in the hands of much more competent persons. Let us face it, I was only a parasite in your house. You had entered into legal obligations that prevented you from turning me adrift, but I owe you a debt of gratitude for never letting me see by word or gesture that I was no more than a costly and at times inconvenient ornament.

JOHN: I never looked upon you as an inconvenient ornament. And I don't know what you mean by being a parasite. Have I ever in any way suggested that I grudged a penny that I spent on you?

CONSTANCE (*with mock amazement*): Do you mean to say that I ascribed to your beautiful manners what was only due to your stupidity? Are you as great a fool as the average man who falls for the average woman's stupendous bluff that just because he's married her he must provide for her wants and her luxuries, sacrifice his pleasures and comfort and convenience, and that he must look upon it as a privilege that she allows him to be her slave and bondman? Come, come, John, pull yourself together. You're a hundred years behind the times. Now that women have broken down the walls of the harem they must take the rough-and-tumble of the street.

JOHN: You forget all sorts of things. Don't you think a

man may have gratitude to a woman for the love he has had for her in the past?

CONSTANCE: I think gratitude is often very strong in men so long as it demands from them no particular sacrifices.

JOHN: Well, it's a curious way of looking at things, but obviously I have reason to be thankful for it. But after all you knew what was going on long before it came out. What happened then that made you make up your mind to go into business?

CONSTANCE: I am naturally a lazy woman. So long as appearances were saved I was prepared to take all I could get and give nothing in return. I was a parasite, but I knew it. But when we reached a situation where only your politeness or your lack of intelligence prevented you from throwing the fact in my teeth, I changed my mind. I thought that I should very much like to be in a position where, if I felt inclined to, I could tell you, with calm and courtesy, but with determination —to go to hell.

JOHN: And are you in that position now?

CONSTANCE: Precisely. I owe you nothing. I am able to keep myself. For the last year I have paid my way. There is only one freedom that is really important and that is economic freedom, for in the long run the man who pays the piper calls the tune. Well, I have that freedom, and upon my soul it's the most enjoyable sensation I can remember since I ate my first strawberry ice.

JOHN: You know, I would sooner you had made me scenes for a month on end like any ordinary woman and nagged my life out than that you should harbor this cold rancour against me.

CONSTANCE: My poor darling, what are you talking about? Have you known me for fifteen years and do you think me capable of the commonness of insincerity? I harbour no rancour. Why, my dear, I'm devoted to you.

JOHN: Do you mean to tell me that you've done all this without any intention of making me feel a perfect cad?

CONSTANCE: On my honour. If I look in my heart I can only find in it affection for you and the most kindly and charitable feelings. Don't you believe me?

(*He looks at her for a moment and then makes a little gesture of bewilderment.*)

JOHN: Yes, oddly enough, I do. You are a remarkable woman, Constance.

CONSTANCE: I know, but keep it to yourself. You don't want to give a dog a bad name.

JOHN (*with an affectionate smile*): I wish I could get away. I don't half like the idea of your travelling by yourself.

CONSTANCE: Oh, but I'm not. Didn't I tell you?

JOHN: No.

CONSTANCE: I meant to. I'm going with Bernard.

JOHN: Oh! You never said so. Who else?

CONSTANCE: Nobody.

JOHN: Oh! (*He is rather taken aback at the news.*) Isn't that rather odd?

CONSTANCE: No. Why?

JOHN (*not knowing at all how to take it*): Well, it's not usual for a young woman to take a six weeks' holiday with a man who can hardly be described as old enough to be her father.

CONSTANCE: Bernard's just about the same age as you.

JOHN: Don't you think it'll make people gossip a bit?

CONSTANCE: I haven't gone out of my way to spread the news. In fact, now I come to think of it, I haven't told anyone but you, and you, I am sure, will be discreet.

(JOHN *suddenly feels that his collar is a little too tight for him, and with his fingers he tries to loosen it.*)

JOHN: You're pretty certain to be seen by someone who knows you and they're bound to talk.

CONSTANCE: Oh, I don't think so. You see we're motoring all the way and we neither of us care for frequented places. One of the advantages of having really nice friends like ours is that you can always be certain of finding them at the fashionable resorts at the very moment when everybody you know is there.

JOHN: Of course I am not so silly as to think that because a man and a woman go away together it is necessary to believe the worst about them, but you can't deny that it is rather unconventional. I wouldn't for a moment suggest that there'll be anything between you, but it's inevitable that ordinary persons should think there was.

CONSTANCE (*as cool as a cucumber*): I've always thought that ordinary persons had more sense than the clever ones are ready to credit them with.

JOHN (*deliberately*): What on earth do you mean?

CONSTANCE: Why, of course we're going as man and wife, John.

JOHN: Don't be a fool, Constance. You don't know what you're talking about. That's not funny at all.

CONSTANCE: But, my poor John, whom do you take us for? Am I so unattractive that what I'm telling you is incredible? Why else should I go with Bernard? If I merely wanted a companion I'd go with a woman. We could have headaches together and have our hair washed at the same place and copy one another's nightdresses. A woman's a much better travelling companion than a man.

JOHN: I may be very stupid, but I don't seem to be able to understand what you're saying. Do you really mean me to believe that Bernard Kersal is your lover?

CONSTANCE: Certainly not.

JOHN: Then what *are* you talking about?

CONSTANCE: My dear, I can't put it any plainer. I'm going away for six weeks' holiday and Bernard has very kindly offered to come with me.

JOHN: And where do I come in?

CONSTANCE: You don't come in. You stay at home and look after your patients.

JOHN (*trying his best to control himself*): I flatter myself I'm a sensible man. I'm not going to fly into a passion. Many men would stamp and rave or break the furniture. I have no intention of being melodramatic, but you must allow me to say that what you've just told me is very surprising.

CONSTANCE: Just for a moment, perhaps, but I'm sure you have only to familiarize yourself with the notion in order to become reconciled to it.

JOHN: I'm doubtful whether I shall have time to do that, for I feel uncommonly as though I were about to have an apoplectic stroke.

CONSTANCE: Undo your collar then. Now I come to look at you I confess that you are more than usually red in the face.

JOHN: What makes you think that I am going to allow you to go?

CONSTANCE (*good-humouredly*): Chiefly the fact that you can't prevent me.

JOHN: I can't bring myself to believe that you mean what you say. I don't know what ever put such an idea into your head.

CONSTANCE (*casually*): I thought a change might do me good.

JOHN: Nonsense.

CONSTANCE: Why? You did. Don't you remember? You were getting rather flat and stale. Then you had an affair with Marie-Louise and you were quite another man. Gay and amusing, full of life, and much more agreeable to live with. The moral effect on you was quite remarkable.

JOHN: It's different for a man than for a woman.

CONSTANCE: Are you thinking of the possible consequences? We have long passed the Victorian Era when asterisks were followed after a certain interval by a baby.

JOHN: That never occurred to me. What I meant was that if a man's unfaithful to his wife she's an object of sympathy, whereas if a woman's unfaithful to her husband he's merely an object of ridicule.

CONSTANCE: That is one of those conventional prejudices that sensible people must strive to ignore.

JOHN: Do you expect me to sit still and let this man take my wife away from under my very nose? I wonder you don't ask me to shake hands with him and wish him good luck.

CONSTANCE: That's just what I am going to do. He's coming here in a few minutes to say good-bye to you.

JOHN: I shall knock him down.

CONSTANCE: I wouldn't take any risks in your place. He's pretty hefty and I'm under the impression that he's very nippy with his left.

JOHN: I shall have great pleasure in telling him exactly what I think of him.

CONSTANCE: Why? Have you forgotten that I was charming to Marie-Louise? We were the best of friends. She never bought a hat without asking me to go and help her choose it.

JOHN: I have red blood in my veins.

CONSTANCE: I'm more concerned at the moment with the grey matter in your brain.

JOHN: Is he in love with you?

CONSTANCE: Madly. Didn't you know?

JOHN: I? How should I?

CONSTANCE: He's been here a great deal during the last year. Were you under the impression that he only came to see you?

JOHN: I never paid any attention to him. I thought him rather dull.

CONSTANCE: He is rather dull. But he's very sweet.

JOHN: What sort of a man is it who eats a fellow's food and drinks his wine and then makes love to his wife behind his back?

CONSTANCE: A man very like you, John, I should say.

JOHN: Not at all. Mortimer is the sort of man who was born to be made a fool of.

CONSTANCE: None of us know for certain the designs of Providence.

JOHN: I see you're bent on driving me to desperation. I shall break something in a minute.

CONSTANCE: There's that blue-and-white bowl that your Uncle Henry gave us as a wedding present. Break that, it's only a modern imitation.

(*He takes the bowl and hurls it on the floor so that it is shattered.*)

JOHN: There.

CONSTANCE: Do you feel better?

JOHN: Not a bit.

CONSTANCE: It's a pity you broke it then. You might have given it away as a wedding present to one of your colleagues at the hospital.

(*The* BUTLER *shows in* MRS. CULVER.)

BUTLER: Mrs. Culver.

CONSTANCE: Oh, mother, how sweet of you to come. I was so hoping I'd see you before I left.

MRS. CULVER: Oh, you've had an accident.

CONSTANCE: No, John's in a temper and he thought it would relieve him if he broke something.

MRS. CULVER: Nonsense, John's never in a temper.

JOHN: That's what you think, Mrs. Culver. Yes, I am in a temper. I'm in a filthy temper. Are you a party to this plan of Constance's?

CONSTANCE: No, mother doesn't know.

JOHN: Can't you do something to stop it? You have some influence over her. You must see that the thing's preposterous.

MRS. CULVER: My dear boy, I haven't the ghost of an idea what you're talking about.

JOHN: She's going to Italy with Bernard Kersal. Alone.

MRS. CULVER (*with a stare*): It's not true: how d'you know?

JOHN: She's just told me so, as bold as brass, out of a

blue sky. She mentioned it in the course of conversation as if she were saying, Darling, your coat wants brushing.

Mrs. Culver: Is it true, Constance?

Constance: Quite.

Mrs. Culver: But haven't you been getting on with John? I always thought you two were as happy as the day is long.

John: So did I. We've never had the shadow of a quarrel. We've always got on.

Mrs. Culver: Don't you love John any more, darling?

Constance: Yes, I'm devoted to him.

John: How can you be devoted to a man when you're going to do him the greatest injury that a woman can do to a man?

Constance: Don't be idiotic, John. I'm going to do you no more injury than you did me a year ago.

John (*striding up to her, thinking quite erroneously that he sees light*): Are you doing this in order to pay me out for Marie-Louise?

Constance: Don't be such a fool, John. Nothing is further from my thoughts.

Mrs. Culver: The circumstances are entirely different. It was very naughty of John to deceive you, but he's sorry for what he did and he's been punished for it. It was all very dreadful and caused us a great deal of pain. But a man's a man and you expect that kind of thing from him. There are excuses for him. There are none for a woman. Men are naturally polygamous and sensible women have always made allowances for their occasional lapse from a condition which modern civilization has forced on them. Women are monogamous. They do not naturally desire more than one man and that is why the common sense of the world has heaped obloquy upon them when they have overstepped the natural limitations of their sex.

Constance (*smiling*): It seems rather hard that what is sauce for the gander shouldn't also be sauce for the goose.

Mrs. Culver: We all know that unchastity has no moral effect on men. They can be perfectly promiscuous and remain upright, industrious and reliable. It's quite different with women. It ruins their character. They become untruthful and dissipated, lazy, shiftless and dishonest. That is why the experience of ten thousand years has demanded chastity in women. Because it has learnt that this virtue is the key to all others.

CONSTANCE: They were dishonest because they were giving away something that wasn't theirs to give. They had sold themselves for board, lodging and protection. They were chattels. They were dependent on their husbands and when they were unfaithful to them they were liars and thieves. I'm not dependent on John. I am economically independent and therefore I claim my sexual independence. I have this afternoon paid into John's account one thousand pounds for my year's keep.

JOHN: I refuse to take it.

CONSTANCE: Well, you'll damned well have to.

MRS. CULVER: There's no object in losing your temper.

CONSTANCE: I have mine under perfect control.

JOHN: If you think what they call free love is fun you're mistaken. Believe me, it's the most overrated amusement that was ever invented.

CONSTANCE: In that case, I wonder why people continue to indulge in it.

JOHN: I ought to know what I'm talking about, hang it all. It has all the inconveniences of marriage and none of its advantages. I assure you, my dear, the game is not worth the candle.

CONSTANCE: You may be right, but you know how hard it is to profit by anybody's experience. I think I'd like to see for myself.

MRS. CULVER: Are you in love with Bernard?

CONSTANCE: To tell you the truth I haven't quite made up my mind. How does one know if one's in love?

MRS. CULVER: My dear, I only know one test. Could you use his tooth-brush?

CONSTANCE: No.

MRS. CULVER: Then you're not in love with him.

CONSTANCE: He's adored me for fifteen years. There's

something in that long devotion which gives me a funny little feeling in my heart. I should like to do something to show him that I'm not ungrateful. You see, in six weeks he goes back to Japan. There is no chance of his coming to England again for seven years. I'm thirty-six now and he adores me; in seven years I shall be forty-three. A woman of forty-three is often charming, but it's seldom that a man of fifty-five is crazy about her. I came to the conclusion that it must be now or never and so I asked him if he'd like me to spend these last six weeks with him in Italy. When I wave my handkerchief to him as the ship that takes him sails out of the harbour at Naples I hope that he will feel that all those years of unselfish love have been well worth the while.

JOHN: Six weeks. Do you intend to leave him at the end of six weeks?

CONSTANCE: Oh, yes, of course. It's because I'm putting a limit to our love that I think it may achieve the perfection of something that is beautiful and transitory. Why, John, what is it that makes a rose so lovely but that its petals fall as soon as it is full blown?

JOHN: It's all come as such a shock and a surprise that I hardly know what to say. You've got me at a complete disadvantage.

(MRS. CULVER, *who has been standing at the window, gives a little cry.*)

CONSTANCE: What is it?

MRS. CULVER: Here is Bernard. He's just driven up to the door.

JOHN: Do you expect me to receive him as if I were blissfully unconscious of your plans?

CONSTANCE: It would be more comfortable. It would be stupid to make a scene and it wouldn't prevent my going on this little jaunt with him.

JOHN: I have my dignity to think of.

CONSTANCE: One often preserves that best by putting it in one's pocket. It would be kind of you, John, to treat him just as pleasantly as I treated Marie-Louise when I knew she was your mistress.

JOHN: Does he know that I know?

CONSTANCE: Of course not. He's a little conventional, you know, and he couldn't happily deceive a friend if he thought there was no deception.

MRS. CULVER: Constance, is there nothing I can say to make you reconsider your decision?

CONSTANCE: Nothing, darling.

MRS. CULVER: Then I may just as well save my breath. I'll slip away before he comes.

CONSTANCE: Oh, all right. Good-bye, Mother. I'll send you a lot of picture post-cards.

MRS. CULVER: I don't approve of you, Constance, and I can't pretend that I do. No good will come of it. Men were meant by nature to be wicked and delightful and deceive their wives, and women were meant to be virtuous and forgiving and to suffer verbosely. That was ordained from all eternity and none of your new-fangled notions can alter the decrees of Providence.

(*The* BUTLER *enters, followed by* BERNARD.)

BENTLEY: Mr. Kersal.

MRS. CULVER: How do you do, Bernard, and good-bye. I'm just going.

BERNARD: Oh, I'm sorry. Good-bye.

(*She goes out.*)

CONSTANCE (*to* BERNARD): How d'you do? Just one moment. (*to the* BUTLER) Oh, Bentley, get my things downstairs and put them in a taxi, will you?

BENTLEY: Very good, madam.

BERNARD: Are you just starting? It's lucky I came when I did. I should have hated to miss you.

CONSTANCE: And let me know when the taxi's here.

BENTLEY: Yes, madam.

CONSTANCE: Now I can attend to you.

(*The* Butler *goes out.*)

Bernard: Are you looking forward to your holiday?

Constance: Immensely. I've never gone on a jaunt like this before, and I'm really quite excited.

Bernard: You're going alone, aren't you?

Constance: Oh, yes, quite alone.

Bernard: It's rotten for you not to be able to get away, old man.

John: Rotten.

Bernard: I suppose these are the penalties of greatness. I can quite understand that you have to think of your patients first.

John: Quite.

Constance: Of course John doesn't very much care for Italy.

Bernard: Oh, are you going to Italy? I thought you said Spain.

John: No, she always said Italy.

Bernard: Oh, well, that's hardly your mark, is it, old boy? Though I believe there are some sporting links on the Lake of Como.

John: Are there?

Bernard: I suppose there's no chance of your being anywhere near Naples towards the end of July?

Constance: I don't really know. My plans are quite vague.

Bernard: I was only asking because I'm sailing from Naples. It would be fun if we met there.

John: Great fun.

Constance: I hope you'll see a lot of John while I'm away. I'm afraid he'll be a trifle lonely, poor darling. Why don't you dine together one day next week?

Bernard: I'm terribly sorry, but you know I'm going away.

Constance: Oh, are you? I thought you were going to stay in London till you had to start for Japan.

BERNARD: I meant to, but my doctor has ordered me to go and do a cure.

JOHN: What sort of a cure?

BERNARD: Oh, just a cure. He says I want bucking up.

JOHN: Oh, does he? What's the name of your doctor?

BERNARD: No one you ever heard of. A man I used to know in the war.

JOHN: Oh!

BERNARD: So I'm afraid this is good-bye. Of course, it's a wrench leaving London, especially as I don't expect to be in Europe again for some years, but I always think it rather silly not to take a man's advice when you've asked for it.

JOHN: More especially when he's charged you three guineas.

CONSTANCE: I'm sorry. I was counting on you to keep John out of mischief during my absence.

BERNARD: I'm not sure if I could guarantee to do that. But we might have done a few theatres together and had a game of golf or two.

CONSTANCE: It would have been jolly, wouldn't it, John?

JOHN: Very jolly.

(*The* BUTLER *comes in.*)

BENTLEY: The taxi's waiting, madam.

CONSTANCE: Thank you.

(*The* BUTLER *goes out.*)

BERNARD: I'll take myself off. In case I don't see you again I'd like to thank you now for all your kindness to me during the year I've spent in London.

CONSTANCE: It's been very nice to see you.

BERNARD: You and John have been most awfully good to me. I never imagined I was going to have such a wonderful time.

CONSTANCE: We shall miss you terribly. It's been a

great comfort to John to think that there was someone
to take me out when he had to be away on one of his
operations. Hasn't it, darling?

JOHN: Yes, darling.

CONSTANCE: When he knew I was with you he
never worried. Did you, darling?

JOHN: No, darling.

BERNARD: I'm awfully glad if I've been able to make
myself useful. Don't forget me entirely, will you?

CONSTANCE: We're not likely to do that, are we,
darling?

JOHN: No, darling.

BERNARD: And if you ever have a moment to spare
you will write to me, won't you? You don't know how
much it means to us exiles.

CONSTANCE: Of course we will. We'll both write. Won't
we, darling?

JOHN: Yes, darling.

CONSTANCE: John writes such a good letter. So chatty,
you know, and amusing.

BERNARD: That's a promise. Well, good-bye, old boy.
Have a good time.

JOHN: Thanks, old bean.

BERNARD: Good-bye, Constance. There's so much I
want to say to you that I don't know where to begin.

JOHN: I don't want to hurry you, but the taxi is just
ticking its head off.

BERNARD: John is so matter-of-fact. Well, I'll say
nothing then but God bless you.

CONSTANCE: Au revoir.

BERNARD: If you do go to Naples you will let me
know, won't you? If you send a line to my club, it'll be
forwarded at once.

CONSTANCE: Oh, all right.

BERNARD: Good-bye.

(*He gives them both a friendly nod and goes out.*
CONSTANCE *begins to giggle and soon is seized
with uncontrollable laughter.*)

JOHN: Will you kindly tell me what there is to laugh at? If you think it amuses me to stand here like patience on a monument and have my leg pulled you're mistaken. What did you mean by all that balderdash about meeting you by chance in Naples?

CONSTANCE: He was throwing you off the scent.

JOHN: The man's a drivelling idiot.

CONSTANCE: D'you think so? I thought he was rather ingenious. Considering he hasn't had very much practice in this sort of thing I thought he did very well.

JOHN: Of course if you're determined to find him a pattern of perfection it's useless for me to attempt to argue. But honestly, speaking without prejudice for or against, I'm sorry to think of you throwing yourself away on a man like that.

CONSTANCE: Perhaps it's natural that a man and his wife should differ in their estimate of her prospective lover.

JOHN: You're not going to tell me he's better-looking than I am.

CONSTANCE: No. You have always been my ideal of manly beauty.

JOHN: He's no better dressed than I am.

CONSTANCE: He could hardly expect to be. He goes to the same tailor.

JOHN: I don't think you can honestly say he's more amusing than I am.

CONSTANCE: No, I honestly can't.

JOHN: Then in Heaven's name why do you want to go away with him?

CONSTANCE: Shall I tell you? Once more before it's too late I want to feel about me the arms of a man who adores the ground I walk on. I want to see his face light up when I enter the room. I want to feel the pressure of his hand when we look at the moon together and the pleasantly tickling sensation when his arm tremulously steals around my waist. I want to let my head fall on his shoulder and feel his lips softly touch my hair.

JOHN: The operation is automatically impossible; the poor devil would get such a crick in the neck he wouldn't know what to do.

CONSTANCE: I want to walk along country lanes holding hands and I want to be called by absurd pet names. I want to talk baby-talk by the hour together.

JOHN: Oh, God.

CONSTANCE: I want to know that I'm eloquent and witty when I'm dead silent. For ten years I've been very happy in your affection, John we've been the best and dearest friends, but now just for a little while I hanker for something else. Do you grudge it me? I want to be loved.

JOHN: But, my dear, I'll love you. I've been a brute, I've neglected you, it's not too late and you're the only woman I've ever really cared for. I'll chuck everything and we'll go away together.

CONSTANCE: The prospect does not thrill me.

JOHN: Come, darling, have a heart. I gave up Marie-Louise. Surely you can give up Bernard.

CONSTANCE: But you gave up Marie-Louise to please yourself, not to please me.

JOHN: Don't be a little beast, Constance. Come away with me. We'll have such a lark.

CONSTANCE: Oh, my poor John, I didn't work so hard to gain my economic independence in order to go on a honeymoon with my own husband.

JOHN: Do you think I can't be a lover as well as a husband?

CONSTANCE: My dear, no one can make yesterday's cold mutton into tomorrow's lamb cutlets.

JOHN: You know what you're doing. I was determined in future to be a model husband and you're driving me right into the arms of Marie-Louise. I give you my word of honour that the moment you leave this house I shall drive straight to her door.

CONSTANCE: I should hate you to have a fruitless

journey. I'm afraid you won't find her at home. She has a new young man and she says he's too divine.

JOHN: What!

CONSTANCE: He's the A.D.C. of a Colonial Governor. She came here today to ask me to break the news to you that henceforth everything was over between you.

JOHN: I hope you told her first that I was firmly resolved to terminate a connection that could only cause you pain.

CONSTANCE: I couldn't. She was in such a blooming hurry to give me her message.

JOHN: Really, Constance, for your own pride I should have thought you wouldn't like her to make a perfect fool of me. Any other woman would have said, What a strange coincidence. Why it's only half an hour since John told me he had made up his mind never to see you again. But of course you don't care two straws for me any more, that's quite evident.

CONSTANCE: Oh, don't be unjust, darling. I shall always care for you. I may be unfaithful, but I am constant. I always think that's my most endearing quality.

(*The* BUTLER *opens the door.*)

JOHN (*irritably*): What is it?

BENTLEY: I thought madam had forgotten that the taxi was at the door.

JOHN: Go to hell.

BENTLEY: Very good, sir.

(*He goes out.*)

CONSTANCE: I don't see why you should be rude to him. Bernard will pay the taxi. Anyhow I must go now or he'll begin to think I'm not coming. Good-bye, darling. I hope you'll get on all right in my absence. Just give the cook her head and you'll have no trouble. Won't you say good-bye to me?

JOHN: Go to the devil.

CONSTANCE: All right. I shall be back in six weeks.

JOHN: Back? Where?

CONSTANCE: Here.

JOHN: Here? Here? Do you think I'm going to take you back?

CONSTANCE: I don't see why not. When you've had time to reflect you'll realize that you have no reason to blame me. After all, I'm taking from you nothing that you want.

JOHN: Are you aware that I can divorce you for this?

CONSTANCE: Quite. But I married very prudently. I took the precaution to marry a gentleman and I know that you could never bring yourself to divorce me for doing no more than you did yourself.

JOHN: I wouldn't divorce you. I wouldn't expose my worst enemy to the risk of marrying a woman who's capable of treating her husband as you're treating me.

CONSTANCE (*at the door*): Well, then, shall I come back?

JOHN (*after a moment's hesitation*): You are the most maddening, wilful, capricious, wrong-headed, delightful and enchanting woman man was ever cursed with having for a wife. Yes, damn you, come back.

(*She lightly kisses her hand to him and slips out, slamming the door behind her.*)

# Important Drama Collections

**Fifteen American One-Act Plays:** *The Lottery, The Devil and Daniel Webster* and thirteen other outstanding plays (46867 75¢)

**Three Comedies of American Family Life:** *I Remember Mama, Life with Father, You Can't Take It with You* (46853 75¢)

**Three Dramas of American Realism:** *Idiot's Delight, Street Scene, The Time of Your Life* (W0652 60¢)

**Three Plays About Business in America:** *The Adding Machine, Beggar on Horseback, All My Sons* (46852 75¢)

**Three Plays About Marriage:** *Craig's Wife, They Knew What They Wanted, Holiday* (W0659 60¢)

**Three Plays About Crime and Criminals:** *Arsenic and Old Lace, Kind Lady, Detective Story* (W0934 75¢)

**Three Plays About Doctors:** *An Enemy of the People, Men in White, Yellow Jack* (46855 75¢)

**Three Plays by Maxwell Anderson:** *Valley Forge, Joan of Lorraine, Journey to Jerusalem* (W0670 60¢)

**Three Plays by Victor Hugo:** *Hernani, Ruy Blas, The King Amuses Himself* (W0662 60¢)

**Three Classic Spanish Plays:** *The Sheep Well, None Beneath the King, Life Is a Dream* (W0660 60¢)

**Three Scandinavian Plays:** *The Father, The Lady from the Sea, The Wild Duck* (W0657 60¢)

**Three Dramas of W. Somerset Maugham:** *The Letter, The Sacred Flame, For Services Rendered* (47487 90¢)

**Four Plays by Bernard Shaw:** *Caesar and Cleopatra, The Devil's Disciple, Man and Superman, Candida* (W•935 75¢)

---

# WSP WSP *Collateral Classics* WSP WSP

Unique editions of literary masterpieces containing a 48-64 page illustrated Supplement to enrich your understanding and reading experience

*Pictorial Background*—authentic material illustrating significant plot highlights

*Picture Quiz*—illustrations of items that are to be matched with their corresponding words

*Allusions and Notes*—explanations of literary allusions and historical references

*Vocabulary*—exercises relating unfamiliar vocabulary to the context in which it is used

*Do You Agree with the Critics?*—diverse selections from a variety of critical evaluations of the work

| | | |
|---|---|---|
| THE AUTOBIOGRAPHY OF BENJAMIN FRANKLIN | CC • 501 | 50¢ |
| BILLY BUDD, Herman Melville | CC • 502 | 50¢ |
| CANDIDE, Voltaire | CC • 503 | 50¢ |
| A CHRISTMAS CAROL, Charles Dickens | CC • 504 | 50¢ |
| THE COVERED WAGON, Emerson Hough | CC • 513 | 50¢ |
| CRIME AND PUNISHMENT, Fyodor Dostoevsky | 46753 | 75¢ |
| DR. JEKYLL AND MR. HYDE, Robert Louis Stevenson | CC • 518 | 50¢ |
| DON QUIXOTE, Miguel de Cervantes Saavedra (abr.) | CC • 709 | 75¢ |
| EMMA, Jane Austen | CC • 505 | 50¢ |
| FATHERS AND SONS, Ivan Turgenev | CC • 506 | 50¢ |
| GULLIVER'S TRAVELS, Jonathan Swift | 46018 | 50¢ |
| HEART OF DARKNESS, Joseph Conrad | CC • 516 | 50¢ |
| HENRY ESMOND, William Makepeace Thackeray | CC • 508 | 50¢ |
| LE MORTE D'ARTHUR, Sir Thomas Malory (abr.) | CC • 702 | 75¢ |
| LES MISÉRABLES, Victor Hugo (abr.) | CC • 703 | 75¢ |
| LIFE ON THE MISSISSIPPI, Mark Twain | CC • 519 | 50¢ |
| THE LITTLE WORLD OF DON CAMILLO, Giovanni Guareschi | CC • 514 | 50¢ |
| LUST FOR LIFE, Irving Stone | CC • 707 | 75¢ |
| THE MOON AND SIXPENCE, W. Somerset Maugham | CC • 710 | 75¢ |
| OF HUMAN BONDAGE, W. Somerset Maugham (abr.) | 46762 | 75¢ |
| THE ORDEAL OF RICHARD FEVEREL, George Meredith | CC • 704 | 75¢ |
| PERE GORIOT, Honoré de Balzac | CC • 509 | 50¢ |
| THE PICKWICK PAPERS, Charles Dickens | CC • 904 | 95¢ |
| THE PORTRAIT OF A LADY, Henry James | CC • 901 | 95¢ |
| THE RISE OF SILAS LAPHAM, William Dean Howells | CC • 705 | 75¢ |
| THE SEA WOLF, Jack London | CC • 517 | 50¢ |
| SENSE AND SENSIBILITY, Jane Austen | CC • 510 | 50¢ |
| TESS OF THE D'URBERVILLES, Thomas Hardy | CC • 511 | 50¢ |
| THE THREE MUSKETEERS, Alexandre Dumas | CC • 902 | 95¢ |
| TWO YEARS BEFORE THE MAST, Richard Henry Dana | CC • 520 | 50¢ |
| VANITY FAIR, William Makepeace Thackeray | 47903 | 95¢ |
| THE VICAR OF WAKEFIELD, Oliver Goldsmith | CC • 512 | 50¢ |
| THE WAY OF ALL FLESH, Samuel Butler | CC • 515 | 50¢ |

If your bookseller does not have these titles you may order them by sending retail price, plus 15¢ per book for mailing and handling, to Mail Service Department, Washington Square Press, Inc., 1 West 39th Street, New York, N.Y. 10018. Please send check or money order—*do not send cash.* WSP 11-69